Praise for _50 Women, Book One_

"As you read these stories of women from across the globe in _50 Women, Book One_, you come to understand how much in common we share in our lives. It's why we believe that sisterhood is global."

Katherine Spillar,
executive editor, _Ms. Magazine_ and
executive vice president, Feminist Majority Foundation

"As Americans, we hear and see news stories of famine, poverty and human suffering in third-world countries around the globe. As a result, we often turn a blind eye to these injustices, whether it be intentional or because of ignorance. Through the personal, first-person stories that fill its pages, _50 Women, Book One_ effectively helps us lift lids of misunderstanding and denial by offering an authentic look at the struggles of women we'd otherwise never know."

Michelle Fitzhugh-Craig,
editor in chief/CEO,
Shades Magazine – Celebrating All Women of Color

"_50 Women, Book One_ contains stories of courage, self-determination, and power to survive the difficult experiences of poverty, abuse, hunger, and grief. I am in awe of each woman's dignity and resourcefulness to find ways to better not only their own lives, but also the lives of hundreds of others. In witnessing their truths, we readers can offer our support, compassion, and love to heal their wounds. As I work to serve women and girls in the areas of health, education, and happiness, I will strive harder to serve with a heart like these fifty warriors of light."

Deborah Santana,
CEO and founder, Do A Little

"For too long women's stories have gone untold and their voices hidden. *50 Women, Book One* embraces the heroic journey of everyday women around the world and emphasizes the worth and wisdom *all* women hold. If you ever doubted your personal influence or ability to create a new dream, read *50 Women*. Everything is possible."

Elisa Parker,
co-founder, CEO, host, See Jane Do

"I have been working in the women's rights arena for decades as president and CEO of Women's Intercultural Network. As a United Nations consultative NGO, we strive to elevate the voices of women and girls to ensure they are heard and represented in their communities, governments and economies. *50 Women, Book One* is truly a remarkable anthology as it is shockingly authentic and a vital tool to ensure the lives and strengths of women are documented. We cannot properly advocate for our global sisters until we understand and relate to their tribulations and triumphs. Bravo! Very well done!"

Marilyn Fowler,
president and CEO, Women's Intercultural Network

"While I had been curious to read the stories in *50 Women, Book One*, I was really taken in as soon as I read Jessica's introduction about not only the life of the book's creation, but also about how the project itself transformed her. Each woman's story allows the reader to see and hear the life of another. With each new country, new challenge, new setback, and new accomplishment, the reader is able to make a connection to each and every one of the women. It is through story sharing that we come to realize the connectedness between us all; that we are one, regardless of culture, country, or ethnicity. That is the power and the importance of this book."

Mary Ann Ellison,
executive director, Flowering Hope

"In the world of quick and simplified Facebook and Twitter postings, *50 Women, Book One* is a refreshing, honest and in-depth look at the important lives of women around the world. Despite our supposed increase in connectivity, it is still so difficult to know the true history of women. By using individual stories, this book expands your mind and your heart, while also giving you a vital understanding of the overall issues women are facing around the world. Everyone who cares about women should read this book."

Christine Bronstein,
founder, A Band of Women

"This book connects us to our sisters around the world as we receive the honor of not just witnessing their stories, but also having their stories change our own. What may have simply been headlines of war to us was their reality. What they endured moves me, haunts me, and inspires me. All too often, history has been written from the male perspective and this book ensures that women's voices are heard. *50 Women, Book One* weaves together a beautiful tapestry of women's stories, many who faced the worst that life has to offer, and yet they each emerged with wisdom that benefits us all."

Shasta Nelson,
CEO of GirlfriendCircles.com and author of
Friendships Don't Just Happen!
The Guide to Creating a Meaningful Circle of Girlfriends

Dear Honey

~~Dear Brother, Reader,~~

past:– 1784, December 31st, The Darkest night of Rakhaing people. My great grand Father was the last King of "Mrak-u" now called "Arakan Kingdom of Rakhaing Kingdom 10,000 people died that scary night. what its like to be forced to Flee One's Homeland. & hunted and empowed by Truamas of the past.

present:– Me and my childen 4th generation of struggle — and still .

Our ancestor.

50 Women

Thanks:

BOOK ⟨OF⟩ ONE

Nane oo

COMPILED BY

JESSICA BUCHLEITNER

50 Women, Book One
First Edition

Copyright © 2014 by Jessica Buchleitner

Compiled by Jessica Buchleitner
Editors: Nancee Adams-Taylor, Patricia McKenna and Carol Pott
Cover design by theBook Designers
Map illustrations by Dejan Petrovic
Somali editorial cartoons by Abdul Arts
Layout by Jera Publishing

ISBN: 978-0-9903375-0-8 (print)
        978-0-9903375-1-5 (eBook)
LCCN: 2014910300

Published by:
Nikita Publishing
Alameda, California USA

Please visit www.50womenproject.org

Contents

Introduction

This week, I am wrapping up *50 Women, Book One.*

What a journey.

Six years, over fifty interviews, nearly a hundred new friendships, five immigration cases, one nervous breakdown, three United Nations trips, a complete "turning inside out" of the self, a ninety-two-page book proposal and a manuscript that is hundreds of pages.

The recurring themes of my journey with *50 Women* appear to be vulnerability, surrender, and the authentic self.

Initially I sought to compile *50 Women* to heal from many things. I know what brokenness is like, I know what self-deprecation is like, and, above all, I know what it is like to endure fear, shame, and humiliation. For these reasons, I felt a sense of solidarity with every woman who participated in *50 Women.*

When I was younger, I received the rare opportunity to cultivate friendships with women from across the world. I quickly learned that most women, no matter which country they were from or ethnic background they represented, shared similar experiences. Their stories transformed me and their friendships and cultural sharing gave me a sense of belonging. I wanted to go deeper into their cultures and observe and experience life from their point of view.

In 2009, the idea to compile *50 Women* came to me suddenly as I sat at a desk pondering a documentary I watched about Ahmad Shah Massoud. Subconsciously, I was seeking redemption through fifty other women and over the last several years, I found what I was looking for. I was naïve going into this project. I assumed that it would not affect me as much as it did. Yet the experiences I have encountered through its course forced me to ask introspective questions. At the beginning of 2012, this journey shattered all of my spiritual constructs, leaving me bewildered, raw, and egoless. Every layer, every façade, every notion, and every aspect of me was stripped away. For those fortunate enough to experience a phenomenon of this nature, it is very humbling.

I often say that I wrote this book to "find God" and now that I have the manuscript, I am still striving to see how much closer I am. Can someone tell me if I am still very far?

Once you live so many different experiences and travel through so many different cultural realities, it is difficult to condense yourself back to who you were before. All the beliefs you once held no longer make sense due to the expansion of your character. Evolution and humility are the prizes you gain, yet the prices you pay for curiosity.

In literature, it is believed that there are always a context and a subtext to a person and story. The context represents the cultural circumstances in which the events in a person's life occur. The subtext is the deep-rooted inner conviction and underlying core of a person that defines their beliefs, ethics, and values. I have gone deep inside the cultures and lives of many of these women in *50 Women* on a very ethnographic level. I did so because I wanted to understand them in context and subtext. In order to write a person's story you have to know them inside and out.

After all, this was not just a book, rather immigration cases, policy reform attempts, board of director duties, UN trips, sisterhood connections, tears, fears, a confrontation of demons and all the world's problems.

To craft an effective narrative, one must answer a fundamental question: What is the story about?

This story is not just about fifty women, but also about a young woman, certainly not an ingénue, rather an old soul in a new body—wary and wise to her own long path—who sought to understand the context and subtext of humanity through the tumultuous lives of fifty women from thirty countries. It was not always a comfortable experience or a familiar one, but she was vulnerably ready to be molded and shaped by it as the bits and pieces from every person and culture she interacted with became pieces of her . . .

Jessica Buchleitner
San Francisco, CA
2014

The Little Box

The little box gets her first teeth
And her little length
Little width little emptiness
And all the rest she has
The little box continues growing
The cupboard that she was inside
Is now inside her
And she grows bigger bigger bigger
Now the room is inside her
And the house and the city and the earth
And the world she was in before
The little box remembers her childhood
And by a great great longing
She becomes a little box again
Now in the little box
You have the whole world in miniature
You can easily put it in a pocket
Easily steal it easily lose it
Take care of the little box

—*Vasko Popa*

Acknowledgments

First and foremost, I want to thank all the women in this first book in the series of *50 Women* for their courage. Their courage to be unconquerable, to remain unbroken by circumstances that obliterate so many others, and to relive painful memories and experiences when telling me their stories. I am humbled. You have all completely turned me inside out. Thank you.

Thank you to my three editors who helped this book make sense: Carol Pott, Patricia McKenna, and Nancee Adams-Taylor.

A big nod goes to Alan Hebel and Ian Shimkoviak of *the*Book-Designers for giving *50 Women, Book One* a beautiful cover/face.

Thank you to my parents, Julie and Jerry Buchleitner, for always encouraging me to dream and raising me as an equal. Also my brother, Jason, for using this as an inspiration to manifest his own path.

To all of my Afghan sisters who introduced me to Islam, Afghan food, and *Yak Qadam Pesh*: Ta shakur.

Thank you to Dejan Petrovic for not only believing in me, but for drawing the map illustrations with such a stunning accuracy that you confirmed my belief that you are a reincarnated military general from the 1300s.

Thank you to Jean Claude Musore, author of *Your Promises Stand Forever*, for assisting with Swahili translation and for his partnership with *50 Women Project*. God bless you and your family.

Thank you, Andranik Dedeyan, for adding to the creative process over the years. You are a very talented artist.

Thank you to Linda Fahey, who helped me outline this project in the beginning as I spent countless Saturdays at her kitchen table throwing around ideas while we drank tea and ate mango salsa.

Finally, thank you to all of you who believed in this project over the years. It is through your collective encouragement that it is now born.

Dedication

This book is dedicated to the mad, the perpetrated, the forgotten, the seemingly beaten, the discriminated, the strong of heart, the fierce yet weary souls, the victimized and the 50 warriors of light (my heart and soul embodied).

May all you reading these stories have the strength to choose life.

50 Women

Views expressed in *50 Women, Book One* are solely those of the participants and do not reflect the personal views, beliefs or opinions of the author. This book contains graphic descriptions of violent acts and very sensitive topics. Reader discretion is advised.

AFRICA

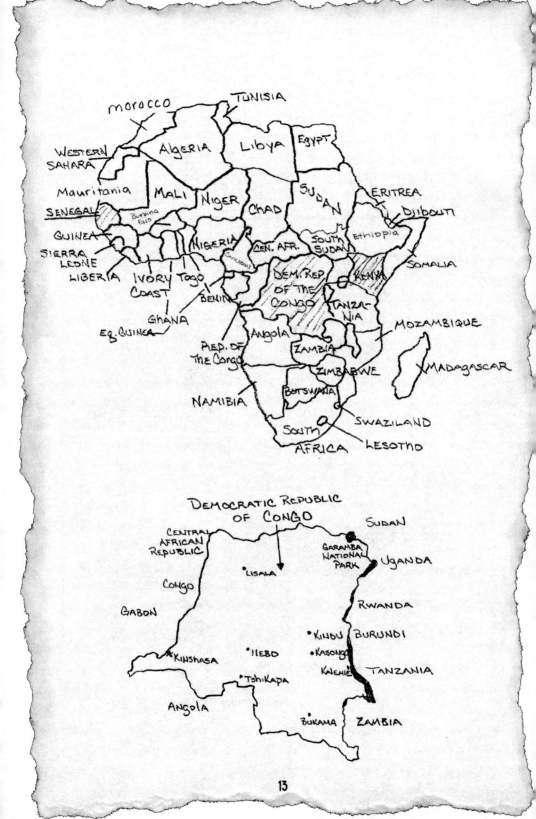

morocco
TUNISIA
WESTERN
SAHARA
Algeria
Libya
Egypt
Mauritania
MaLi
Niger
Burkina
Faso
Chad
SUDAN
ERITREA
DJIBOUTI
SENEGAL
GUINEA
Nigeria
CEN. AFR.
Cameroon
South
SUDAN
Ethiopia
SOMALIA
SIERRA
LEONE
LIBERIA
IVORY
Coast
Togo
BENIN
DEM. REP
OF THE
CONGO
KENYA
TANZA-
NIA
GHANA
Eq. GUINEA
Angola
REP. OF
The Congo
ZAMBIA
ZIMBABWE
MOZAMBIQUE
MADAGASCAR
NAMIBIA
BOTSWANA
SWAZILAND
South
AFRICA
LESOTHO

DEMOCRATIC REPUBLIC
OF CONGO

CENTRAL
AFRICAN
REPUBLIC
SUDAN
GARAMBA
NATIONAL
PARK
UGANDA
CONGO
• LISALA
GABON
RWANDA
BURUNDI
• KINDU
• KINSHASA
• ILEBO
• KASONGO
TANZANIA
• TShiKapa
KALEMIE
ANGOLA
• BUKAMA
ZAMBIA

NEEMA

Democratic Republic of Congo

The Second Congo War began in August 1998 in the Democratic Republic of Congo and officially ended in July 2003 when the transitional government took power. The largest war in modern African history, it directly involved eight African nations. In the aftermath, nearly 5.4 million people were killed, starved, or brutally murdered.

Neema, a Banyamulenge Tutsi widow, narrates her horrific ordeals as a prisoner of war and as a survivor of the August 13, 2004 genocide at the Gatumba Refugee Camp. A force of armed combatants, many of them members of the National Forces of Liberation (FNL), massacred at least 152 Congolese civilians and wounded another 106. Neema recounts how she survived the horrifying ordeal.

BEFORE THIS, I lived a calm, quiet existence. Although I am fortunate to be where I am today, I've experienced many difficulties in the last twenty years. Twice, I have survived intense traumas that should have claimed my life. It was by the grace of God that I did not perish.

Every time I tell my story, I feel very bad. It makes me physically ill. It takes me back to these very traumatic experiences and it is inexplicably difficult for me to recount these memories. These were horrible and shocking experiences. I am telling my story with the hope that someone can help the orphaned children who remain as a result of Gatumba. I miss and worry about them so often. I am telling it because I hope someone will understand what my people have experienced.

I was born in what is now called the Democratic Republic of Congo (DRC) in a town called Mulenge. I was a farmer, like many others who are part of my ethnic group, the Banyamulenge Tutsi. As a young woman, I got married and had five children. Sadly, two of them passed away. I am very thankful that I still have my son and two daughters. They mean so much to me. Two of my children passed away because we did not have access to a hospital nearby and couldn't get them to one in time. In my country, some villages do not have hospitals and you have to travel many miles to the nearest city for medical care. This is a common problem for women and prevents them from getting the care they need. Years after my children died, I lost my husband to the war and I am still a widow.

One day just before the war started in 1998 my husband went traveling for business. He decided to take a large number of cattle to several cities in the states of Shaba and Katanga in Congo and sell them in exchange for money or gold. He traveled with a group and they left the city of Kalemie with the cattle and moved on to another city called Moba where they collected the rest of the herd. Their final destination was Lubumbashi, the second largest city in the country, where they would sell the herd. After they sold the herd, he and the others were planning to retrace their route to Moba and back to Kalemie. Unfortunately tragedy struck before they left Lubumbashi. There was a massacre instigated by a rebel group called the Mai-Mai and my poor husband was in the middle of the city and was killed. At the time, I was devastated that the tragic massacre had left me a widow. Little did I know that losing him was only the beginning of my suffering and that of other Banyamulenge Tutsi.

In my country, when the father in the family dies it is very hard for a widow to support her family. Tradition dictates that the father of the family holds all of the money. In my country most people don't use banks to hold their money, either. My husband's killers stole the money from the sale of the cattle he had just made, leaving our family destitute. None of my late husband's money was given to me.

After my husband died, there was so much pressure and I was under such stress that sometimes I would faint because it was too much for me to process. There was too much grief for my heart and with all the worry I felt helpless. I didn't know how I would take care of my children. I didn't know what to do or even what I could do. I was scared that the war and the massacres would continue. Unfortunately, they did.

In the aftermath of all of this, my son had to go outside the country to find work in order to help the family. Once he was gone, I was responsible for everything in the house, including my two remaining daughters. Life was very difficult and I lost all of my willpower and hope for the future. After my son left, the war started again just as I feared.

LIFE IN JAIL

One evening in the fall of 1998, I was home washing dishes. I did not realize that a call to violence and derogatory propaganda against the Banyamulenge Tutsi was being spread throughout the town and on the radio. Roadblocks were hastily set up and mass violence broke out. The Mai-Mai and other rebel groups, including another called the Interahamwe took me and all the other Banyamulenge Tutsi in Kalemie and put us in jail. The Interahamwe were responsible for the Genocide in Rwanda in 1994. In 1998, they came to the DRC and continued their war crimes. I was taken from my home and forced by soldiers onto a truck filled with other Tutsis and taken far outside of the city of Kalemie to jail. Fortunately, my two daughters escaped to a village called Vyura, so they did not have to experience this awful jail.

Before everyone was taken to jail, the soldiers took certain people and they were hanged and whipped. The Mai-Mai, Interahamwe, non-Tutsi residents of Kalemie, and the prison guards were trying to exterminate us all. The killers would just look at your face and the shape of your nose and if they suspected you to be a Tutsi then you would die or go to jail. It was that simple. There was no argument or debate. Death was inevitable.

I had no contact with my children during the month I was in jail. I was thinking about them all the time. I prayed that they were safe.

In the jail, the women, men, and children were kept in separate cells. We were all afraid of each other because no one knew why we were there. The women were wary of the men because we were afraid of being raped. We did not know if we could trust anyone. We had no information and no understanding of what was happening at the time.

For the entire month that we remained in prison, we were given little to no food or water. I was very worried for my family, deeply depressed, and hungry all the time. All of us were very quiet because we were afraid if we said anything we would attract attention and the soldiers and prison guards would kill us. The conditions at the prison were absolutely horrible. Many chilling and horrifying things happened at the jail and I had to bear witness to all of it. There was one woman who was pregnant and her baby was born in the prison. The guards just took the baby from her and never gave it back. We believe that they killed the baby. It was their way of emotionally manipulating us through torture. One day, I witnessed a prison guard stab a woman with a knife and watched it come out the other side of her body. This was only happening because we were Tutsi.

Every morning, the guards would come and tell us to make a line. They would count everybody—one, two, three, four, five—and tell those people to expect to be killed the next day. They did this for the entire month we were there to manipulate us with fear. The guards told us that food and water were not necessary for us in the prison because we would all be dead in a few days. They did not believe Tutsis were worth anything.

Toward the end of that month, they took people out of the jail and began to load them onto military trucks. They put all the men on one truck and I was put on another truck with the other women and the children. They drove us to a steep cliff and herded the men to a precipice and started pushing them over the edge. The man in charge was just pushing men off the cliff and watching, as they would tumble through the air to the ground below.

For those men who were not pushed over the cliff, the guards tied cords around their ankles, wrists, and arms, binding them, and then hit them with a sledgehammer on their foreheads, cracking their skulls. The guards dug a massive hole in the prison yard and dumped the bodies of all the men on top of each other. I watched it happen. It took them three days to kill all of the men, about seventy-eight men in total. The guard was calling everyone's name, because they had lists of the names of every Tutsi in the city. It was like a death roll call. They massacred all the men at this time. It was their time to die.

After that, the prison guards told the women, "We're going to kill you tomorrow, so be prepared to die. All of you will be dead tomorrow." They told us that five o'clock was the time the rest of us would die.

At five o'clock, they brought all of us into a hall. My spirit was so weak that I was not afraid. For the entire month, I had believed tomorrow was my last day, so I never became frightened. They had often warned us that we would be killed. How could we know if this would be the time? I lost all hope at one point. Knowing that death could happen at any minute meant I was no longer afraid of it. When the Mai-Mai and guards would come into the jail to kill, the prisoners begged for death. They pleaded, "Please kill me! Please kill me!" Sometimes death holds more promise than life. Despite the emotional manipulation and the horrible conditions in the prison, I was very fortunate because I was able to stay alive thanks to the Rwandan soldiers who came by helicopter and landed in the prison yard. They started to fight with the Mai-Mai and eventually the Mai-Mai ran in fear and left us women all behind in prison. We were spared, and right on time!

During the entire time I was held in prison, only one woman was killed. No one knew why she was taken, but I remember the day that the soldiers came and took her. She never returned and no one knew what happened to her but I can only imagine. I thought of her the night the Rwandan military came carrying torches and searching through the jail to rescue us. They never found the body of the woman, only the bodies of the seventy-eight men.

I was freed from prison. But once free, I still had to worry about the Mai-Mai and the other groups who disliked and targeted the Banyamulenge Tutsis. We were not really free because there was no protection and we were looking over our shoulders in fear every day. People were watching everything my people did. The Mai-Mai and Interahamwe killed so many people. I can't remember the number but it was too many.

After jail, all the Tutsi were brought to a village called Uvira and also to Rwanda. I stayed in Uvira where the United Nations High Commissioner for Refugees (UNHCR) helped us set up tents so we could live peacefully. After I was reunited with my children, we remained in Uvira until 2004, when problems for the Tutsi arose again, forcing us to flee to Burundi.

GATUMBA MASSACRE

Life was too difficult in Democratic Republic of Congo, with threats against the Tutsi rising again. Although Uvira was a nice place to live, we feared for our safety. In 2004, the situation had become so bad for the Tutsi that I fled with my son and one of my daughters to Burundi settling nervously into a refugee camp called Gatumba. We felt more secure in the camp, but it's common knowledge that if someone wants to kill you, they will find you no matter how far you run. After two months, on a Friday night, the evil came. They came in the form of civilians and soldiers who desired to exterminate all of the Banyamulenge Tutsi in the Gatumba refugee camp.

It was the night of August 13, 2004, when four groups entered the camp: the Mai-Mai and the Interahamwe came with the Forces Armées Congolaise *(FAC)* and the Forces Nationales de Libération (FNL). Fortunately, my son had just returned to Uvira one week before this happened and my other daughter was also not with us. I was in my tent with my youngest daughter, the only one of my children who was with me at the time. I heard a large group of people entering the camp beating drums and singing pleasant songs. They were carrying machetes and other weapons. In only a few hours, they killed more than 166 camp residents, most of them women and children. They wanted to finish us. As the camp was being attacked, the only place I could hide was under the dying bodies of other people. I just allowed their lifeless bodies to fall on top of me. There were five, six, then ten bodies on top of me. Everyone who tried to run away was brutally murdered.

It was a scene from a horrible nightmare. The soldiers did whatever they could to kill. They were shooting people or using machetes, grenades, even gasoline to kill people. They would pour the gasoline on someone, light a match, and set the person on fire. Many people were burned alive. By the end of the massacre, there were twelve bodies on top of my daughter and me. I hid under the dead and dying bodies from midnight until six o'clock in the morning. I was too afraid to move or make a sound for fear that the killers still roamed the camp. I just stayed there under the pile of bodies to avoid detection. I did not want the killers to know that I was still alive or they would have killed me, too. I was not physically hurt, but my heart and soul were forever wounded.

The next morning, an ambulance came to take the survivors to a hospital. There was blood everywhere and bodies in piles, lifeless and limp. I was covered in blood but the relief workers eventually realized that I was alive. I was very much in shock.

I was taken to the hospital but I didn't know where I was. My mind was lost. All the night I cried out, screaming. I was having nightmares and cold sweats. I knew the hospital staff was around me, but their voices sounded far away from me like echoes in the distance. I was lost in another world; a nightmare.

After the hospital, the only thing I could think about was going to help the children who had been orphaned in the massacre. That was what my life became. It made me feel better to help the children and they needed someone to take care of them. There was a one-year-old baby who needed a mother and I became his mother. Other people helped us as well. I know one pastor who took in many children. He was not a rich man and did not have the financial ability to support all of these children; he just did what he could. He is still in Burundi taking care of fifty-nine orphans. He was not in the camp the night of the massacre. He was in Bujumbura, the capital city of Burundi. He is a man of God and that is why he takes care of these children. The children call the pastor "papa" and the women who care for them "mother." The children became like family to us. We were all they had.

I still think about those orphaned children. I know they have many problems and don't have enough people to take care of them and give them everything they need. Even after I moved to the United States, they still call me from the camp to talk to me. It breaks my heart to feel so powerless. I am praying that one day someone will help me to help them. They are so far away from me now. I don't speak English and am slowly adjusting to my new life in America. It is an awful feeling when you know someone is suffering and you feel powerless to help them.

REUNITING WITH HER CHILDREN AND ARRIVAL IN THE UNITED STATES

I left the camp in Burundi along with one of my daughters and we were soon reunited with my other daughter and my son at a refugee visa interview. You cannot imagine how beautiful it was to see my son and other daughter after being separated from them for so long. I had not known if they were dead or alive until that day. We, as a family, had the option to interview for a refugee visa and were told if we were chosen, then we would receive resettlement in the United States. There were only a certain amount of interviewees chosen for the visas, so we were praying to receive them and thanks to God, we did.

We moved to the United States within the following year as refugees. Now we are all together again and I thank God for that every day. My children are all I have in the world.

I know I am in America now, but I think too much about the orphaned children, families, and the rest of the Banyamulenge who are left behind and still suffer. Sometimes, when I think too much about their suffering, I remember too much about my own. I am very quiet about everything. Sometimes, I don't eat or sleep because of these terrible memories. I have erratic mood swings during the day so I take medication for that and a pill to help me sleep. I am troubled by the fact that there is nothing I can do now to help these children in Burundi. It is also hard for me to go out of my house and see people all around living a normal life. Although my life is so much better now, in many ways it is still a struggle.

I still experience pain from what happened. I still have memories and I still talk to those children I left behind. I don't know if I will ever be the same as I was before this happened to me, but at least now my family is living safely in the United States. At least I know none of my family will ever have to experience these atrocities again. If that is the blessing that I have, then I am thankful for it.

NEEMA'S ADVICE FOR WOMEN

Life is for God. There are a lot of testimonies, but it is only God who knows the lives of the women. My testimony is for the women and the children because, after the husband dies, no one is there to help women or take care of them. After this happened to me, I became very strong. I had to. I hope God will help the women survive everywhere in the world.

PAULINE

Cameroon

Pauline was born in Cameroon and grew up with child abuse, rape, and poverty. Despite all her experiences, she discusses her willpower to move and excel beyond the life she was born into.

IF I ONLY knew what was coming when I was born, I would have chosen not to be in my father's family.

I was born in a country called Cameroon, in a small village named Nkoumadzap, twenty-five kilometers from Yaoundé, the capital of Cameroon. My mother says that she did not have time to walk twenty-five kilometers to the capital city Yaoundé, so I was not born in a hospital. I was born in a cocoa field and wrapped in macabo leaves. During her labor, two farmers assisted her and afterward I was taken to the hospital. I am the second child of seven children. I have five brothers and one older sister. I was born as a member of the Beti-Pahuin group and the subgroup is Beti. My family speaks Ewondo, one of the most common dialects of the languages spoken by the Beti in Cameroon.

According to my mother, I was a small, strong, alert, and very ugly baby who cried a lot. There was nothing she could do to stop my crying. I was always sick and did not eat very well, so my mother had to carry me everywhere on her back like a little monkey. For that reason, I was nicknamed Okende (small monkey). I developed a strong mind and was rebellious from infancy.

For two months after my birth, I was the girl with no name. Like other things in my life, my name came with a lot of struggles. According to Beti culture, a baby is to be immediately named by the father who is also the first person to hold the baby after birth. The naming of the child is symbolic of welcoming a new member into the family and is also a way for the father to accept the newborn child. In our culture, a married woman cannot name her child. She needs her husband's permission. Because my mother already had a girl with the birth of my older sister, my father wanted the next child to be a boy. When I was born, I was viewed as a disappointment and my mother as a failure since she could not produce boys. My birth and arrival was what started the destruction of her marriage to my father.

At the time of my birth, most African men within the Beti sub-group still believed that the mother determined the sex of a child. Many African women were accused of being incapable of producing boys and they were forced to let their husband take another wife who would be able to produce boys. To be considered a powerful wife, your firstborn should be a boy. That way you would not have to share your husband with another woman. Unfortunately for my mother, she had my sister first.

My mother always said that the trouble in paradise started when I was born. Not only was I not welcomed into the family and remained nameless for months, it also took my father nearly a year to hold me in his arms. After several months, my grandmother's older sister came and named me after herself. I was named Evina Marie Seraphine Pauline. Finally, the child that nobody would name had a name.

When I was seven years old, we were forced to leave our little village because my father was physically abusive. He was constantly beating and traumatizing us so my mother decided to save her life and her children's lives and leave him.

My mother's decision was very courageous. Even though most African women are physically and emotionally abused by their husbands, they cannot leave because of our culture. Many women come from abusive situations in their own families and have seen their mothers abused by their fathers and yet their mother never left. To some, physical abuse by the husband is interpreted as a sign of love.

It is also taboo for a woman to divorce. The cultural practices of the majority of Africans prohibit divorce. Divorced women are shunned and singled out by the community. The act of divorce brings shame upon the woman's family and her mother is seen as a bad mother, an incapable person, and a failure in the community. No woman wants to bring such trauma to their family so they stay with the abusive husband until one of them is dead. Culturally, it is difficult for women to file for divorce in African society. Most people believe that divorce is for European cultures and that the marriage is a family affair, not something up for the government's jurisdiction.

Yet by the time I was seven years old, my mother had taken enough abuse. She took us four kids to stay with our dear grandmother for almost a year before the community of Nkoumadzap convinced my father to come and get us and leave my mother. My grandmother did not want us to leave but she did not have the power to fight tradition and my mother did not have any support except for my grandmother. When my father showed up to take us there was nothing they could do. We were taken to his "torture camp" where we were at the mercy of a man without any feelings for us.

To fully understand the extent of the torture we endured at the hands of our father, it is best for me to describe him. My father is six feet tall and weighs about 170 pounds. He is the third child of four in a family of two boys and two girls. He had brown skin, brown eyes, and black hair. He was a good-looking African man and was always desired by women. He was also very spoiled as a child and was used to other people taking care of him. He never learned to do anything for himself. He was a player.

After my father took us from my mother, he moved out of our house and went to live with a woman fifteen years older than him. Soon after, we went to live with him and this woman. She owned a house and was working as a secretary for a manufacturing company. She was very beautiful and she had the heart of a mother. Even though she did not have kids of her own, she loved us and took care of us all. Yet, that relationship was just the beginning of our father's distancing himself from his wife and children.

After that woman left us, he moved us into a house shared with several other people. He just dumped us there and went back to live with the woman. He only came to visit every once in a while until he finally broke up with her. Then he came to live in the house with us, gave himself the nicest room, and left us in a very dirty, small room. Another man who shared the same house with us had a sister and my dad fell in love with her. After that, we were moved into a very abusive situation with that woman and her three kids. Eventually, when I was nine years old, I went to live with my mother because his abuse was so bad. But leaving his home did not stop the abuse.

The big problem was that my father would visit my mother regularly and force her to perform her sexual duties. If the sex was not to his liking he would beat her. During my father's visits, my siblings and I were not allowed to play, talk, ask questions, eat, or move. You can imagine how impossible it was for us to stay still for hours.

I was not my father's favorite child, so it was easy for him to find a reason to come after me. I think he experienced some kind of pleasure in beating his children, especially in beating my younger brother and me. My father thought that using a belt or spanking a child was a game. To him, grabbing me by my small legs and slamming me on the ground or shoving my head into the wall was proportional to whatever I did to offend him. I cannot remember how many times I passed out due to his beatings and had to be revived with cold water. After a while, I developed resistance to the violence. Believe it or not, his punishment did not stop me from doing things he forbade me from doing. I decided I would do what I wanted, take the beating, and move on to the next thing.

I have a lot of scars on my body. Each one of them represents the "love" of my father. The beatings I endured also led to my being nearly blind in one eye. From his treatment, I learned to stand on my own two feet and fight for what I want in life. Later in my adult life, I used that lesson to survive in a country that gave me more than life.

In my adult years, because of my father's beatings and the emotional abuse I suffered from him, I am always in a state of fear and stress concerning anything that I do. I have very low self-esteem. I am not able to be creative due to the fact that I was not allowed to play or have any kind of fun when I was a child. I was not able to express my opinions, ask anything of my father, or move around when he was near me. It is by the grace of God that I survived the hardships of my early childhood. I think I am a winner. As I emerged into my teenage years, many other situations arose that changed me. But my father's abuse had already built a thick outer shell.

MY EVOLVING TEEN YEARS

My teen and adolescent years were times where I learned a lot about myself. After I returned to live with my mother when I was about nine years old, we bounced from shack to shack because she had such a rough time supporting me and my four other siblings. What makes my teen years particularly memorable is the fact that I was able to see beyond my circumstances and set the course for the rest of my life. I was able to take care of myself and to help my mother with my siblings by selling things or braiding hair since my mother was working as a housekeeper trying to support us. Besides working, I also had different groups of friends and even started to have fun and learn more about life. It was at the age of fourteen years that I learned that the brutality of men went beyond that of my father.

I became involved with a group of friends, the first I'd ever had outside my family. They were older, wiser, and bolder than I was. They were able to tell me things that my mother did not want me to know. I was learning through mistakes I saw them make. At that time, because I was younger, I was a messenger girl to many of them. I was always carrying a message to a married man or protecting someone's secret that they did not want other people to know. I came to believe that a secret is a secret when nobody else is aware of it. Even today, I keep to myself, but I am about to reveal something painful that resulted from my days as a messenger girl. I never told anyone about it because I felt they would not believe me and would blame me. So here it is: I was raped.

The man who raped me was in the Cameroon army and was in a very powerful position. When the president of Cameroon would walk around, this man was the one standing behind him. He was a responsible officer and was very respected among his friends and family. His wife was my friend. At the time of my rape, she had just given birth and was staying with her mother, as our culture requires a woman stay with her extended family for the first three months after having her first child, especially if the husband has no mother. After many days without seeing her husband, my friend sent me to go and check on him. In those days, there were no cell phones and very few people owned home telephones. Most people communicated by writing letters or sending someone to relay a message directly. In this case, I carried a sealed envelope to my friend's husband. He got the letter and something else—my body.

On my way home, I thought about telling my friend, but I knew the consequences of telling her. Her family was very proud of their new son-in-law. How could I destroy her happiness and her trust in me? Would I be able to live with the guilt of ruining something so good? What would be said about me? Would she believe me?

In Africa, if you are raped, it is always your fault. The fact that I put myself in the vulnerable position to be raped meant that I had to take all the blame, and I have held the pain with me until now. At birth, I was the girl with no name and at age fourteen I became the girl with no face and no voice who was raped. I always worried that I would be asked to deliver a message to him again and that if we were in a secluded area, he would rape me again. When a powerful man takes advantage of a woman like me in my culture, she can't say anything. Everyone would look at me like I was a liar or assume I was trying to destroy his reputation. If I had told my friends, they would have said that I was jealous of my friend's rich husband and that I desired to take him away from her. After all, I was the message girl; who would care if I'd been raped? For two months following that rape, I gravely feared that I was pregnant because my monthly period was late. I was relieved when my menstrual cycle started again.

My silence about my rape has given me a lot of grief over the years, but my friend's happiness seemed more important than my own emotional state. Unfortunately, her marriage ended in divorce. Her husband could not keep his pants zipped and his actions even ultimately resulted in the death of her son. To be honest, I was happy years later when I heard that he'd died of a heart attack, but sad because I did not have a chance to confront him and let him know that he did me wrong. He used his human force, authority, and influence and relied upon my naïve trust and took advantage of me.

A year later, when I was fifteen, I was introduced to a lavish lifestyle and that forever changed me and allowed me to raise my standards and expectations for my life. In each family there are always people who reach the top level and end up with admirers. In my family there is no exception to that rule. My cousins lived in a beautiful city called Douala and I thought they had it all!

Douala is the largest city in Cameroon and it is also the commercial capital of the country. After the Second World War, the city grew rapidly, attracting business and commerce. Douala had the first international airport and was the port of entry as well as the primary port for exportation and importation. For that reason, as a young poor girl, I heard people say that people who lived in Douala were rich, so in my mind, I could not imagine seeing poor people there. At the age of fifteen, I used to visit my second cousin and would, at times, stay for weeks before going back home. I liked visiting because I could take a shower, instead of taking a bath with only ten liters of water. Since there was always electricity, I developed a reading habit. Everyone could do whatever he or she chose without causing problems for the rest of the family in the household.

I assumed that everyone in Douala lived in beautiful homes that were clean and organized. Their children went to good schools, had all the books they needed, and had an after-school teacher. I knew that they all celebrated Christmas with toys and gifts. Each individual had his or her own shoes and clothes. They even had their own beds and didn't have to share beds like we did in my mother's house. Even though many of my friends in Douala had attitudes and were self-centered, arrogant people, I was happy to be part of their group and be given the opportunity to hang out with them. Hanging out with them made me feel like I had moved from the lower class to the middle class. By my midteen years, I was on my way up in this world, determined to change my situation because I knew I could have more in life.

THE SUCCESS CODE

After my visits to Douala, my living standards changed. I returned to Yaoundé and formed "the team group" with my two best friends in my late teen years.

My two best friends and I set some rules to follow in our lives. We were so disappointed by our fathers that we decided to live differently than our mothers. A lot of young girls we knew wanted to marry a man like their fathers by their late teen years. We did not want poor African men who were uneducated because the lifestyle they could afford would leave us with no options or alternatives. So we studied our options and chances of meeting better men and noticed there were a few things we had to do. First priority, we would not go to low-class nightclubs. We knew we would only find low-class boyfriends at those places. Second, we changed our dress code. We decided to dress clean, neat, and conservative yet sexy to attract higher-class men. In Africa, only rich people can enjoy the luxury of books, swimming pools, tennis courts, and other expensive activities, so our third objective was to engage in those activities.

I had a lot of homework to do at first. I had to figure out how to read and speak French, learn how to swim, and take dance lessons. In order to do all of that, I needed money so I had to get a job no matter how low the pay was. My friends and I needed work just to save a few pennies every payday. When there was no work for us, we would sell things on the side of the road to earn some extra money. I worked hard and sold things to scrape together any money I could and was able to save enough for two or three complete outfits, one good bathing suit, and two beautiful pairs of shoes. I will say this, for all women in search of a smart man, you must first be smart yourself. That is the most important lesson when you are looking for a good man. Learn things that attract smart, classy people by reading books, following sports, and learning about economics and politics.

Behave as a civil person by carrying yourself with dignity and pride. When you speak, answer in confidence with what you know but do not speak if you do not know the answer.

I decided to read everything that I could get my hands on. I found that I was enjoying books, so I started reading almost every day. I read everything—newspapers, magazines, and classic novels. I was educating myself so I was able to inform my friends about things that were happening beyond the borders of Cameroon. I knew the leaders of all the European countries, the United States, and the African countries and studied up on major athletes, fashion designers, and thought leaders. When we were in a group with other people, I always had something interesting to say. People used to tell me I was well-informed. African men think that African women can't be well-informed. The real reason why many women are not well-informed is that we lack the opportunity to cultivate ourselves. African women are just as capable as any other women to cultivate knowledge and use it to our advantage.

In Africa, when a young woman portrays herself as smart, intelligent, outspoken, educated, well-groomed, and freethinking, people call her names and try to destroy her. Because of my father's abuse, I was not afraid of what they would say. So I kept educating myself.

My friends and I did not want to date low-class men, so aside from our lifestyle rules, we created rules about the types of men we would date. Most African men do not like a woman who questions their social status, honesty, loyalty, and intelligence. Back then, my friend and I succeeded in eliminating certain groups of men in our lives and that made it difficult to find a good, single, educated man. Life in high-class society can be lonely in Africa, especially when you only have a few members in your circle. My life was about to change dramatically. Soon, I would meet an American man and move to the United States.

FROM GABON TO THE UNITED STATES: MEETING MY HUSBAND

When I was twenty-two, I went to Gabon in West Africa to visit one of my friends. This visit was a much-needed break for my soul. Two years before I went to Gabon, I had traveled to Italy to visit an Italian boyfriend, but returned home to Cameroon since I caught him using drugs. I felt like a failure upon my return since everyone expected me to stay abroad. I was depressed for nearly one year after that trip. The opportunity to go to Gabon was just what I needed! I would never have imagined that during my stay I would meet my husband. During that time, I was given a new and different view of life. I knew that, no matter what, I was going to change my circumstances. I had the ability to think very straight. One of my friends lived in Libreville, the capital city of Gabon, and she told me I could stay with her as long as I wanted. Her husband owned his own company and was doing very well financially, affording her a nice lifestyle, a big house, a driver, and two cars. During my stay, I took care of her children and started to feel like I was moving forward. My friend really supported and encouraged me to pursue new opportunities. I was very comfortable with this living situation.

Ironically, my husband and I both arrived in Libreville in September 1993, only one week apart. We met exactly two weeks after I arrived. People always say that life is full of surprises and I found out that some surprises are remarkable and precious. The day we met, the sun was shining bright. My friend's husband told me to take their child out because he had a business meeting and wanted the house to himself. So I decided to go to the private swimming pool. The pool was at a classy hotel and access to it cost an equivalent of five dollars. Some hotel rooms had a view of the pool and my husband's room was among those rooms. When we got there I did not know that there was a young man looking at people from his hotel room window. According to him, he saw me coming and from the moment he laid eyes on me, he knew he wanted to talk to me. He put on his bathing suit and joined the swimmers in the pool, immediately befriending the child whom I was with. As a protective aunty, I had to make sure that she did not talk to strangers so I approached him. Little did I know that was his plan to lure me in. It worked very well! His name was John and he was American.

After I met John, I did not want to go back home to Cameroon. My friend encouraged me to stay and even got me a job in a café. John and I clicked very quickly and although I spoke no English, I taught him French so we could communicate. After two or three months, John was sent to work in Mayumba and he wanted me to go with him. I was hesitant because it was a remote village and I was so happy to finally be in a big city. John was feeling lonely there by himself so I eventually agreed to go. We stayed there together for almost one year and our relationship grew even stronger.

When we returned to Libreville, I got a visa to travel to the United States through his classmate who worked in the embassy. I worried that traveling to his home with him meant that things were moving too quickly and I was not sure if our relationship would last. I worried that something would happen to us when he took me to the United States since I did not speak English and was not educated. I saw his family in pictures and assumed that they were all rich. He told me that his family had never really been close to a black person and I was shocked since we always saw beautiful African American women in the media. I was scared to meet them after that. I feared when I came to the United States he would abandon me. Funnily enough, he secretly thought I would abandon him. We both had the same fears but never talked about them.

Before I left for the United States in August 1994, John and I traveled to Cameroon. I was hesitant to introduce him to my family, especially my father. My concerns ended up being very valid! Upon meeting him, my father, assuming John was rich because he is a white American, treated John like he was his personal bank account. My father did not ask John anything about himself. He did not care about John's hobbies or interests. Instead, less than an hour after they met, my dad wanted John to buy him a watch and a new car. I was horrified by his selfish behavior and relieved that we were moving to the United States. Little did I know, many years later my father's indecent selfishness would resurface when I returned to Cameroon for my wedding celebration.

I have to say that most young girls have dreams about their future and about what they strive to become in their lives. Some of them dream about being a doctor, a princess, a mother, a politician, or a big lawyer. For me, there was no sense in having fancy dreams of the future when you are forced to survive day by day. When I was growing up, I did not have the luxury to lie flat in my bed and dream about the future. Everything was so uncertain for me. What I needed the most was a place to sleep, a decent meal, and an education like everybody else my age. Africa could not give me those luxuries.

You can imagine when I flew to New York in August 1994 that these memories of my tumultuous upbringing were racing through my mind. It was such a long trip! I ended up getting sick in the plane. I had to fly from Africa to New York, New York to Phoenix, then from Phoenix to San Diego. I was a nervous wreck—I could not sleep or eat. I am a small woman and when I worry it affects every part of me. My biggest fear was failing in my relationship and having to return to Cameroon. I worried John would already have a girlfriend or a wife here. I was used to African men.

By the time I arrived in San Diego, I was very tired and scared that John would not be waiting for me. I was dressed in traditional African clothes that he had bought for me back in Gabon and my heart raced with anticipation to see him. He was there as he had promised.

He took me to his mother's house and she was so excited to see me. She hugged me and I knew from the beginning that she truly wanted me there. She had traveled to Africa before so she was very happy to welcome me to the new country. She asked me if I wanted to eat but my nerves were on fire and I had no appetite. In my culture, if you are offered food and you refuse it, it is an insult; so I ate a little bit although I was not hungry. Then I took a shower and went to sleep. I awoke in the morning to sprinklers in their garden and was amazed to see water shooting up in the air. I had never seen sprinklers before. We stayed in San Diego for a week or two and then we left to move to Oakland, California.

John was very honest with me though the process. He had informed me that he did not have a job and that we were going to start a new life from scratch. In the beginning of that new life, we lived in a bedroom and did not even have a bed! We borrowed the mattress we slept on from the manager of our apartment building and borrowed money from John's mother. I told John that I knew how to braid hair and that I could do that during the day while he went to school. There were so many uncertainties and because of that I was frightened. Yet I felt safe being with John. No matter what happened, I was happy to be with him. I felt so good all the time that I did not care that we were sleeping on the floor. Coming from Africa, I was used to that.

When John would leave to go to school I had to find my way around the city of Oakland. I did not know how to read maps or the street signs so in the evenings I would ask him to show me. I set goals for myself every day and learned to walk from my apartment to certain landmarks in the downtown area. I also started braiding hair seven days a week at home. Each day, after finishing work, I would walk a little in Oakland to acquaint myself with the city and observe my surroundings.

One thing that particularly shocked me when I arrived in the United States was identifying people who were poor. Growing up in poverty, I was accustomed to a certain low standard of living and was shocked to see that poor people in America have electricity, home telephones, color televisions, and running water. From the perspective of a young lady from Africa, there are no "poor" people here. Being poor in Cameroon meant that I did not have running water in my home and did not see a water fountain until I was a teenager when the Cameroon government was able to install running water in most districts of Yaoundé. I used to walk two miles on foot to get drinking water. Electricity was also only for rich people. We had one small kerosene lamp and my mother used to light it late to save fuel. I did not see a telephone until I was about twenty years old and I certainly did not know how to use it. I was very surprised to hear that someone can speak to another person who is far away and even in another country. No one in my family had a car, but I did know what one was. I used to think that you had to be Bill Gates to own a car. Yet in Oakland, California, there were cars everywhere! Even poor people had them! That said, I never really felt poor in my life with John.

As time progressed, our lives gradually improved. I started to attend school to work as a nurse and John was working in a restaurant at night and attending school during the day. He was also working as a substitute teacher. I finally felt like I'd arrived—I'd found the most ideal life for myself. I was pursuing an education, I had a wonderful husband, and I'd moved to a new country to thrive in. I was blessed and I was grateful every day for everything.

DOWRY AND MY FATHER'S DEMANDS

John and I had two weddings in the United States, one in 1996 in civil court and another in 1997 that was a very religious, traditional catholic ceremony. When these marriages took place, I had no relationship with my father and I did not speak with him until nearly ten years after. My family did not participate in these ceremonies as they were held in the United States.

In 2007, I received a call informing me that everyone from my village wanted my siblings and me to reconcile with my father. My father called me and we spoke for the first time in twenty years. He said that he desired to make peace with me. I felt that this occurrence would give me an opportunity to respect my culture, so I initiated a form of dowry for myself. My culture is a dowry culture, meaning when a woman gets married, her future husband is expected to pay the family money in order to marry her. She also throws a big party and feeds the whole village. I promised my village that I would return and give them food to celebrate my wedding and meet the requirements of my dowry.

So I returned to Nkoumadzap, Cameroon, in 2011 to make peace with my dad, see my family, and allow them to participate in a ceremony in honor of my marriage. I returned without John because I did not want people to try to exploit him, which is what my father had attempted to do when he met John in 1994. I did not want my father anywhere near my husband. The rest of my family are good people and I still wanted to participate in my culture and not appear too westernized when I interacted with them. I asked people to make a list of what they wanted as a dowry. I said that I would give people food to celebrate but that I was not giving anybody a motorcycle or a suit. My dad wrote how much money each dowry envelope should contain then asked me to forget about everyone else in my village back home and buy him a Mercedes car and a house. I asked him why I would do that when I already told a whole village that I would give them food. I could not believe he wanted me to erase all those people just to give him a Mercedes!

Knowing how I feel about my father, you can imagine that I was against paying him anything or buying anything for him. I am not against my culture, but considering how my father treated my siblings and me, I didn't see why he deserved the money.

I respect a father who takes care of his children, loves them, and puts them through school. You don't have to be rich to love your children. It is natural for children to seek approval from their fathers, so I was greatly impacted by my father's rejection and abusive treatment. When you don't get love from your father, you never feel that you are good enough. I felt that way my entire life. If I was not good enough, why did I succeed in my life? I succeeded on my own without any help from my father. Why would I force my husband to pay my father a dowry for me? My father did not help me succeed.

Many African families want their daughters to marry white men because they believe it will make them rich. They only want to exploit white men as a source of wealth. American families are about individualism; your father may have money but that doesn't mean he will give it to you and instead may require that you earn if for yourself. Not all white men are rich. My father does not understand this. If he was a good father, I would have tried to explain this aspect of American culture to him. But for a man who had rejected me from the moment I took my first breath, a man who physically abused me so badly that I almost lost my eyesight, he didn't deserve the luxury of an explanation, in my opinion. He is a very selfish man. My visit back home in 2011 resulted in a party for my village and food to celebrate my life. My father got nothing.

When I returned to the United States I got into a fight with my father and we are not speaking to this day. I do not let John talk to him, either. If he wants to talk to my husband, he has to go through me. Living in the United States has made me more linear in dealing with the people back home, especially with my father and brothers. I have five brothers. Some of them are hard workers and some of them are lazy. They ask me for money, but most have done nothing to deserve it. If they were trying to advance in life and were struggling, I would have no problem helping them. One of my brothers lies on a couch all day and yet he wants me to give him money. My father used to call me and tell me stories about things my brother needed and try to guilt me for not giving him money. One day, my father called and told me my brother's child was in the hospital. He said that

I should send money. I explained to him that he is the father and the grandfather, and asked why he doesn't send money to the child if the situation is so desperate. I bluntly said, "I did not fuck that woman. Why should I have to pay for that child?" Then my father told me that the child was named after me though my brother had never told me that. Some of my brothers assume they can play and do whatever they want because at the end of the month, I am going to pay the bills. They are wrong. I will not pay people who are lying around doing nothing. At this point, I have had enough of this behavior and the entitlement that some of the people back home have.

My dad victimized me from the day I was born, and as an adult, I have always told myself that I would never be a victim. When you have many hardships in your life, they tend to follow you. But you can always try to make the best of things and see what life has to offer. I got help from God. God gave me a new country where I could try my best to succeed. I am thankful for that. I am very thankful. I owe God more than anything. I also owe many thanks to my husband who is very supportive. From the beginning, he motivated me to go to school. I got a degree in nursing which gave me the opportunity to earn a good living.

Looking back at my upbringing gives me a lot of motivation. I am so happy with myself and I want to hug my husband because he did so much for me. It is because of him that I am where I am now and I appreciate him for that. I think I love my husband more every day. Every day I grow older with him, I appreciate all the opportunities he brought into my life and everything he has done for me.

PAULINE'S ADVICE FOR WOMEN

I have fallen down many times in my life, but here is what I have learned: When you fall down and wait for someone else to pick you up, you will get walked on before you will get any help. So when you fall, get up and dust yourself off. If you lie there complaining about how you fell and don't get up and figure things out for yourself, you will stay on the ground. I will always get up, dust myself off, and keep walking. The girl with no name has come a long way. My father did not give me a name. I have earned my name by being a fighter and by being strong. My name is Pauline Evina.

I would like to tell all women to be stubborn, sassy, and smart. Set goals, keep a realistic perspective on your life, and don't expect things to fall from the sky for you because they will not. Don't be a victim. Don't put yourself down.

BINETA

Senegal

Bineta was awarded the opportunity to get a college education in the United States. Shortly after arriving, she became a victim of human trafficking and was forced into intensive labor by a family member. Her story describes how she found the means to free herself and pursue her dreams through realizing her own strength and great determination.

A T THIS POINT, having the opportunity to tell my story is like opening a door. I have never spoken about it, but I feel that now I must. Too many women are uneducated or have no access to education in this world and suffer because of it. I want my story to illustrate why women need an education. If there is anything in the world that I wish for, it is for all women to be educated. Muhammad, the prophet of Islam, said, "Go and seek knowledge, even if you have to go all the way to another land, because that is the only power that you have."

I am from Senegal, a small country in West Africa next to Mali, Guinea, and Mauritania. I came to the United States when I was twenty years old with the promise of getting a quality education. I had no idea how difficult my journey would be! All of my struggles on that path have made me into the woman I am today. I hope my story shows how important it is to educate women.

EARLY LIFE IN SENEGAL: PROMISE OF AN EDUCATION

I grew up in a very large, very poor Muslim family. My mother and father made it clear to me that education was the only thing that could set me free. From a very early age, education was my priority. Girls in Africa are often overlooked for education and parents prefer to keep them home to work in the house. When my mother was teaching me how to cook, my father came to the kitchen and told my mother, "Leave her alone. This girl is not a kitchen girl, this girl is a book girl." When I gave him my schoolwork with A+ marks, he told me that I could do better. Even though I told him that I could not do any better and explained that I was doing the best I could, he said, "You can always do more."

I have five brothers, one sister, and one adopted sister who is more like a daughter to me. My father lost his mother when he was sixteen and was left with nine siblings that he had to care for. At age sixteen, he was forced to quit school and raise his family by himself. I grew up witnessing the tight family bond that his sacrifice and devotion created. My uncle and my aunt had no one but my mother to rely on. When I grew up, I often saw my mother and my father struggling, but my mother used to tell me, "Bineta, I don't care what I have to do. I will do whatever it takes to make sure that you have a quality education." From a young age, I knew

I wanted to be educated and understood that a good education was also my family's goal for me.

As a young girl in Africa, I lived a life sheltered by my large, extended family. In Africa, if you are not married then you always have your family no matter how old you are. That is how I learned about giving to people and developed a strong sense of community. I remember when I was nine years old I began to realize the importance of giving to others. I started helping the little *talibé* children from my country. The *talibé* beg in the street and many of them are orphans. Even though we were very poor, my father and I used to take the children to our house, give them clothes, and make sure they had something to eat. That is where I first realized the importance of giving back to society. It is interesting how generous the poor can actually be.

After I received my high school diploma, I had a talk with my father and he said, "Bineta, you are all we have. You are nineteen years old and we don't have any hope except you. We want you to get an education and do amazing things in your life." When he told me that, I felt like the weight of the world was on my nineteen-year-old shoulders. He told me that my family was willing to make a huge sacrifice for me to go to college. My mother has twenty-six siblings and my father has nine. Out of all of them, I am the only woman to go to college.

Around this time, my relative offered to help me get a student visa to come to the United States to study at a university. I did not believe him at first. I felt that I was not special enough to be given that opportunity. For a girl from Africa, that is like a dream come true. My relative did what he promised and when my student visa application was approved for a college in Cincinnati, Ohio, my mother was holding me and crying. She was beside herself with absolute joy. She said to me, "Bineta, I know you will go far one day. When you were born and your grandfather held you he said, 'I may not live to see this, but this girl will be so powerful one day.' He was so proud of you then and would be even prouder today."

I never knew my grandfather because he passed away when I was five years old. My mother never believed what he'd said until I was leaving to go to the United States. She told me that one day I would be a strong woman leading many women. I never fully believed her. It was hard for me to believe that I, a simple Muslim girl from Africa, could be a leader. Right after I received my acceptance letter, I went to a local mosque, handed them my passport, and asked them to pray for me so that I could prepare myself for my journey. When I returned home my mother was crying. She told me that she did not have the $800 needed to buy a plane ticket.

The only way that my mother could help me get the ticket was to sell a piece of land that was a part of my inheritance. I went to my bedroom and cried because for them to sell this for me was huge. I felt like it was too much and that I could not take it from them. Not only would I be taking all they had, but I was also taking my siblings' inheritance, too. I went back and told my mother that I could not do that to my brothers and sisters. I said I should stay in Africa, and no matter where I ended up, I would always make the best of my situation.

Despite what I'd said, she decided to sell her jewelry. She sold rings, bracelets, necklaces—everything she had. You have to understand, for African women, jewelry is your value and a symbol of your status. We take gold jewelry very seriously because people are poor and gold is very difficult to come by. It was a big sacrifice for my mother to strip herself of her jewelry for my sake. I remember she came back crying and said, "Bineta, I worked so hard to earn this jewelry and sold it for nothing. They took advantage of me and did not even pay a third of its value. I should feel cheated but for me this is the best day in the world because I can now send you to the United States to study."

My journey to the United States was like realizing my calling. Sometimes you receive a sign, yet you might not understand it is for you. I never once in my life pictured that I would be in the United States. It was a country I never really thought about.

On my final night in Africa, I remember my father came to my room and sat me down and told me that I was the only one in the family to have this opportunity and said he was happy to give me this chance. The whole family said that they believed in me and recognized the change I can bring to the rest of the world, to other women, and to the family.

I left for America the following day with only $200 in my pocket. It was right before Christmas in December of 2002. I arrived in a country I knew little about where people spoke a language that I barely knew. Before I left, my mother gathered more money and gave it to my relative so he could keep it for me. That would end up being a mistake.

INTENSIVE LABOR

After landing in the United States, I was supposed to be staying with my relative's friends until he arrived from Africa. My family allowed this because he was practically raised by my mother. As the eldest, she'd been there for him, helped him get an education, and supported him through high school.

When I arrived, I spoke to my relative on the phone and he told me that even though I had been accepted to a school and had come to the United States to study, I would not be able to go to college until I understood English. He said that he'd arranged for me to work with some of his friends who would take good care of me, so I went to live with them in the state of Michigan. The day after I arrived, things seemed to be okay. I rested a little bit and tried to adjust to my surroundings. I missed my family terribly but was excited to think that I was closer to getting a college education.

At that point, I spoke no English but I was skilled at African-style hair braiding. I could do any style. My relative's friends saw that and put it to their own use. The day after I arrived, they took me to a hair salon and told me that clients were paying $300 for African braids. They said that they would give me half of the money to save for school. Not long after, I began working seven days a week from eight o'clock in the morning until two o'clock the next morning.

I was kept very isolated and was not allowed to go anywhere by myself. In the morning, they would come and pick me up from the apartment where I lived and would drive me straight to the salon. I lived in a one-bedroom apartment with four other girls and paid my portion of the rent out of my earnings. My relative's friends controlled everything we did. At eight o'clock every morning, we were taken out of the house to the hair salon. I would braid women's hair and each job would take me about six to seven hours from start to finish. I would work until two o'clock the following morning and then I would go home. Since I only had a few hours between my long shifts, if the bathroom was full, I did not get to take a shower and if I did not cook, I did not eat. It did not take me long to realize that my relative's friends did not care very much for my well-being.

All of the money I made working was taken by my relative and the people who owned the business. My relative said that he would keep the money for me. He told me that I could not keep it because I did not have any papers and because of my poor language skills and my immigration status, I could not open a bank account. Whenever I got paid, I was instructed to purchase a money order with all my earnings and send it to him in Africa.

In February of 2003, nearly three months after I'd arrived, my relative finally came from Africa to the United States. When he arrived, I was still living in the one-bedroom apartment with the four other girls from work. Shortly after he arrived, I called him and explained that I had come here for an education but instead found myself working full-time. He reassured me and told me that the time would come for me to go to school but that it was not the right time yet. I asked him when it would be the right time and reminded him that the only reason my family had sent me here was to get an education. I told him that the money he was keeping for me was to be used to pay for my education. I asked him to please call the university that I was supposed to attend and make sure that I could get there. He had said that when he came to the United States he would see that I got to school, but he never followed through on that promise.

The people whom I was working for at the hair salon took me from one state to another in the months before I went to live with my relative. Every time they would open a new hair salon they would take me to a different state to work. I started in Detroit, Michigan, and worked in many cities in Michigan before they took me to Montgomery, Alabama. From Alabama, I called my relative again and told him that I was tired and that I did not want to live that life. He told me I would be in school very soon. Yet from Alabama, I was taken to Cincinnati, Ohio where I continued to work braiding hair.

One day, they told me to do someone's hair and, because I was so exhausted, I told them that I could not do the job. Because I refused that one client, I did not get paid for an entire week. I was just too exhausted to work on that person's hair and I lost an entire week's pay because of that. Since I had no money, I had nothing to buy food with to eat. Later, when I returned to the house where I was living, all of my gold jewelry had been taken from my room. I did not feel that I was in a position to say anything to them. I didn't know anything about this country and I was fearful that my relative's friends might hurt me if I brought it up. I felt very vulnerable.

Eventually, I called my relative and told him that I needed to leave and come to live with him, my only family in the United States. I told him what had happened and explained the terrible working and living conditions. He told me not to worry and claimed that he would take care of me, so in August of 2003, I went to live with him. When I arrived at his home, he warned me not to go outside, explaining that American people would kill me for as little as twenty dollars. I saw dead people and drug addicts on television all the time and that gave me the wrong idea about Americans. I was so afraid that I would not go outside. My relative was also clear that I had to pay the rent if I stayed with him. All the money that I earned went to him; I was not in school, and I felt like I was failing my family and myself. It was devastating.

One day during that time, I was doing a woman's braids, and, after talking to her for some time, she said that I was so smart and asked me why I was not in school. I told her that I wanted to go to school but that my relative had said my English was not good enough to attend a university. She told me about English as a Second Language (ESL) classes that would help me learn English. She said that she was an attorney and could help me get to school. She told me to get the name of the university I wanted to attend and said that she would call the school for me.

That night, I went through my relative's things, found the name of the school, and gave all the information to the woman. The next day she called the university on my behalf and found out that I was supposed to have started classes in January 2003, just after I'd arrived in the United States. She also found out that my student visa had expired and told me that I could not be readmitted to the university. I felt like my dream had disappeared; that everything my mother and father had fought so hard for was completely wasted because they had trusted my relative.

That day, I cried and cried. I wondered why I was so unlucky, why I was suffering so much just to go to school, and why it was so hard for me to get a quality education when some other people are even paid to go to school. I told myself no matter what happens I was going to make sure that I went to college. Despite everything, I did not lose hope. I knew that there was something better waiting for me.

When my relative finally arrived home, I confronted him. He had just bought a new Mercedes. I complimented his choice and said it was odd he could afford a car so expensive even though he did not work. He said nothing. I told him that I'd called the school and knew I was supposed to be there nearly eight months ago. I accused him of forcing me to continue braiding hair to pay his expenses. I demanded all the money he was keeping for me and told him that I'd kept track of how much money I'd given to him over the last year and I knew it was about $12,000. He told me, "I'm sorry, Bineta, but there is no money." When I asked him what had happened to all of the money orders I'd sent to him, he said, "Those were gifts you were giving me, don't you remember?"

I felt my world crumble at that moment. I had worked for over a year and had sent all my money to my relative—everything—even the money my mother had scraped together for me before I left Africa. I had been working more than eighteen hours a day every day without any rest or time off, and, because of my relative's greed, I had nothing to show for it. All that time, I had believed I was going places and was on my way to getting an education but that was all just an illusion. Obviously, my relative was only there for himself. I had been so naïve and trusting and now, at twenty years old, alone in a foreign country, I was completely unprepared for all of this.

I went to the Internet to a Senegalese chat room where I started speaking with a guy named Amar. I told him, "I know you are a stranger but I have faith in you." I told him all of my troubles and explained that I wanted to get out. He told me to come to him and explained that he was living in North Carolina. He told me he could help me to go to school if I wanted. I did not even think twice. I did not even consider what danger I might be putting myself in. I did not know Amar, but I was so desperate to get out of my situation that I was willing to do almost anything.

I told my relative that I was leaving. He told me that I needed to pay $700 for bills and the apartment before I left. In my culture, a relative should never ask you for money to pay their bills. If they take you into their home, they are supposed to care for you. It is considered very improper to make such demands. Regardless, I gave him all the money that I had and told him that I would be working for a few more days to pay for a bus ticket and then I would leave.

Soon after, I left my relative's house and went to live with Amar in North Carolina. Although Amar was from Senegal and attending a local university, I really didn't see any other option other than taking a risk and going to another state to live with a man I'd never met. I am a Muslim woman and it was a big leap of faith for me especially since living with a man that you are not married to is frowned upon in my culture. It was also a big leap of faith because I did not know what he was capable of and what his intentions were. Thanks be to Allah, he was very kind, understanding, and respectful; and at that point, he was all I had.

After moving to Amar's house, I went and visited several universities and tried to get into school. Every time I would speak with the admissions people, they would shut the door in my face. They would tell me that I could not attend school because I had overstayed my visa in the United States. This was very painful for me to hear because I felt like I was not smart enough, good enough, or driven enough to have a quality education. The more I tried, the more I realized there was more to it than just being smart. Being smart was not enough. Being good was not enough.

I went to speak with a university and a man working there assured me that he could help me with my visa if I had sex with him. He also asked me to give him my laptop. I was horrified! As if my body was not enough for him, he wanted my computer as well! I decided if my body was the cost of my education, then I was no longer interested in pursuing it. I went to his supervisor, the director of the international center, and told him what that man had proposed. The director informed me he could do nothing about my complaint because he had only been in his position for two weeks. He also told me that any mention of this could reflect poorly on his career. He denied me access to the university claiming that my complaint meant that he could not admit me.

After that, I went back to hair braiding because that was the only way I knew how to earn money. At least I was not working for the greedy, selfish men my relative had forced me to work for. This time, it was my business, my time, and my money.

OPPORTUNITY FOR AN EDUCATION

One day I was braiding the hair of an African American girl named Rakia. It took me about six hours to finish her hair, and when I was done, she started crying. She told me, "Bineta, I know it took you six hours to do my hair but I won't be able to pay you." I told her, "Please don't do this to me. I have bills and rent to pay and I have to save for my education." She told me that she couldn't pay at that moment because she'd been tossed out of her grandmother's house because she did not pay the rent.

I was shocked! My grandmother in Africa would never throw me out for not paying rent. Rakia told me that things worked differently here and that she'd paid rent to her grandmother since she was fifteen years old. I told her not to worry about paying me now; we would go and get her things and she could stay with me. She could pay me later for her hair. That is how we do things in my culture. When someone is in need, we take them in. After that, Rakia and I became sisters. We started caring for each other. Little did I know that my generosity was the best blessing of my entire life and that it would open the doors to receiving the education I craved.

One day, Rakia asked me to tell her my story about coming to America. I told her that the only thing I ever wanted in life was an education and explained that I had come all the way from Africa to get one. I also told her why it hadn't happened. Shortly after that, Rakia took me to her mother's house and told her mother that I'd invited her into my home without even knowing her. I told her mother my story and explained how my relative had exploited me. I asked her, "Is it such a crime for me to learn? That is all I ever wanted to do." I told her about the days when I would eat only French fries and ketchup for lunch because I could not afford any other food and explained that the money I was earning now was not only being sent back to Africa to help my family but was also was being saved for my education.

Her mother was shocked by all of my struggles and told me about a small university in South Carolina where she was sure I would be accepted. It had a very diverse student body and a lot of foreign students. Soon after, her mother drove me down to South Carolina to see the school and talk with the administrators. I remember when we arrived I broke down crying. The campus was so beautiful with sidewalks lined with oak trees and flowers. It was like a heaven of sorts; a dream realized.

We went to the university's international center and met Laurie, the director. She was blonde and blue-eyed and I was a little intimidated because I feared that she would not want to help me because she was white. If she told me that I could not get an education, I decided that I was going to return to Senegal. Sitting in front of her that day, I said, "Before you tell me 'no' please listen to my story." I told her about coming to America, being exploited by my relative and the people I worked for until I escaped and explained how I went from school to school and was rejected by all of them. "I did not come here to harm anyone, I just want to go to school."

I then asked her, "Do you know why it means so much to me? Because my aunt tried and failed as did my mother and my sister and now I am the only one with the opportunity to attend college. Why is it so hard for me? When people look at me, they see an African, a Muslim woman, a poor black woman—no one ever sees me as the educated woman that I want to be. Why is it such a crime for me to want to be a successful woman just like anyone else? I survived exploitation and have worked so hard only because of my hope for an education."

Laurie looked at me and said, "I know that you can make it. I see the drive in you, but unfortunately you don't have enough money to pay for school at this point. The only thing I can do is let you apply, encourage you to write your story in the application, and see if that can get you a scholarship for international students."

There was hope! She was willing to help me! I started crying. Laurie said that she believed in me; she was the first person outside of my family to tell me that! That took all the pain of the last few years away. When she said she believed in me my outlook changed and I realized that my dream of getting an education was possible.

I was admitted to the university with a scholarship to help pay for my classes. When I started, I told Laurie that everything I did in school would be to please her because she believed in me. When everyone else did not believe in me, she was right there. She has no idea what a difference she made in my life. I wish to this day that I could tell her how much she changed my world.

I attended that university and it was wonderful. Since we were all so far from home, the international students from around the world acted like a surrogate family. It was the first time since coming to the United States that I felt connected to a community. I was finally where I wanted to be and my family in Senegal was so proud of me.

I used to go to school from nine o'clock in the morning until eight o'clock in the evening and then I would go home and braid hair until around four o'clock in the morning only to get up the next morning and go to school. That was the sacrifice I had to make to pay for my education. Although the international center provided me with a scholarship, I had to pay my rent and expenses with money from my hair-braiding business. I worked so much but it was a sacrifice I was willing to make. Working my way through school taught me useful entrepreneurial skills that have helped me build, grow, and expand my life in so many ways.

When I look back on all those hard years, I remember how my spirit suffered because I was so discredited and unfortunate. But I never gave up and developed an iron will. Some people don't appreciate having access to education and that fills me with sorrow. I think back to the days that I could not afford to eat because I had to pay for school. I also think about the many years I spent away from my family just because I wanted to go to school. What many people see as simply a thing to do, I saw as a challenge I had to overcome for my family. I always thought it would be wonderful to go back to Africa and have them say, "Wow! We have a woman in our family who is educated." I remember the days when my grandmother was chased from the radio station because she did not speak French so they said she was uneducated. My sister was also ridiculed because she was not educated and could not speak French.

Attending college was a dream come true. I met many people who changed my life and made me into the woman I am today. They showed me that I am more than what I thought I was and taught me that I could represent others and be a voice for women. That dream is still in the making. I managed to finish three years of college, but had to stop because of the pressures of money, parenting two young children, and running a business.

Even though I did not get my degree, the experience I gained in the process was very valuable. My formal education empowered me and led me to create a foundation to give to those *talibé* kids whom my father and I used to take into our home and feed. I want them to have the opportunity to go to school because I believe that all a person has is intelligence and education. If everything in my life is taken away from me, then all I have is the knowledge in my head.

Someday, I will finish my degree. I am a wife and a busy mother of two, I run a business and a charity, yet I still know that I can finish my education. Education is freedom. No matter how much it costs you, do whatever you can to get it. Growing up, I witnessed many African women being denied an education because the culture doesn't allow them to pursue it. With an education, people can combat stereotypes and teach others compassion and that is why I am such an advocate.

My story illustrates the plight of a lot of immigrant women. When I was working for my relative, I did not immediately understand that I had been sold into a forced-labor situation. It was not until I escaped that I understood that the harsh conditions I was subjected to were abusive and illegal. I think many women in my situation misunderstand, naïvely trust, and assume people will not take such advantage. I empathize with all of them, because when I left Africa I thought I was coming to the land of milk and honey! When I was forced to work exhausting hours under harsh conditions, I still had the promise of my education burning inside me like a light. That kept me going. Even though I worked very hard, once I was in school and still working, I felt like I'd made it because I was that much closer to getting an education. Being naïve is part of a growth process, something else to overcome, especially in a forced-labor situation. Women in this circumstance eventually have to realize that they are being taken advantage of and figure out how to escape, no matter how frightening that choice might be.

Perhaps I had to experience this in order to be able to help others. For example, I have a friend who was subjected to female genital mutilation, was emotionally broken, and had a terrible marriage. She had no education and limited opportunities. She joined a program that I hosted offering computer training courses to immigrant women. Later, she received a high school diploma because I taught her how to use a computer. After learning those skills, she was unstoppable. She took an online course, learned medical billing and coding, and is now able to earn a decent income. Her education ultimately allowed her to leave her marriage and save her daughter from barbaric cultural and religious practices. This is why I believe so strongly in the freedom provided by education. After hearing her success story, I realized all I want to do is educate other women and children. When you give someone an education, you place the world in their hands.

Every day, Allah is educating me. Yet this form of education is coming to me through all the people in my life. As long as I know that I am touching everyone's life in my own special way, I am satisfied. I now take gratification in the things I do like educating women through my college program or sending soap and books to the *talibé* kids in Senegal. When I touch another person's life, I can then measure my achievements. It is then that I have truly arrived.

BINETA'S ADVICE FOR WOMEN

I advise all women to reach deep within and find their inner power. I want all women to find strength and show how strong they really are. Never give up. Many times, when I was in college, I had to find a job so that I could pay tuition. Once I went to a hotel to inquire about a job. The manager asked me to take my hijab off. I told her that I would be a model employee, that I speak English, French, Spanish, and many other languages, and that I am a very talented individual. She told me that was not enough. She pointed out that the fact that I was black and dressed like a Muslim woman meant that she could not put me in the front of her hotel because I could scare away her customers. I told her thank you very much and refused the job.

People will always see me as a black Muslim woman and judge me. It's my job to show them that their judgment is wrong and be the wonderful person that I am. I think a lot of people are afraid of me before they meet me but after they befriend me and know who

I really am, then those judgments fall away. I am proud to be that African woman, I am proud to be that poor woman, and I am proud to be that Muslim woman.

If a label is given to you, don't try to push it away. It's part of you. Instead, use it to your advantage. Use it as a mechanism of change where you take it and raise it proudly. You can make something positive out of a stereotype and change the world forever.

JANE

Kenya

The Kibera region of Nairobi, Kenya, constitutes the second largest slum in Africa. Within its boundaries are women and girls struggling to get an education and move beyond their situation. Jane Anyango works in a grassroots way to mobilize women in Kibera. In 2010, she was invited to the United States to attend the International Visitor Leadership Program where she was nominated for the International Women of Courage Award. In 2011, she received the Young Women of Achievement Award from the Women's Information Network. She is currently in charge of the Polycom Development Project where she works to educate and empower young girls living in Kibera.

I WAS BORN IN 1970 as the fourth child in a family of ten. My father loved me dearly. I grew up in a rural setting doing everything that rural children do: playing in the garden, fetching water, and collecting firewood. My village did not have electricity so we used small kerosene lamps to provide light.

Before I turned eighteen, I moved to Kibera, a slum in Nairobi, Kenya, and that is where I ended up getting married. It was a very boring life and a filthy environment. I was not happy with the turn my life took. The village I grew up in was beautiful and I ended up living somewhere that was very dirty and crowded. For years, I locked myself in the house and would only leave to go to the toilet outside. It took me quite some time to start talking to the neighbors. I only started talking to them when I had my first baby and needed advice since I was a young mother with no one around to help me.

The Kibera Slums where I live house 1.5 million people. That is nearly fifty percent of Nairobi's total population. We live on less than five percent of Nairobi's landmass. The Kibera slum is about the size of Central Park in New York City and it is one of the most densely populated places on the planet. Life expectancy in Kibera is thirty years of age compared to fifty years in the rest of Kenya—and half of all the people living there are under the age of fifteen. Considering the conditions we live in, it is no surprise that one out of five babies born in Kibera does not live to see their fifth birthday.

Here in Kibera, there is no running water in most homes. To obtain water, we must purchase water from private vendors, paying two to ten times what is paid by a Nairobi resident outside the slums. But drinking water is not the only issue—a lack of proper plumbing affects us, too. Kibera's 1.5 million residents share only 600 toilets. On average, one toilet serves 1,300 people. Although these issues break my heart, the issue surrounding women and girls of Kibera is more heartbreaking.

Sixty-six percent of girls in Kibera routinely trade sex for food by the age of sixteen. Many begin this method of survival as early as age six. Young women in Kibera contract HIV at a rate five times that of their male counterparts. Studies show that only forty-one percent of boys and thirty-two percent of girls in Kibera know that condoms are effective in preventing HIV transmission.

Only eight percent of girls in Kibera have the opportunity to go to school. One of the subject areas I am most concerned about as a woman working with grassroots mobilization is working to improve the lives of Kibera's women. Educating a girl in places like Kibera means she will earn more, be more likely to invest her earnings in her family, be three times less likely to contract AIDS, and have fewer, healthier children who are also more likely to survive past the age of five.

I got married when I was barely eighteen to a stranger. I celebrated my eighteenth birthday as a married woman, yet married to a man I'd just met and living in a place very different from my home village. My husband wasn't a very patient man. He could be very arrogant so he often lost his employment. I went through so much to ensure my children got an education. I sold groceries and would also do laundry for people.

I have come very far to be where I am today. I used to wake up at five o'clock in the morning and go to bed later than ten o'clock at night just doing any work to put food on the table for my four children. I would beg for torn, used books for my kids, and I even asked my son's teachers if he could only attend half-day lessons as I could not afford the full tuition. He still performed well, but it badly interfered with his self-esteem. His friends used to laugh at him when he was growing up because he came from a very poor family. They would make fun of his clothes and torn books. One of the most difficult challenges in my life was watching him go through this.

In 2004, tired of watching the women and girls around me make bad choices and suffer, I started a campaign to empower girls in Kibera.

I was living with my eleven-year-old niece and she was sleeping with a thirty-nine-year-old man. When I learned about this relationship, that was it for me. In Kenya, that relationship is not considered rape, it is consensual and to me that is a very disturbing thing.

Often in Kibera, grown men are able to coax young girls to have sex with them. Most girls, like my niece, do not understand that what these men do to them is wrong. These girls don't have any self-esteem or self-respect. They do not understand what these concepts are. That was why I had to do something to empower girls to take control of their lives and manage them positively. I couldn't believe these things were happening right under my nose. I realized that many of the girls and women of Kibera do not understand how to have self-respect and respect for their bodies. They lack proper role models and education encouraging them to have respect for themselves. Since this is the case, men often take advantage of them. There are so many girls who are coerced into sex and even their own parents are not aware. There is a serious need for girls to understand themselves and their bodies.

As a result of everything I observed, I started the Polycom Development Project, a self-help and self-improvement program for women and girls. We meet with the girls and provide them a platform to talk about abuse, no matter how traumatic. We do exercises to help them gain self-esteem and self-respect. We also teach them proper personal hygiene.

Ever since then, I have not stopped. My efforts have only grown stronger. After Kenya's post-election violence in 2007 and 2008, I became very active. Chaos erupted in Kenya after the result of the presidential election was disputed. The incumbent, President Mwai Kibaki, was declared the winner of the election held on December 27, 2007. Supporters of Kibaki's opponent, Raila Odinga, alleged electoral manipulation. Women and children in Kibera and other areas of Kenya were caught in the crossfire of the upheaval and suffered extensively. Unfortunately, one of my girls was killed during an incident of ethnic violence. She was a fifteen-year-old girl I had mentored for a long time. In an effort to stop the violence, my friends and I mobilized hundreds of women to go to the district officer and request that First Lady Lucy Kibaki, and Ida Odinga, the wife of the Prime Minister Raila Odinga, talk to their husbands about the suffering of the women and children.

We ended up creating Kibera Women for Peace and Fairness and I managed to mobilize more than eight hundred women across tribes that were fighting and killing each other. My powerful message was that we all have a right to live in Kenya and we have to respect one another and live peacefully.

The fact that I was able to bring women from different communities together and to convince people to throw down their weapons and embrace peace attracted the attention of the American Embassy in Nairobi. I was invited to visit the United States in 2010 for an exchange program called the International Visitor Leadership Program where I received a nomination for the prestigious International Women of Courage Award. Although I did not win, I was honored to receive a nomination. I received a Young Women of Achievement Award for leadership by The Women's Information Network in 2011 and again traveled to the United States, though this time having to raise money for my travel.

Having the funds to travel is always a barrier for me. Women working in grassroots organizations like me do not get much visibility at big international conferences about women because we cannot afford the airfare and accommodations necessary to participate. In 2012, I desperately wanted to attend the United Nations 56th Session of the Commission on the Status of Women but could not go because I did not have the money. The subject was rural women and technology use and as a rural woman fighting technology obstacles every day, I was a perfect representative for that meeting. I must work around many obstacles to organize large groups of women here in Kibera. It seems that affluent women always get their travel paid for by institutions, but what about the voices of the women working in the field? We need to be at the table, too, so we can all work together.

Part of my reason for wanting to tell my story is that I want the world to know how many opportunities women like myself miss because they do not have money. People are more willing to send a university professor to such conferences. It's as though we are forgotten but we are working on the ground in our countries and communities to bring about the change that must happen. I worked very hard with my girls by selling jewelry to help raise the money to come to the United States in order to talk about the issues affecting them. The girls thought my coming could help bring solutions to most of their problems. Women working in the field are less exposed and empowered these days. "Experts" and other advocates like to talk about the issues of women like me, but realistically we are rarely given a chance to participate and represent ourselves.

There is increasing social acceptance of violence among these girls in Kibera who lack an understanding of their fundamental rights. Several needy girls have been coming to me to ask for help for their school fees and currently some of my Facebook friends assist. Currently, two girls who are not my own are staying with me. I owe this to our girls who helped me to sell jewelry and many of my Facebook friends have been so good to us. One has even "adopted" one of the girls. Through networking, I have fourteen girls in high school with their fees paid by charitable contributors but it is still a challenge for me to keep them in school. I will always try to find more sponsors so these bright girls can stay in school. It is their best hope and will bring them the best opportunities.

I have recently organized a march of women called the Justice for Angel Project in response to a court case. In this case, a six-year-old girl was brutally raped and defiled by a fifty-year-old neighbor. This man was only charged with attempted rape and was immediately released on bail for less than $45 US (4,000 Kenya Shillings). The women of Kibera were disgusted! The police in charge and many other people attempted to convince the mother of the young girl to accept 50,000 Kenya Shillings (a little more than $500 US) to drop the case. I have been mobilizing the women since June 2012 to march to the courts but the police are delaying the case and this man continues to brag to everyone about his conquests.

The police threatened to arrest and detain Kibera women if they showed up in court on September 4, 2012, the date the trial was supposed to start. I wanted to mobilize more than three hundred women to march to the courthouse on that day to demand change. We cannot sit back as our children are abused everywhere! The case was delayed again and eventually pushed to November 27, 2012. The women were very mad and staged a big protest at the Kibera Law Court, which the media covered.

After several corrupt occurrences involving this case, I am now mobilizing the women to march to Kilimani Police Station to push for further charges. I have been very frustrated with the case and the women are giving up, because there is so little hope for justice. All of the women in Kibera live from hand to mouth. If the women come to court or join a protest, it means that they will go without food on that day. My efforts to get funds have not been fruitful, so I am also collecting signatures on a petition to support our cause. I don't care if we fail to convince the police to further prosecute the perpetrator. Regardless of the outcome, a lesson will be learned from this. This poor girl will always be very close to my heart. My reason for pushing this issue so far is to set a precedent in our community that sexual violence should not be accepted or go unpunished. This case is just one example of the issues I and many other women working on grassroots mobilization around the globe constantly undertake.

I believe the Kibera women are leading the way for all women in even the poorest communities to stand up for themselves. That case is just one example. There are many things that women can collectively push for. We are going to see empowered women standing strong to defend their rights, participating in women's issues locally, regionally, and internationally, and we will build a powerful resource center where we can access information. If women can bring peace to Kibera, what can't we do? For years people have come here offering solutions for us, but I know all we need is empowerment and we can deal with our own problems. Many people think the inhabitants of Kibera are poor because they are lazy or do not want to work. The people of Kibera work very hard for very little pay and make up a large portion of the labor force in Nairobi. If there is one thing I want people to take away from my story, it's that people in Kibera are not incompetent or lazy. I will never stop the fight for Kibera women and women everywhere. Even if I have to go without food, I will never stop all of my efforts. We can create change and we have proven that time and time again.

JANE'S ADVICE FOR WOMEN
Believe in yourself and have self-respect. You are very powerful and through that power you can change this world in so many unique ways.

BITA

Senegal

Female Genital Mutilation (FGM), otherwise known as female genital cutting, comprises all procedures that involve partial or total removal of the external female genitalia, or other injury to the female genital organs for non-medical reasons. Often carried out by traditional circumcisers, the practice is recognized internationally as a violation of human rights and an extreme form of discrimination against women. The practice is generally carried out on minors between the ages of four and puberty.

Bita details her personal experience with FGM and discusses the real-life consequences of being subjected to this form of abusive gender persecution.

MY NAME IS Bita and I am from Senegal. I want to share my story about how, as a young girl, I was forced to have my genitals mutilated and was persecuted in this way only because I am female. While female circumcision is not practiced among all the ethnic groups in Senegal it remains widely practiced among my ethnic group, the Fulani. It's something that nearly all Fulani girls have done to them by their families. It is a ritual and is a tradition in our culture.

When I was about seven years old, I was mutilated. It was my mother who wanted it done to me, although I didn't know what was going to happen until moments before. My mother invited a lady to our house. She was there for three days. One morning after breakfast, my cousin was brought into the bathroom by my father's first wife and my mother, his second wife. They were in the bathroom with the lady who was visiting us. Soon after, I heard my cousin screaming. I was frightened. I didn't know what was happening to her and I didn't know that the same thing was going to happen to me.

When I was brought into the bathroom, I saw the visiting lady holding a bloody razor blade. My mother and my father's first wife held my arms and legs down to prevent me from moving and the lady cut my clitoris out with the bloody razor blade. It was apparently the same razor blade used to cut my cousin just moments before. Afterward, I remember that I was bleeding a lot and I had severe pain. I continued bleeding for a long time after that. I was told to sit in hot water to urinate but I didn't receive any antibiotics or medication to relieve the pain. After that, I developed an infection and eventually my mother had to take me to the doctor for treatment. It took me a long while to recover.

Years after that experience, I am still suffering. I have a lot of pain during menstruation and the loss of my clitoris makes sexual relations painful and unpleasant. I believe that I have more infections because of the circumcision. Also, when I gave birth to my two children, the deliveries were more difficult than if I had not been circumcised. To this day, I still have horrible reminders of what happened to me as a young girl.

I have a young daughter and I don't ever want the same thing happen to her. That is why I am ready to do everything in my power to fight that and help others to stop this violence against women. No other girl should have to have this experience.

BITA'S ADVICE FOR WOMEN
Please do not allow this terrible practice to continue. It is cruel and harsh. After the birth of my daughter, I knew that I wanted no other woman to suffer through this like I did.

SOMALIA

in Cartoons

Women's rights are a key issue in Somalia, particularly in the lower part of the country where Mogadishu has fallen into the control of rebel groups who have imposed strict Sharia law. Female genital mutilation (FGM) is also a widely practiced custom.

Abdul Muhiadin is a Somali artist specializing in editorial cartoons. As a boy growing up in war-torn Mogadishu, he started making cartoon drawings to understand the complicated political situation and societal upheaval happening in his country. After posting graffiti peace messages on the streets of Mogadishu, he was invited to publish his work in local newspapers where he drew editorial cartoons. Due to their overt criticisms of ruling warlords and radical groups, he received threats and became exiled in Egypt.

Abdul is now a guest cartoonist in Norway. His work has been exhibited in libraries and other public institutions.

"My cartoons depict important messages about the situation in Somalia and are important for the Somali audience because of the high rate of illiteracy among our population. This way people who cannot read can receive the messages and enjoy the humor the cartoons reveal. I wish for Somalia to have peace and freedom since my people have suffered for decades. I will never give up defending our human rights and will defend them with my pen each time I draw."

71

Abdul's work can be viewed at
http://abdularts.blogspot.com and on Afrikanation.

Child: Dad, where is my brother's grave?
Dad: It is right there next to your mother's
grave and behind your sister's grave.

MIDDLE EAST

TURKEY
SYRIA
IRAQ
IRAN
JORDAN
KUWAIT
SAUDI
ARABIA
U.A.E
OMAN
RED SEA
YEMEN
ARABIAN
SEA

ISRAEL
AND
OCCUPIED
TERRITORIES

LEBANON
GOLAN
SYRIA
HAIFA
WEST
BANK
TEL
AVIV
JERUSALEM
JORDAN
DEAD
SEA
GAZA

EGYPT

NADIA

Yemen

In February 2011, the citizens of Yemen started an uprising as a result of their frustration with high unemployment, poverty-stricken economic conditions, and political corruption. Their demands soon escalated to calls for Yemeni President Ali Abdullah Saleh to resign. The uprising followed the initial stages of the Tunisian Revolution and occurred simultaneously with the Egyptian Revolution. Nadia Al-Sakkaf, editor in chief of the Yemen Times, the first English-speaking newspaper in the country, discusses some of the hardships the paper fell under during these critical times, challenges she faced in order to remain an ethical journalist, and her hope for a new Yemen.

S INCE I WAS a young girl, I have always wanted to write. I used to love stringing words together to create sentences and the simple act of using language. At the age of fourteen, I aspired to write books and other creative pursuits. When I was going to college, I told my father I wanted to be a writer, and he told me, "No. Study something that will earn you a good living." When I think of this now, I smile because, although I listened to him in pursuing my studies in computer science engineering, journalism eventually became my career, anyway. You can't fight against or overlook what you were meant to do.

Since 2005 I have been the editor in chief of the *Yemen Times*, the first and most widespread English-language newspaper in Yemen. The story of how I came into this role is an interesting one. The *Yemen Times* has had quite a history since my father, Professor Abdulaziz Al-Saqqaf, established it in 1990 and the first issue came out in 1991. Until today, it is the only independent English newspaper in Yemen. It came from his vision for Yemen to be an important part of the world, even though it was 1990 and before the Internet turned the world into a small village; he had already understood the importance of having an independent source of information on Yemen in a global language, as a way to bridge the gap between Yemen and the rest of the world. In addition to the language (English), the structure and style in which the paper is produced also speaks to rest of the world.

In 1999, my father was killed in a car accident, which we have reasons to believe was actually an assassination. He was doing a lot of critical reporting of the government at the time. He had been abducted before and was tortured and imprisoned for his involvement in such criticism. The paper was also closed by state political security more than three times between 1991 and 1999. After his death, my brother took over until 2005, when I became publisher and editor in chief.

My father was killed during my third year of university studies. When I graduated in 2000 I joined the *Yemen Times* to support my brother in running the paper. Watching my brother manage everything daily, I quickly realized that it takes more than just journalism skills to manage a paper. You need to know management specifics, too. I got a scholarship through the British Council to study Management Information Systems in the United Kingdom.

From 2001 to 2002, I earned my master's degree in Management Information Systems to build a bridge between my technical background and the management training I needed. When I came back, I started working on my practical experience in the real world outside of the *Yemen Times* and worked for a year as a systems analyst before I moved on to work with Oxfam, an international confederation of seventeen organizations networked together in more than ninety countries, to build a future free from the injustice of poverty, while still keeping my ties with the *Yemen Times* as a reporter and part-time translator. Working with Oxfam exposed me to development, poverty, and gender issues which I focused on when I later ran the newspaper.

Finally, in 2005, my brother had to leave the country to earn his PhD in Sweden, and that is when I assumed the full-time role with the *Yemen Times* as editor in chief. You could say that I have been writing for the paper and contributing to it since 2000, but it became my life in 2005.

When I became the editor in chief, I was living under two men's shadows: my father's and my brother's. To me, these two men before me were very great and having to live up to those expectations was difficult. Journalism is a new profession for many Yemeni women. Generally, the culture still does not accept women working in public, but I have seen the interest grow. Women who decide to be journalists in Yemen are still facing the glass ceiling; it's very difficult for them to climb up the ladder and become managers or editors. A lot of people thought I would not be able to run the paper; because I was a young woman, they didn't believe I would be able to run a project as huge as the *Yemen Times*. We are actually one of the only independent media institutions with a business model in the whole country; the rest of them are either supported by the state or by political parties. Our policy is to provide readers with objective information and always write objective coverage. Sometimes it becomes very, very difficult, especially in times of political instability like what Yemen went through in the past few years. For example, during our coverage of the 2011 uprising, although our heart was with the revolution and change, we had to make sure we covered all stakeholders and make sure that we produced a balanced story covering all sides. Even if we hate the other side, we always have to stick to the commitment of the *Yemen Times* to be an independent, objective newspaper.

In fact, the press in Yemen is very uncertain. There is no fixed system or mechanism for handling journalists or media. There are three types of media in Yemen: state media, which is the majority; political parties' media, affiliated with a certain line of thought; and independent outlets, which are the minority. The latter is the category that we fall under.

In January 2011, I met some of the most extensive challenges in my career as a journalist and editor. These issues arose about the same time as Yemen's revolution when a series of revolutionary uprisings began across the Middle East.

The uprising in Yemen occurred in February 2011, but in many ways, it actually started much before the January uprisings in Tunisia or Egypt. You could say the revolution was happening for a few years prior to its actual occurrence. Yemen is a country where there is a lot of poverty. Around 40 percent of its people live around the food poverty line, meaning these people don't have enough food to eat. Half of the people are also illiterate, especially the women. There are many injustices; the law is not the same for everybody, and there is favoritism and so much corruption and humiliation. The average Yemeni citizen lives under much humiliation because they have few basic necessities and rights.

In Yemen, we have always had a much wider democratic space in the Gulf region, in terms of our press being freer and being able to write much more openly, than the rest of the Gulf countries. We even have a strong civil society. However, whether the issue is political parties other than civil society organizations, political development, or charity, these processes were not something the common man or woman related to. So politics, until 2011, was mainly the business of the elite or the intellectuals; the layman or laywoman would not relate to politics and, therefore, did not participate in the political process.

This was also the case in Tunisia and one of the reasons for their revolution. Tunisia's revolution began when a vegetable vendor named Mohamed Bouazizi burned himself alive because his vegetable cart and other wares that were his livelihood were thrown away by a municipal officer. At that point, he believed there was no point in living because he would be forced to live in poverty and humiliation. His action not only triggered the revolutions in Tunisia and Egypt, but in Yemen, as well, because we have millions of people like him who don't have anything to live for and don't have anything to lose. Many Yemenis are so poor that when the revolution began they started living in protest areas where there were tents that provide better living arrangements than the streets where they used to live. This gave legitimacy to the revolution. In the beginning, there were tens of thousands of people coming together; soon, thousands became millions of people for one cause all around the nation. There were people from all walks of life—professionals, students, and political parties. Within this revolutionary spirit, the cultural gaps were bridged.

This was the turning point in Yemen's recent history. The society today has never been so empowered. There is a strong sense of optimism, but a lot of uncertainty.

Our challenges in 2011 at the *Yemen Times* began with the revolution. In February 2011, advertising started to diminish. However, this is natural in any country where there is instability because the first elements that run away are money and investments. The private business sector was the first sector to close down. A lot of people pulled their money from the banks, and many international companies withdrew their people and funds back to their original countries. Basically, business life stopped, so we didn't have any advertisements, which we rely on heavily. That is ultimately when money became short. Our objective position on everything also affected us in these areas. For example, we wrote about atrocities that happened against the protestors, and this angered the regime at the time, so we were even deprived of government ads. It became a nightmare. In April 2011, we started laying off people, beginning with freelancers and part-time employees. We then started assigning people to double jobs. We had to outsource our distribution, too, because, in the beginning, it was more efficient for us. For example, a time came when we had to use our personal cars for distributing the paper. It was the same with phones and laptops—we were relying on our own resources and were actually taking money from our own pockets to make sure the paper survived.

Sending reporters to the protests was always very difficult for me. It's quite natural for a reporter covering a protest to be subjected to clashes from thugs and security or even get killed by a stray bullet. Those clashes used to be with sticks or knives. There were also exchanges of gunfire. In these particular incidents, a reporter trying to take photos can become the victim of a ricocheted stray bullet or be shot directly. There were so many vicious attacks in these protests. They happened from rooftops and inside houses. They were unpredictable, and became very difficult to hide from.

I remember when one of my reporters returned to the office in shock. He said that the man standing next to him was shot dead. The reporter was traumatized and kept repeating, "It could have been me!"

Any time I ever send reporters to protests, my hand is on my heart until they all come back to the office and I know they are safe. At the same time, we cannot NOT send them. If we don't tell the story, who will? I thank God and cross my fingers that we have not lost any reporters, though one was hurt by broken glass during one protest. Another had to stay home for a few days because of tear gas. In one traumatizing attack, our office in Taiz was closed because it was surrounded, and everyone was locked in by state security for about four hours. In another incident, two of my reporters were prevented from traveling. I was also stopped and interrogated by political security in Sanaa's airport on my way to a conference in Jordan, but was eventually let go.

In our profession, these things happen, and they are sometimes rattling. We used to get threats and receive calls and emails telling us we were traitors and that we were anti-legitimacy. We even got hate calls from the opposition when we covered the pro-regime news, because there were millions of people supporting Saleh at the time and as professional independent media we had to cover those rallies. The opposition didn't like it because they didn't want us, as an English newspaper, to say that there were people who support Saleh.

This is a major problem in Yemen in general because the press is extremely politicized. Nobody reported, for example, that protesters at one point were armed with metal bottles, but we did. At another time, protesters tried protesting near the TV station. I am not sure if they wanted to take it over, but that was a red line and it was very likely that thousands would be killed if they tried to; it was more like a suicide attempt sacrificing thousands in order to get the world's sympathy. The organized uprising of 2011 had what we call an "escalation committee," whose job was to take over key places, and spread the protest grounds to new streets and areas, sort of like a takeover scheme. In Taiz, protestors burned a police station, took over the education and financial offices, and occupied those places. They wrote "closed by the people" on the doors.

During a revolution, these things are expected. Peace no longer seemed to be an option. But this was not received lightly by the pro-regime forces, who took vicious actions against the expanding protests. In Taiz also, the tents in the revolution square were burned down by state security causing some people to die in the fire or suffocate.

In the midst of all this turmoil, our job as an independent press was and always will be to be the ones to say who did what and when. This is not reflected by the protestors or the pro-revolution media and is also not reflected by the state media. It is up to us to be objective, and we can never stray from that.

One thing I know is that if I don't objectively tell these stories, nobody will. My staff and I feel like we are contributing valuable information to our society and the world through our journalism, especially in our coverage of the 2011 revolution.

The last few years have proven to be exciting times to be in Yemen as we are on the verge of a new nation. I feel the international community has really supported us during our times of need. We received emails and phone calls from people in other countries who said they were praying for us. While traveling in Jordan, I met an activist from the Egyptian movement who helped create the Egyptian Revolution. She talked about what happened to the protestors and activists and the suffering they went through. We shared a moment and cried together. We understood one another through all of the change.

The support I have received from all over the world and the dream of what will happen next kept me going for the last few years. Once I was with a few friends from the women's movement in Yemen, and we asked, "What do we want in the new Yemen?" As we dreamed together, I realized for the first time that we can dream and feel that it is possible. Our dreams were simple: Education, basic health services, and electricity that does not cut off suddenly—things that we thought were not possible—are now just across the road. We only need to cross the bridge.

I remember in 2011, my five-year-old daughter heard the protestors outside one day. There were thousands of people marching and protesting in unison. There were also the anti-change rallies where the pro-regime protests were usually accompanied by thugs who carried sticks and looked very intimidating. She saw one of those aggressive protests and ran home in a panic, crying that we had to close the windows and doors because they were coming to kill us.

I tried to tell her they were not, but she was in a frenzy, so I did what she asked. Eventually she said, "We have to stay here! We have to arm ourselves and protect ourselves!" We talked about it, and I reassured her that they were not coming for us. I used a metaphor, telling her that the citizens of Yemen don't like their "teacher," and they all want a new "teacher." But she then said, "I like my teacher." "Okay," I said. "So you don't have to go out in the street and demand a new "teacher" like them. They just have a very mean teacher, and they don't like him. That's all they want." I reassured her she was safe and I was there to protect her.

I am sure there are so many other kids who were traumatized by the protests. I may be educated and calm enough to be able to handle the upheaval, but how many children do not have that sense of security? How many children live on the streets and suddenly had this commotion all around them? How many families are broken because of relatives in conflict positions? There are so many people, especially the younger ones, who will be scarred for life by these experiences. I am sure we will have to deal with the aftermath of this revolution for many, many years to come.

That is why I have a lot of hope for Yemen and the *Yemen Times*. The *Yemen Times* did not stop when my father died; we kept the paper going. When I took over, we kept on despite all odds and people who speculated that I would not be able to run it being a young woman. When finances were tight in 2011 we felt it was a shame to go down because of the economy. We suffered and lived through political oppression and other challenges. But we did get support from others and from so many unlikely places such as European newspapers like the *Politiken* in Denmark and *Der Standard* in Austria, who raised funds from their people for us.

We got past that phase and we are in a much better shape now. We even started Yemen's first community radio station in the end of 2012 with the support of the Open Society Foundation.

The public loves us and I hope they learn from our message that journalism is a responsibility, a commitment, and a privilege, not just a job.

I hope the dreams we possess for a better country come true. When my daughter remembers these days, I hope we have a developed country and she understands why we had to go through this revolution. Yemen is a rich country in terms of natural resources, and I want to enjoy a good life and enjoy our resources. I know so many Yemenis who would sell a kidney just to go abroad. I am dreaming of the day where the people of Yemen don't think like that because they want to stay in their own country and they feel appreciated as citizens.

This is a very unbelievable time in history. There is much turmoil now, but I hope this transition phase results in something much more prosperous in the end. Although it was a defining moment for Yemen, this revolution was also an opportunity to unveil the other faces of Yemen and break all the stereotypes the international community had of us. I am glad that this revolution has resulted in the world knowing more about Yemen and other Arab countries. In many ways, it has brought the world closer together to our region and in a kindred spirit to our people.

Nobody is going to do my job for me. I know I have to do my own job, but it feels good to know that there is support. I would not be able to do the things that I do without my team. I have a lot of great people and a larger community with me now. For that reason, I am strong and will remain strong as will the *Yemen Times*.

NADIA'S ADVICE FOR WOMEN

Surround yourself with a good support system. Reach out—don't try to do things on your own or assume that nobody will understand what you are going through. It's amazing how much help, goodwill, and kindness there is if you just reach out and tell others what you are going through. Even good words will boost your emotional condition and make you feel so much better. Never feel that you are alone. There is always somebody who will share with you and is willing to help you. It is very comforting to know that people are there for you, as such a notion gives you the strength to carry on.

ZAFIRA

Jordan

There is a scientific way to study happiness—it is called Positive Psychology, and includes a focus on cultivating strengths, self-esteem, and optimism. Positive Psychology is an emerging branch of psychology that emphasizes using traditional practices of the scientific method in order to understand how certain mental processes, such as changes in happiness levels and brain function, occur. In essence, it is the study of human thriving. Such ideas are slightly radical in the Middle East, where Zafira shares her experience of creating a coaching program founded on these values. She describes the challenge of being a forward thinker and the obstacles she has confronted in her life due to her intellectual perspectives.

FROM THE TIME I was a child, I felt that I never fully belonged to my family or community. I thought that I was adopted. Even now, I still feel like I came from another place. This difference seems to be visible to locals and nonlocals, as I get asked frequently why I'm different.

Certainly there were many factors that contributed to and shaped my personality and my life. The first factor was that I have been very blessed to have inherited intellectual genes and characteristics from my father. He had an insatiable curiosity for knowledge and wisdom and was always reading and studying. Anybody was welcome in our home, even those who had different beliefs from his because he was open-minded. He always talked and explained things calmly and patiently. He was a determined truth-seeker. He studied Islam at Al-Azhar University in Cairo, so he understood and practiced its principles, such as "There is no compulsion in Islam," which means that you cannot force anyone to practice religion. He never forced me to practice religious rituals or to cover up. He did all he could to protect me from the injustice of society. For example, he had my passport issued as soon as I became fourteen, which was the legal age to have one, so that I would never need anybody else's permission to obtain one. Until very recently, women needed permission from a male relative—their father, husband, or brother—to have their passport issued.

I had an unusual childhood because my family moved from one city to another every couple of years due to my father's profession as a court judge. As a result, I had to change schools often, sometimes every year. I was alone most of the time. Forming friendships and acclimating to a new city or town takes time, and we never lived in the same place long enough for me to acclimate. Fortunately, television was very limited, so I spent a lot of my time in my room reading. Books were my best friends and literally my window to the world.

I read a lot, and this has influenced and cultivated my intellectual development.

I was very blessed to have many great teachers all through my life. The first one I remember very clearly was in middle school. She encouraged me to read because she was connected to the school library. I read the biographies of the great philosophers, like Nietzsche, Kant, and Descartes, in addition to all the geniuses in history, like Albert Einstein, Leonardo da Vinci, Gandhi, Thomas Edison, and Helen Keller. I loved them all and was inspired by their courage. They were different and unfit in their societies, yet possessed brilliant ideas that inspired and changed the world. I was hungry for knowledge and wanted to know everything about life. This led me to study the latest discoveries in science, as well as philosophy. I was particularly searching for the meaning of true freedom, love, happiness, joy, peace, and wisdom. Freedom, one of my core values, was the most challenging. Although I could get away with many things, I still felt suffocated by the old ways of thinking and traditions.

I had a breakthrough when I managed to convince my family to allow me to travel to Italy for the first time in 1985. I continued to travel almost every summer for over a decade. This opened a whole new world for me.

Another major turning point happened in 1989 when I moved out of the family's house and rented my own apartment. At that time, it was very rare for a single woman to live alone. Usually, women and men lived with their families until they got married. Moving out alienated most of my relatives, because they did not understand why I made that choice. However, I was very happy with the arrangement and enjoyed having my own place and the freedom. Finally, I started gaining control over my life. This was a huge step for me, and even though there was a lot of opposition and many difficulties, I'm glad that I chose my own happiness. One of my favorite quotes is:

"To go against the dominant thinking of your friends, of most of the people you see every day, is perhaps the most difficult act of heroism you can perform." —Theodore H. White

Living on my own allowed me to follow my passions, like traveling and studying. I traveled extensively in most west European countries. The many museums and historical monuments I visited, the people I met, and friendships I made over the years have enriched my life. Besides that, I have studied several languages, including English, French, and German, and this has opened new opportunities for me. They say knowledge is power, and I believe that, especially when we apply it.

I was introduced to a higher level of understanding when I came across the teachings of the Indian philosopher J. Krishnamurti in the early 1990s. His definition of love, joy, truth, and freedom was different from anything I had read before, and it resonated with me. He explained the true meaning of these values, as well as the reason why it is hard for most people to understand them. According to him, our understanding is limited because we are heavily conditioned by the values of our families and societies. We seek validation from others, while the truth lies within us. I learned a great deal from him, and a lot of the concepts that I was struggling with became crystal clear.

Another turning point was in 1998, when I bought my first computer and had access to the Internet at home. This opened another window. Then in 1999, after I completed a coaching program, I received an email announcing a new field of study called Positive Psychology. I was thrilled because this was what I was looking for all my life through my readings and intellectual pursuits. So I delved into studying Positive Psychology. It is true that what we seek, also seeks us.

I was introduced to a whole new world in 2003 when I became a member of SERVAS International, a voluntary organization that was founded in Europe after the Second World War for the purpose of helping students travel and work. Later, it became recognized and represented in the United Nations Economic and Social Council (ECOSOC). As a host, I have received many SERVAS travelers from all over the world. These cultural exchanges with people from different cultural backgrounds have enriched my life. Although the encounters were brief, from a couple of hours to a couple of days, the discussions I had with SERVAS travelers were interesting. These are the kind of people I like to interact with, and I am still in touch with many of them.

In 2004, I gained another level of understanding when I came across an American spiritual teacher who was living in Amman. She introduced me to new fields of science such as quantum physics, which was eye-opening for me, and led me to pursue further these fields to deepen my understanding.

In 2007, I quit my job as a human resources manager, and focused on studying Positive Psychology, or the Science of Happiness, as I prefer to call it. Even though it is a new field of science, its roots go back to Aristotle. Then I considered coaching as a profession, because it resonated with me, as it is a higher level of training and helps people reach their full potential. After taking several courses on how to coach others, including having my own coach from the United States, who helped me through her program to expand my knowledge and start my own coaching program, I started offering my services as a happiness coach. I reached a point where I thought it was time to share with people, especially women, what I have learned through the years about how to be happy.

One day, while I was searching the Internet, I came across the Happiness Club and thought it was a great idea to spread happiness. I contacted the founder of the Happiness Club, and he was very supportive and provided me with the information I needed to start a Happiness Club. My first attempts were unsuccessful: nobody showed up. It is still a new concept and most people are skeptical about new ideas, especially those that challenge their paradigms. Besides that, they have no idea what happiness is. They think that it depends only on having lots of money and material possessions. This doesn't mean that poverty will make us happy; however, if we don't have inner contentment, material possessions will only make us happy for a short period of time.

There were many interesting studies in Positive Psychology. For example, we now know that there are three factors that determine our happiness; 50 percent is determined by our genes, 40 percent is determined by our intentional activities and the choices we make every day, which are under our control, and only 10 percent is due to our circumstances. Another fascinating discovery is that happiness is contagious. When we are happy, we affect everybody we know, their friends, and the friends of their friends, even if we have never met them. I think this is very important; that is why I keep working on spreading these concepts.

One of the most amazing discoveries in neuroscience, which made everything we knew previously about the brain obsolete, is the brain's plasticity, or the brain's ability to change its structure, as we learn new things. Whenever we do a specific task over and over again, it takes less effort. This is the basis for changing our behavior for the better. To understand how this works, think of when you first started to learn how to drive; you had to think about every move you made. After several repetitions, you could drive without thinking about it. The same thing happens when we learn new skills; they sink into the subconscious mind and become habits, and we do them automatically without being aware of our behavior.

Our brain is involved in everything we do: in every thought, in every word we speak, and in every move we make. There is a famous quote from the Upanishads that sums this up beautifully: "Watch your thoughts; they become words. Watch your words; they become actions. Watch your actions; they become habits. Watch your habits;

they become character. Watch your character; for it becomes your destiny."

Another fascinating discovery is that we actually have three brains: besides the one in the head, there is one in the heart, and one in the gut. It's interesting that the heart stores some of our characteristics in its cellular memory. One example of this is how people who have a heart transplant begin exhibiting some characteristics of the donor after the operation. They even go as far as adopting their likes and dislikes.

I would like to focus on helping women to be happy. Most women are unhappy because they do not have the freedom to make their own decisions and choices or even to express themselves. Family always comes first, and they have to sacrifice their needs and wants to serve their family. Besides that, women comprise half of the population, and they raise the other half. When women are happy, their families and the whole society will benefit.

Another reason why teaching happiness skills is very important to me is because happiness is the key to world peace. Only happy people can create peace. In addition to that, happiness is the ultimate goal in life. Everything we do, we do it because we believe it will make us happy. As Aristotle said, "Happiness is the meaning and the purpose of life."

I teach practical skills that have been proven to help raise our happiness. One of the most basic for our well-being is to adopt a healthy lifestyle and practice happiness every day. Another important aspect is to shift our negative paradigms to positive ones. By changing our old beliefs and ways of thinking, we can ultimately change our lives.

These are just a few of the basic concepts that my coaching program is based upon. My biggest wish is for everyone to learn how to be happy. Happiness is a skill that can be learned and it is the most practical and intelligent thing to do. You just need to open your heart and mind to these new concepts, be willing to change, and believe that happiness is possible.

ZAFIRA'S ADVICE FOR WOMEN

The most important advice I have for women is to be honest with themselves. This helped me throughout my life, especially in difficult situations and when making important decisions. The second thing is to STOP pleasing everybody at the expense of their needs. They become resentful, and, as a result, get sick. Learn to say "No." The third thing is to learn how to be happy. May all beings be happy, always!

SAHAR

Palestine

As the daughter of renowned peace activist Nuha Nafal, Sahar discusses the continuing conflict between Palestine and Israel and tells the story of how she arrived to her sense of purpose through her escape from an emotionally abusive marriage and through her will to continue the important activism work of her mother.

I SPENT THE FIRST twelve years of my life with my family, traveling from country to country in search of a place to belong. Every country I lived in, every school I attended, and every person I met only made me feel a lesser sense of belonging. There was always something—my religion, my culture, my accent, my fair complexion, or even the color of my hair—that alienated me from others, no matter what setting I was in.

My name is Sahar. I am Palestinian and the daughter of peace activist Nuha Nafal. After escaping an emotionally abusive marriage, I feel more alive than ever and am prepared to take on the path that my mother carved for me. Let me first tell you about where I came from and the greatest inspiration in my life: my beloved mother.

EARLY LIFE

My mother was from the West Bank from a city called Birzeit. It has one of the largest universities in the Arab world and a radical, liberal energy very similar to the town of Berkeley, California. It was the perfect setting for a woman like my mother.

My father was working in Kuwait before he married my mother. Just like a typical Palestinian man, when he was in his midtwenties, he decided it was time to get married. My mother was seventeen years old when they met and was already very active. She had such bright, wide, incredible energy, and my father liked that a lot. She acted in her school theater and was very good at sports. As a child, she wrote poetry and performed as a gymnast. In fact, she almost competed in the German Olympics, but her brother would not allow her to travel. My grandmother had passed away when my mother was fifteen years old, and she had been forced to live with her brothers, who were very strict. She knew she needed a way out of that household in order to spread her wings, and my father appeared to be the most readily available solution.

Honestly, I think my mother was a smart woman for choosing to marry my father. She saw that he was financially comfortable because he lived in Kuwait and worked in the airline industry. More important, he had the opportunity to take her out of Palestine, so she could harvest her talents. He was more open-minded than the typical Arab man because he worked with the British; thus, he was not strict or traditional. He liked her feistiness and the fact she didn't agree with everything he said. He knew he was marrying someone special.

They married and moved to Kuwait. I was born in Kuwait in 1964, but that is honestly just a stamp on my passport. My father's business took us all over the Arab world. In 1966, he received an opportunity to transfer to Jordan, but due to a brewing war between the Palestinians and Israelis, we moved to Saudi Arabia. Moving to Saudi Arabia was difficult because we were Palestinian, Greek Orthodox Christians and had very light complexions and light eyes. Because my father feared we would be discriminated against for our appearance and religion, my brother and I stayed in Jordan to attend a Catholic boarding school.

In 1970, I was in Jordan, enrolled in the Catholic boarding school, when the Black September war between the Palestinians and the Jordanians started. I was a little girl caught in the middle of a war. It was horrific and confusing. There were bullets, killings, and terrible, inhumane things that I did not understand because I was so young. My dad had to come and literally confiscate me. They hid me in an army truck and took me out from where I was. Then my dad decided that the family needed to be together, which prompted us to move to Saudi Arabia. Meanwhile, my mother started a television show in Jordan. She did a lot of work for the Palestinians during the war, while she was pregnant with my sister, to hide weapons in our home. This lady, I'm telling you, was a patriot and an activist! She would act as a decoy in front of our home and pretend she needed help from the Jordanian army so the Palestinians could hide weapons in our house. Only recently have I been able to talk about this act, and I can only now openly discuss it since I live in the United States. My mother had a very rare blood type. While she was seven months pregnant, she would go and give her blood for injured Palestinians. Anytime there was a Palestinian who needed help she was there to support that person. They were our people, our blood.

From Jordan, we moved to Saudi Arabia, and my story returned to its recurring theme of "belonging." I really felt like an outcast there! When I lived there, I was called an infidel, had rocks thrown at me, and girls would not share anything with me. It was not because I was Christian and Palestinian, but due to my physical appearance. Teachers would ask, "When your mother gives you a shower, do you see any color in the water?" When I told them that my mother did not color my hair and that I was an Arab, they would try to trick me and ask me questions. Because of the remarks and taunting, I had to be veiled at age eleven. Although I was Christian and Palestinian, I had no other choice. Most of my friends were veiled later, by ages twelve and thirteen. I attended an all-girls school, and the law dictated that I could not be shown as a woman by age twelve. I despised the veil and felt they were trying to hide me and erase my identity.

Fortunately in 1976, my family decided to move to the United States. It was the most incredible day of my life. I was so excited because there were Christians, Muslims, and all different people living there. There was even freedom! For once I would belong! I was wrong. I came to America and did not speak English, so I had to start from the beginning. A lot of people helped me and supported me.

I used to hate it when people asked me where I was from. That question haunted me for a long, long time. I wasn't able to say where I was from until three or four years ago. Imagine being a Palestinian, born in Kuwait to a mother who was an activist with the Palestinians, living in Saudi Arabia as a Christian, and living in Jordan in a Catholic school as a Palestinian citizen. I can't say I'm Jordanian, I can't say that I'm Saudi Arabian, and I can't say I'm Kuwaiti, because I am not. In fact, the word "Arabia" became my enemy. "Did you ride your camel to school? Did your parents live in a tent?" These kinds of questions would always be asked by other children. There was little to no diversity in Castro Valley, California, when we moved there. Besides another Persian family, we were the only ethnic people in the entire city.

In my late teens, I went off to college, which is what my mother always wanted me to do. There, my social life revolved around different ethnic groups. I liked them because they were more colorful and diverse. I realize now that I strived to belong to people who did not belong. I felt I could connect with them as we all shared the same sense of displacement.

I started an Arabic club in college and world Arab fashion shows. I was so proud of being an Arab. It was my avenue of exploring and sharing my ethnicity with others. That period of my life was amazing because I started to embrace who I was.

ESCAPE FROM AN EMOTIONALLY OPPRESSIVE MARRIAGE

After college, I met my ex-husband. He was Lebanese and effortlessly charming. In the beginning, he gave me anything I desired. He swept me off my feet with his chivalry and charisma. I was blinded by it because I was only twenty-three years old and my parents pressured me, emphasizing that I was getting old and needed to get married fast. I believed them.

When I agreed to the marriage, my family did not know much about this man. His family had fought and killed Palestinians! His mother was Maronite and hated the Palestinians. Maronites were at war with the Palestinians in Lebanon for many years. How could I marry someone like that? I thought I was in love. I was completely seduced by this man, his supposed kindness, and his beautiful blue eyes.

As the years passed during our marriage, I started to realize the control and abuse I was living under. He cheated on me and dishonored my family as Palestinian by telling me that I needed to be Lebanese. Back in college, I had finally found my Arab voice and for the first time in my life was proud of who I was and of my culture. Yet I was married to someone who felt my identity embarrassed his family. He even told our daughters to never say they are half Palestinian and to identify themselves as Lebanese. Once again, I found myself in a predicament of not belonging. His verbal and emotional abuse escalated until I felt like he was trying to erase me.

In 2007, I made one of the biggest decisions of my life. I had to leave that marriage, and I knew it would not be easy. My daughters were teenagers, and I knew that marriage no longer belonged to me or to them. For a long time, we had money, a vacation home overlooking the Mediterranean Sea in Lebanon, lavish vacations, investment properties, a million-dollar home, and a very successful real-estate business. Those things did not improve my situation. My real issue was the sense of feeling safe, belonging, and love.

Midway through the marriage, I started to call myself Sarah as an attempt to convince myself that everything was okay by creating another identity. Sarah was "the happy one," "the pretender," and "woman in denial." No one knew that "Sarah" had drama or problems because she was very talented at covering it all up. I was not allowed to express "Sahar," say that I was Palestinian, or be myself. I was not allowed to do things that I secretly wanted to do. For years, I didn't belong to Sahar and longed to return to her.

The meaning of the name Sahar is "dawn." I made a decision to leave that marriage and "awaken to the dawn" within me. After I left, I chose to help women awaken to the dawn in them. So many women have a Sarah in them, and she needs to leave so they can express who they really are. They need to be authentic. If they are in a situation where they do not have the freedom to be authentic, they need to find the strength to leave. People never suspected that I was in an abusive relationship. I knew how to hide it. I was such a great actress.

When I made the decision to leave, I began to read inspirational books. I was attending personal development seminars and workshops behind my husband's back, and got to a point where I felt "Sahar" was ready to express who she was!

When I left, I was attending a yearlong training with an amazing coach. We had monthly meetings centered around learning to be accountable for our actions and ensuring the life we chose to live would be congruent with who we are. One day, I was very sad and opened my heart and shared with everybody what I felt. I finally said, "I think I am in an abusive relationship" and everyone else just looked at me and exclaimed, "You think!" I was afraid to admit that I was in an abusive relationship, because I was terrified of being accountable to leave. When I communicated this, the women in the group encouraged me to get help so I went to an abuse center. I realized that was the first step in admitting to myself that the marriage was completely toxic.

At the center, I had to complete a questionnaire about my marriage, listing all the different types of abuse. To my surprise, I answered "yes" to all of them. It was a big awakening for me. In the yearlong training, I was asked a series of questions: "What would it take for you to leave? What, specifically, would have to happen for you to be able to leave?" In fact, when I was asked that question, I attended a seminar where I was asked questions concerning three things that I wanted to achieve. One of them was for me to leave my marriage in 2006.

One year later in 2007, I had to answer that same question from my women's group again: What would it take to get me to leave? A few weeks after that meeting, the final incident occurred. On that final morning, I had just put on a new shirt while my husband was in the bathroom getting ready. He became angry and pushed me. Then he wiped shaving cream all over the shirt and said horrible things to me. The hardest part of that experience was when my daughter came in the room and witnessed it. I realized suddenly that it was over. I realized that I was accountable and it was time for me to leave that negative space. I went and put on another shirt and went for a drive. I thought, "Today is my freedom day, and today I will belong to Sahar!"

Later, I called him and pretended that everything was okay, because I did not want to come home to a fight. Sure enough, that evening, Sarah went out to dinner with him. It was smooth after that, but from August to October, Sahar was strategizing. I got a coaching certification and looked for a place to move.

Women who are in a similar situation and desire to leave must come up with a strategy. I did leave that relationship in 2007 and I am very happy now. There were financial challenges in the beginning, but my girls are very happy, and we live in a very positive space now. In many ways, I did it for them. I wanted to set an example.

No woman should be in an abusive relationship. I hope all women reading this decide they no longer want to be a "Sarah" and would rather be "Sahar." I feel now that I am really alive. In fact, now I know what direction I need to go in, and my mother was a big inspiration in rerouting me back on track and toward my calling.

FINDING LIFE AGAIN

When I was seventeen years old, my mother went to live in Palestine for two years to serve her people. She worked for the Palestine Red Crescent Society, a national humanitarian organization catering to the welfare and health of the Palestinian people, with Yasser Arafat's brother. She also worked in collaboration with the Palestine Liberation Organization. She did extensive social work with the refugees in Gaza and listened to their everyday struggles of war and conflict. She was particularly focused on the people of Gaza because she felt they did not have an outlet to express themselves.

At the time, I did not understand why my mother would leave us and go back to Palestine. I understand that passion now. When she was vice president of our local Arab Cultural Center in the 1980s, she would tell me stories of speaking in Iraq with all the dignitaries, including Yasser Arafat and Saddam Hussein. She would open up opportunities for us to travel to different countries and learn more about the Arab world. She took us to Syria, Lebanon, Jordan, and Egypt, and we got to witness her in action on home soil. She took me everywhere, because I think she knew deep down inside I would somehow take over her work when she passed on.

I remember several occasions when she went to Libya to speak for the Palestinian people on stage with President Muammar Gaddafi. She was a Christian woman, yet consistently in the presence of the Muslim world. She respected and honored every individual, regardless of their religious or social background. She started every speech with the words *bismi-llāhi r-raḥmāni r-raḥīm* (in the name of God most gracious and most merciful). She did this to publicly honor the Islamic nations in the Arab world.

In fact, she taught the Quran to Islamic African Americans. She was a Christian woman, yet knew being an Arab woman meant that she needed to honor and respect the Quran.

In the late 1980s, it was considered very taboo for Jews and Arabs to speak. There was too much political turmoil in the Holy Land, and we all felt the effects of the ethnic hatred. At a time when people avoided the subject of Israel/Palestine, my mother spearheaded an underground mastermind group with Senator Dianne Feinstein, encouraging Israelis and Palestinians to establish dialogue. During this time, she became more open to working and learning more about the Jewish-American community. She always believed collaboration, rather than hatred and blame, was key to overcoming war and conflict. She was working with the "enemy," and what an example that was! It's hard to open your heart and not come from a place of judgment, especially when your people are suffering in front of your eyes. Yet through the wars my mother witnessed and the refugees she visited, she always refused to hate.

In 1996, my mother and I attended the United Nations anniversary in San Francisco, representing the costumes and dress of the first seven Arab nations to join the United Nations. Presidents Carter and Ford were honorary guests at the event.

In 2001, not long after September 11, I helped my mother and a few women in the local Arab community form an outreach panel called Castro Valley Citizens for Middle Eastern Awareness. We were Muslim and Christian Palestinian women but later invited one of our Jewish friends to join us on the panel. We spoke of the cultural stigma of being Arabs in America. Our panel did an excellent job of debunking cultural myths and assumptions. There are so many false stories about Arabs and Israelis in the media. For the first time, I was able to see that the media makes all of us villains.

In 2004, my mother made a decision to go back to her homeland and live in Jordan permanently. She said it was a calling to be with her people, where she most felt she belonged; her journey in America was complete. Although in the United States she was afforded a platform to speak her messages in the open and the freedom to speak without threats, whereas if she had tried to do the same in Palestine she would have had a much more difficult time and less access to the dignitaries and politicians she had access to in the United States, she nevertheless felt she was a prisoner living in the United States because she was unavailable to her people. Thus, her "bars" were internal in nature. She wrote a book about this called *Prisoner Without Bars*.

Two years after my mother returned to Jordan, I witnessed an incident that forever changed my perception on the conflict between Israel and Palestine. My brother got married in 2006 and I went to Jerusalem for the ceremony. As I was walking into my family's house there was a bucket of rocks on the porch. When I asked about it, my mother told me something was going to erupt early in the morning. She told me that I should not worry about it because it would pass. I sat up in my bed that night and witnessed big tankers driving through the streets with teenaged Israeli soldiers yelling and shooting guns into the air. It was an attempt by the Israeli government to intimidate and degrade the Palestinian people and to give the message that we are not safe in the West Bank. It was purely a message of humiliation. There were young Palestinian children throwing rocks at the tankers. That was my turning point. I got home and decided that I wanted nothing to do with the conflict in terms of politics. I decided it was no longer a matter of "who is right and who is wrong." That incident was just an example of generation after generation of hate that had to settle. I realized that I could just sit on the sidelines, watch and be a Palestinian victim, or I could reach out to the other side and suggest that we hold hands together and do something about this sickness as a team. I vowed that I would never hate another Israeli again.

In 2007, my mother was asked to go to the Kabbalah convention in Jerusalem, where she represented the PLO (Palestine Liberation Organization). She courageously spoke in a room where 99 percent of the people were Jewish and Israelis! She was the only Arab Palestinian! From a Palestinian perspective, being in this space is very meaningful.

In 2010, I had the opportunity to be onstage with her in Jordan. I was able to speak from my perspective, where I encourage people not to judge, but to love. Through my mother, I learned the real power of love. I learned how exhausting hatred is. Honestly, it takes much more energy to hate than to love.

In the final years of her life, her work caught up with her. She had diabetes, and in August 2010, she underwent heart surgery, consisting of four bypasses and two arteries. Unfortunately, her body could not handle the surgery. On October 22, 2010, my best friend and hero passed away. She was so loved and respected in the community that hundreds of people showed up at her funeral. It was unbelievable to see the diversity of people who attended.

At one of the ceremonies honoring her, my sister and I wore her Palestinian dresses in all their beautiful colors to honor her. Her passing really had an impact on my life. I went through a deep depression and had to really reflect and understand what I was doing here on Earth. As I held the last book she published in my hands, I asked myself, "Am I taking my mom's legacy? Will I continue to work with women?" I have the Bright Side of Life women's gathering where 80 to 250 women celebrate diversity and connectivity on a monthly basis. I was happy doing that, but I knew that there was a greatness that I needed to share with the world. I realized I was ready to take on a bigger mission. It is my vision to bring both the Palestinian and the Jewish community together to understand and honor one another as human beings. In 2011, I founded the Gift of Acceptance Movement with an Israeli woman named Tzvia. She had not only served in the Israeli military but also survived cancer. Supposedly, I should hate her, but we believe that by working together, side by side, we can encourage people to stop hating and start accepting and honoring one another. Together, we want to turn the bullets being shed in the Holy Land into bullets of peace and the rocks being thrown into the rocks of connection. I am meeting incredible Israelis and we are doing work together by speaking and sharing the same stage. We are encouraged by the wonderful support from some of our Jewish and Arab communities. My true essence and purpose is to translate judgment into love; to be the bridge of healing from pain to love. We need to be an example for our communities.

After witnessing the living example of my mother, this has become my mission. I personally believe that women working together will take back the world. Women working together is where all change starts. I want to emphasize this point as I feel it is one of the most important things I have ever learned: Being a leader is not about having people follow you. Being a leader is being the first to do something that you stand for; being the first to take action on something that you stand for. My leadership initiative is for me to step into that role as a Palestinian woman who is ready to change minds.

In the Holy Land there are a lot of Israelis and Palestinians working together to make change. There are a lot of things that we don't see in the mainstream media, and I want the world to know about the good things that Israelis and Palestinians are doing together.

I believe each person has the power to accept.

I am grateful to my mother for the woman that she was. I am grateful on behalf of every man, woman, and child she served, and in whose lives she made a huge difference. I want to thank her on behalf of the world. She is continuing to serve from a bigger, more universal space. I love her, and I want to make her proud and carry on the torch.

SAHAR'S ADVICE FOR WOMEN

It does not matter where you come from or what you look like, you belong to this universe. No one, no country, no culture dictates whether you belong or not. Only you dictate that. Once you belong to yourself, then you belong to anything and everything.

TZVIA

Israel

The long-standing feud between Israel and Palestine is a brutal one, complete with a military occupation now lasting decades, millions of refugees with no right of return, and complicated politics. The situation has led to generations of hatred between the Palestinians and Israelis, sparking random acts of violence and tense living environments.

In Israel, military service is mandatory for men and women. Tzvia discusses her experience with the Israeli military, surviving thyroid cancer, and the bold initiative she is presently undertaking concerning the situation between Israel and Palestine.

ALTHOUGH I WAS born in Canada, I am Israeli. Israel is my home and where I grew up from the age of six years old. When I first moved to Israel, I wore long, ugly dresses and didn't speak a word of Hebrew.

In addition to my silly attire, I had a brother who was extremely overweight. My brother and I had a challenging beginning between the language, the climate, and our appearance. It took us about a year to become acquainted to our new life.

We moved to Israel because my Jewish parents became very pro-Israel. It was the Jewish state, the haven for all of us. Ideally, we moved to Israel to settle down, but we did anything but that! My mom, whom I often describe as a gypsy, would move us to another city or village every year. I never understood her motivation in the constant shuffling around.

My current husband was actually my very first friend. When I was seven years old, my dad participated in research, and my current husband's father was one of his researchers. When we were seven years old, my husband and I played together, and twenty years later we met again. My parents met his parents by chance at an airport in England, and the situation produced the usual dialogue of "How is your son doing? How is your daughter doing? Is she married to anyone yet?" The Jewish culture is very matchmaking, so it is common for the family of a Jewish girl to try to set her up. I didn't remember him when he called me, but his dad used to make 8mm movies with us, so we have a lot of our earlier moments captured on film. He was my first friend and is my best friend today, as well as my husband and the father of my kids.

When I was in seventh grade, my mom decided to leave my dad and go out on her own. One year later in 1982 when I was in eighth grade, the Israel-Lebanon war started. My brother fought in that war. It was a big war and a big deal for an eighth grader. I don't think I really understood what war meant; I just knew something bad was happening, and that notion produced a lot of fear. Israel is such a small country that it would only take about six hours to drive north to south, and east to west is a one-hour drive. At times, the war was only a few hours away. It really felt close to home. Everybody I knew was there or involved somehow or was somehow affected by it. Everyone knew when someone died. At the time, the population in Israel was only about five million, and everybody knew everybody. It's a very small community, so when a soldier died, you likely knew him or her or one of your friends did.

After the war ended, things were better. My parents decided to get back together, so we moved again to a place called a Kibbutz. It is a community living arrangement where about five hundred people live in a small village. They milk cows together, eat together, and the kids are separated from the parents in different homes when they sleep. A Kibbutz is based on social economic theory. Nobody has their own money because the community provides for itself. You get what you need in terms of basic needs, but that is it. Everything is done as a community. There is little space for individualization.

The basic philosophy of the Kibbutz is "your life is my life, and if you do something, then I'll know about it." There are no secrets. For me, this was challenging. I was fourteen years old, and I was suddenly in a position where I had to sleep away from home and do what I was told to do. I only saw my parents twice a week between the hours of four and seven. As a kid, I didn't like being away from my parents. Even when I was sent to camp, I hated it. I did not want to eat with four hundred people, sleep in the same room as other kids, or share all my free time with large groups of people. The privacy aspect was gone. When that aspect disappears, you get the urge to rebel, especially as a teenager, because you are trying to figure yourself out. I lived in the Kibbutz from ninth grade to the end of twelfth. When you finish twelfth grade in Israel, young women are required to serve in the military for two years, and young men go for three years. I have never had the desire to set foot in that Kibbutz again once I left to enter the Israeli army.

The only way to get out of the mandatory army service is to get married or become very religious. Growing up in Israel, the army and the wars are part of our daily existence. If a man or woman refused to enter the army, society would perceive there to be something wrong with that person. You would not be able to find a job if you didn't serve your term. There is automatically a black stain on you for turning your back on your duties as a citizen of Israel. Even young children talk about it in grade school. I have observed that people are getting more upset with the system today. I think it's the social-media phase of this world that is making our youth more reluctant to join. I will be interested to see how the younger generations will react to the practice of conscription.

Entering the army was quite a highlight for me after spending all those years in a Kibbutz. Upon entering, I was fortunate to get help from a family friend who placed me in a good unit. Being part of a good unit means a better experience, and the one I served in was quite small. It was only three girls and one hundred boys. Can you imagine? Me. The girl who never really had a boyfriend in her teenage years, and suddenly there were one hundred boys everywhere!

My specific position was to take care of the soldiers. We had to give them emotional support, much like a "girl Friday." I was their point of contact for just about everything. We would bake cakes for the boys and care for them as though we were the mothers of the unit.

I gained a lot of self-confidence from that role. It was fun, yet very challenging. The boys in the unit were actually fighters who trained for war. For example, if there were alleged terrorists around, then they would have to investigate the situation and capture them.

I served in the army for the mandatory two years. Often in military situations, you see things you hope to never see again. I will never forget going to settlements and places where Arabs lived, knocking at their door in the middle of the night, and pulling the families out to check them when they were suspected of something. Today, I honestly think there has to be another way. I don't know if one exists. I don't know what happens above me in ranks or with the government. All I know is, for me, I imagine what it must feel like for a kid when army soldiers knock at the door in the middle of the night. I feel sorry for those families. Today, I don't think I could do what I did or see what I saw back then. I was not a fighter in the army, but I think it would really be a hard position for someone to be a fighter. In Israel, we don't have the choice of what kind of army service we prefer to do. You don't know until the last minute where you will be after basic training.

After our unit disbanded at the end of the service, most of us remained in touch and are friends for life. In our adult years, if any of us need help, we are all there for each other. Those are the kinds of bonds the army creates. This is true for all military situations or team-oriented environments.

THE FILM INDUSTRY AND INTIFADA

After my required appointment in the army expired, I was not accepted to the officer course I applied to, so I decided to visit my brother in California. He lived in Los Angeles, and I more or less fell in love with the movie industry. When I returned to Israel, I decided to check into who the important people were in the movie industry and discovered one big company that produced all the action movies made in Israel. I knew I had to get in.

I started bugging a man in charge of the extras for the movies for a job, and my persistence paid off. One day he called and told me to come to the set in Tel Aviv at 4:00 AM. I was twenty-one years old and on my way to a career path! I was responsible for finding extras, organizing them, bringing them to the set, and taking care of them. My military experience served me well in this job. When one movie was over, they took me to another, and I slowly built a reputation. Shortly after that, I became an assistant director for one movie, and then I continued to another movie, slowly, but surely, moving up the ranks to assistant director, until I got into production.

I did this until the Intifada started. This was when the Palestinian population began an uprising in protest of the Israeli occupation of Palestinian territories. It does not take much to spark something in Palestine or Israel, and when it happens, everything blows up and out of proportion. In one incident, a taxi driver was killed, and that lit up the country, sparking a new war between Israel and Palestine. It was a mess. There were bombings of malls and parks in Israel. During the Intifada, all the movies left and never came back because Morocco offered them much more than we did. My last big experience in the movie industry occurred when I worked as an assistant director on *Schindler's List*. I transitioned to television with a large advertising agency, who opened the first commercial television station in Israel. I produced more than six hundred commercials over a period of about seven years, until I decided to move to the United States.

I did not want to leave Israel, but when my daughter was born, there was so much fighting going on in Israel that it was never safe to take her to the mall or the park. There was always tension in the air. I suppose when you don't have children, this kind of environment is seen from a different angle. Suddenly, knowing there were alleged terrorists around, I didn't want to be there anymore. Times had changed too drastically and were too dangerous. For example, if you were in public and noticed a bag sitting on the ground, you would immediately call the police for fear that it was an explosive device. You were constantly on high alert. Anywhere you would walk, you wondered who people were and what they were doing. It is a very paranoid mentality. Every coffee shop you went into, your bag would be checked, and everyone would walk around with an air of suspicion toward everything. When I had my daughter, I questioned whether

Israel was the right place for her and for us. I remember one of our parent arguments at her pre-school was whether or not there should be a bodyguard. It was a big argument and a turning point. Why did I need that environment?

I became pregnant with my second child when we decided to move to the United States. We wanted to go to a place where everyday life was calmer and held less violence.

CHANGE OF SENTIMENT

In moving to the United States, I really learned a lot about myself and about Israel. Where you live ultimately does affect how you think and what you think. Culture is always the underlying theme for all perception. There were several occurrences where God appeared to be checking me. He gave me two teachers for my children who were Arabs. One was from Jordan, and one was from Syria. In Israel, I would never have had a Muslim teacher teaching my son. My son was two at the time, and the thought of a Muslim woman changing his diapers and taking care of him made me very uncomfortable. They were very traditional Muslim women, too, and I wondered how I would handle it.

It was very therapeutic, because I had to break through a lot of resistance that came from where I was raised. I had to ask myself what the resistance was about regarding those two Muslim women. When I did, I found it was about growing up in a place where these women could never be my friends; yet in the United States, they could be without any problem. That fear was instilled in me by the Israeli culture. In the end, we became very good friends, simply because we knew we could never be friends back home. We all moved to the United States for one main reason—to have a better life or a different life. Now we have Lebanese friends, Jordanian friends, and I even have a friend named Yasser, which is shocking for an Israeli!

BACK TO ISRAEL

When I decided to move back to Israel a few years ago, I wondered how to take these new friendships with me. How would they translate in my homeland, especially with all the negative sentiment toward the Arab population? When I landed in Israel on my move back, I still believed Israelis and Palestinians could be friends. My connection with the two teachers changed me, or so I thought. After about two or three weeks, I changed back to my old views because the hatred and the tension are so strong from both sides. There is a lot of blame and hatred for the events of the last sixty years. They throw a bomb, then we throw a bomb. We take their family away, then they take our family away. It never ends. Until there is leadership that will make the atrocities end, they will continue. It's so far away from that progressive end. When you live in an environment like that, you become a product of those ideals. I observed that in my own psyche.

For example, when my daughter started going to school in Israel, she never even knew of an Arab-Palestinian issue. It's something that we never spoke about, especially while we were living in the United States with Arab friends. We always taught our children to accept everybody, no matter what or who they are.

She was in school for about three weeks and came home saying negative things about Palestinians. I saw how the shift was happening in her young mind. The hatred was there, like it was being pumped in daily, whether by friends, radio, or news. In Israel the news runs every half hour, so you are always on the alert. That makes everyone in the culture very nervous. The day-to-day in Israel is similar to American life, but with added tension in anticipation for war or bombing. After only a few months, we decided that we did not want to stay; although we had made such a huge shift to move back there, it was not the right decision. Overall, I am grateful I did that shift. I am grateful that I was able to decide for myself the right life that I wanted. It was tough for my children because the shift between being an American kid and living in Israel was about 180 degrees apart.

Israel had always been my Plan B. When I moved back, I realized I did not have that option anymore. I always have to learn the hardest way, by trying things out. Until I try it and "get burned by it," I don't learn.

FIGHTING CANCER

After we decided Israel was not the right place for us, my doctor found a lump in my neck. I stood in front of the mirror and saw it, surprised I never noticed it before.

My doctor warned me there was a small percentage of a chance I had cancer, and they decided to do a biopsy. He said that he would let me know in a few weeks. In the meantime, my husband and I were planning our move back to the United States. One day, we were sitting in a coffee shop that we really loved when the phone rang. It was the doctor, and he delivered some devastating news: I had thyroid cancer. Right away, I started crying in the middle of the coffee shop. I felt like I was dying. The impact of such news feels like a hammer dropping on your head. There is a lot of shock and disbelief. He said I had a 2.5-centimeter lump near my thyroid and they needed to take it out right away. At the beginning, I kept thinking, *why me?* Then the fight became me wrestling with the word itself.

The word "cancer" is difficult to come to terms with. I never actually believed I could have it. I was healthy, played sports, and ate the recommended foods. Once I understood what having cancer meant, it became less daunting. "Cancer" is just a word, yet we give that word all of its destructive power. I realized if we did not do that, it would not be so frightening.

After my experience, I certainly advise others struggling with cancer not to give the word so much power. Look at the treatment as a routine. It's not as easy as it sounds, but giving it so much meaning makes it harder to confront. Be confident that it can be fixed. Be confident that your body has the power to heal itself. I was lucky because there are terrible cancers, and thyroid cancer is one of the easier ones to treat. The way I look at the situation is if it comes back, at least now I know what the treatment is like and what I need to do. I think one of the hardest things to deal with is the uncertainty. What is it going to feel like getting the radiation treatment? What is it going to feel like telling the kids? Now I know the process. It's interesting how the fog surrounding certain things we don't know or understand is so huge. Worrying does not serve us positively in anything. We need to focus on what needs to be done and not worry. Once we get past the uncertainty, everything is clearer.

The best advice I can give people just diagnosed with cancer is to call it cancer. Call it what it is. There are a lot of good doctors today who know how to treat cancer. The meaning we give that word is practically prophetic. Get over that and work on what needs to be taken care of. I was in mourning for about three days when I was diagnosed, but after I stopped feeling sorry for myself, I was able to move on. None of us choose to have cancer. I always thought that forty-one years old was too young to get cancer, and then I was diagnosed with it.

ISRAEL AND PALESTINE

After my battle with cancer, I met my friend Sahar, a Palestinian woman who also shares her story in this book. We both became a team toward a new initiative called the Gift of Acceptance Movement, where we facilitate dialogue between the Israeli and Palestinian communities. I grew up in an Israeli family, and she grew up in a Palestinian family, and we supposedly should have learned to hate each other. On the contrary, we accept and love each other and believe that others can do the same.

My personal belief is that Palestinians and Israelis don't have to love each other. Trying to force such emotions is overkill. To start, we need to just accept each other and listen to each other and the pain each of us experienced at the hands of each other. When we take this approach, we see another human being who has their own suffering, their own happiness, and their own kids and family. Once we see that we are human beings and we are all the same, then we can begin to love. The second level is love, but first there has to be a level of looking someone in the eye and making an effort to understand that person as another human being. In Palestine and Israel, we can't even do that right now. We need to start with that as a foundation. I have a very good friend named Yasser who is Egyptian. The first time he sat next to me, I was nervous. In talking to him, I learned he was actually very kind, funny, and had kids the same age as my own. If we can just make a connection like that in the first stage, we are already on our way. First, we want to get something going, planting a small seed so the tree can grow.

For us, the gift of acceptance is so important. If we can get a lot of women to follow us, we can solve so many issues that men can't solve because they have egos. There is no way two men will solve the problems in the Middle East; it will take the women who have sensibility and possess motherly care. If women raise their voices, life could eventually be a little nicer in Israel and Palestine. This concept does not exclusively apply to Palestine and Israel. It can apply to Scotland and Ireland or Pakistan and India. There is no shortage of hatred in the world in need of positive intervention.

The Gift of Acceptance Movement is about coming together and seeing things from a human perspective. All of the events in my life have led me to this mission, and I am very excited to see it develop and spread. I believe we can do incredible things and break many barriers.

TZVIA'S ADVICE FOR WOMEN

Keep your power, because once you give away your power, you are doomed. Trust your power and trust yourself. A woman's guts are the strongest guts. So many women are told what to do by society or by their husbands that they lose their power. Women seek approval too often. Take your strengths and use them. When you ride a horse, you control a horse; I would like to see more women riding that metaphorical horse and telling it where to go.

WARDA

Palestine

The long-standing feud between Israel and Palestine is a brutal one, with a military occupation now lasting decades, millions of refugees with no right of return, and complicated politics. Warda discusses her family's experience during the 1948 and 1967 wars, the current situation in Palestine, and her battle with severe arthritis that has crippled her since childhood.

M Y STORY IS a fascinating tapestry of culture, history, courage, and strength. I am blessed by God to come from a wonderful, loving, and close family. Things have not always been easy for me, but when I tell my story, I tell it with pride for my family, our origins, and our closeness.

I will begin with my family. I am an Arab Palestinian. My entire family is from Palestine, and my mother is specifically from Jerusalem. When I say "Palestine," I am referring to two parts of the Middle

East known as West Bank and Gaza. The history of this part of the world is very complicated.

To this day, I still have a lot of family back home in the West Bank area of Palestine, but because of a ban, my family lives in the United States. We're not allowed to live in the Holy Land anymore, even though both of my parents were born and raised on the land. Although born in Jerusalem, my mother does not have a birth certificate. She was denied one because of the political changes that divided East and West Jerusalem at the time of her birth and following the 1948 Arab-Israeli War. At this time, Jerusalem was divided into two parts—the West, or "Jewish" portion, came under Israeli rule, while East Jerusalem, populated mainly by Muslim and Christian Palestinians, came under Jordanian rule. Arabs living in certain western Jerusalem neighborhoods were forced to leave. Although East Jerusalem was captured and annexed by Jordan after the 1948 Arab-Israeli War, after the 1967 Six-Day War, the eastern part of Jerusalem came under Israeli rule, along with the entire West Bank of Palestine.

As of the 19th century, the Palestinian land was inhabited by a multicultural population that lived relatively in harmony with one another. There were mostly Muslims and small percentages of Christians and Jews. After the Holocaust of World War II, a group of Jewish Zionists examined nearly the entire world to find a place to establish a Jewish state, including Africa and the Americas, before settling on Palestine. Their immigration to Palestine caused countless issues and fighting broke out all along the Holy Land. The United Nations intervened in 1947, giving half of the land to the budding Jewish nation in the UN Partition Plan, leading to what is known as the 1948 Arab-Israeli War. Many Palestinians refer to this as "the 48." Hundreds of thousands of Palestinians fled and became refugees in border countries like Syria, Jordan, and Lebanon. The refugees created from this war still, in present day, do not have the "right of return" to go back to their lands and are not considered Palestinian citizens.

In the 1967 Six-Day War, otherwise known as "the 67," more refugees spilled out of Palestine. As a result, the Palestinian territory began to shrink further. Now, only the West Bank and Gaza strip territories of what used to be Palestine remain and are under Israeli military occupation, causing daily conflict in the land. Several Palestinian rebel groups have emerged in the past decades in response to the occupation and refugee situation, including the Intifada in 2000, where the Palestinian population began an uprising.

The complicated politics in this part of the world can make family visits very difficult. Arabs who are American citizens are only allowed to visit once a year and only for the amount of time allotted on the American passport.

Even though we have a lot of family back in Palestine, some are in areas that we cannot go into. Israel has set up border checkpoints between the West Bank and Jordan that are nearly impossible to cross. We need permission, which we have to apply for months in advance. People waiting to cross the border are literally out in the sun in sweltering heat with no shelter, bathrooms, or water. My brothers tried to cross the checkpoint between the West Bank and Jordan once and were sent away and had to return to the border the next morning before dawn. Even then, they still did not arrive at the checkpoint until evening. It's very tiring for healthy people to make this journey under those circumstances, but for those who are sick or elderly, it can be fatal. I am not in the greatest health, so a process like this is far too strenuous for me. With my health problems and my wheelchair, I can't make it because I cannot carry all of my possessions or sit for long periods of time in the heat.

My family is not in the minority concerning this split existence. In fact, Palestinian families have been divided for quite some time due to the long-standing debate about the "right of return." Since the war in 1948, there are Palestinian refugees living in camps on the Lebanese border and in Syria. Our refugees are not given citizenship in these border countries because the goal is to eventually send them back to Palestine with the Palestinian right of return policy, otherwise known as UN General Assembly Resolution 194. This policy asserts that Palestinian refugees, both first generation refugees and their descendants, have a right to return to the land they were forced to leave during the 1948 and 1967 wars in what is now Israel and the Palestinian territories of West Bank and Gaza. The problem is this policy is still debated heavily, and thus these refugees have since remained without the ability to return or citizenship in either Lebanon or Syria.

This has broken up Palestinian families for generations, and it's very tragic.

There are still family members whom we can visit in Palestine and have traveled to see. When I visit, I feel safe and welcomed, but there is not much to do because we are limited to the occupied territories where Arab American citizens are permitted to be. We are lucky to have American citizenship. Surprisingly, having a foreign nationality gives us more rights than our real nationality in our own land.

I won't lie. Sometimes, I am slightly afraid to visit my family in Palestine because of everything I know and observe in the news. The news never gets any better in my homeland. Once I am there, however, I remember how much I love my people. I would go every summer to visit my family if my health permitted it.

My health issues have been a significant part of my life. Most important, they have never stopped me from living it to the fullest extent possible. I have juvenile rheumatoid arthritis. This is not a genetic condition, but rather the result of an allergic reaction to the MMR2 vaccine that aims to prevent measles, mumps, and rubella. When I received the shot, my immune system was too weak to fight the disease that was injected into my tiny baby body. In Palestine, they didn't have vaccines, so when the doctors in the United States told my mother to vaccinate me, she thought she was protecting me. It is strongly suspected by parent activist groups that the particular vaccine I received causes my condition, as well as autism and in more severe cases, potentially brain damage. My advice to mothers: Don't trust vaccines; research them before agreeing to administer them to your babies or small children.

Due to my condition, doctors and hospitals were a part of my childhood since I was about two years old. Every year until I was thirteen years old, I spent three months in the children's hospital receiving physical therapy. At the age of sixteen, I had my first operation where both of my hips were replaced. Then I had two more surgeries to replace both of my knees. I never got to experience anything "normal" in my youth—nothing normal in Arab culture and nothing normal in American culture.

I was wheelchair bound for ten years. I could not stand or walk and was stuck in the same position from my hips and knees. After the surgery, I had extensive therapy and came out walking, which was a surprise to my doctors. I was never supposed to walk, finish high school, or go to college. I have a track record of proving people wrong. It's actually become a talent of mine to do the things that they said I would never do.

My physical health issues caused me problems within the school system. Teachers attempted to place me in special education classes for people with learning disabilities who cannot excel independently. My mother had to fight the system and continuously explain to them that there was nothing wrong with my mind; I only had physical disabilities. If my mother had not fought for me, I never would have been put in mainstream classrooms, attended college, or obtained a master's degree. In the 1980s, people like me were considered a disturbance for the other students. There was nothing wrong with my mind, just my body, but they figured since I was "disabled," I MUST be mentally disabled, too.

One of the most important times my mother advocated for me was when I was sent to a hospital in another state around the age of seven years old. It turned out to be a mental institution for children experiencing severe mental disorders. I noticed the parents would take their children there, leave them, and never come back. They would be completely abandoned. It was a very physically abusive hospital, and I was the only vocal one since impairments often left the other children unable to speak. I saw kids being pulled by their hair and thrown down. Some were beaten for crying or throwing a fit. I was the voice for these kids. I take pride in being the voice of someone who can't speak for themselves. I don't know how I could understand them, but I could and would tell the nurse what they needed or wanted. Of course, I would also be yelled at and sent to my room without food; once, I was not allowed to call my family for several weeks. I also remember telling the nurse that I could not go into the water because the cold temperature would inflame my arthritis. According to her, I was being contentious, so she asked the aides to throw me into the water.

When my mother was finally allowed to visit, she took me back home. When she arrived, I was crying to her and hiding under her feet, talking to her in Arabic as I described the behavior of the nurses and staff. She was appalled and threatened to call the police if the doctors didn't sign me out.

I was in such bad shape from the treatment I was literally a board, stuck like a rock. You could not touch or move me. My mother admitted me for emergency care, where I stayed for almost four months to gain mobility back.

After the hospital situation, my mother was too scared to leave me alone again, until I was about sixteen years old. She was always very devoted to me, and so was my father. My parents are wonderful to me and always have been.

My mother was not used to the views people in the United States have of the disabled, because they are not so looked down on in Palestine. In the holy Quran, the prophet says that God desires for us to care for the disabled and the elderly and ensure they are always properly provided for. God wants us to provide for them at any cost, be it money or medicine. In Islam, this care is looked upon as a test of faith from God. At a very young age, I was taught that God chose me to be the way I am because He loves me. He is not only testing my faith and love for Him, but He also wants me to be with Him in the end. I believe this is a way of cleansing in this lifetime. Maybe I suffer now, but in the afterlife, I will be free of the suffering.

For example, in Islam, we believe if you are blind, you will be one of the few who are allowed to see God in His true nature at the end of your life. I believe in the end I will be pain-free. I will have everything I didn't have in this life and will be with the few who get to see God with their bare eyes, hear his voice, and speak to him—the first of all, other than the prophet Muhammad.

Those with illness suffer in this life because God chose them to suffer. The sick and meek do not go through the trials and tribulations in the afterlife that healthy people must go through. The healthy in this life must answer to their actions in the afterlife because God gave them their health as a gift. I try to keep this thought in mind when I suffer because of my illness. Maybe things are not easy now for me, but when it really matters, things will be easier. The thought of seeing God in the end helps with the depression due to my chronic pain. It will never go away. My whole body hurts, especially my joints. I am in pain from my past surgeries. My joints that were replaced are not supposed to hurt, but they do because they have bone from real joint around them. Sometimes the pain becomes so severe that I don't sleep and I cry. I have to take medication to control the pain. It's been that way for me for years and is slowly getting worse. I have always tried not to let the pain hold me back.

When it was time for me to go to college I claimed my independence. The day I told my doctor I was accepted into college, his staff's jaws dropped to the floor. I am the kind of person who will do anything to prove you wrong if you tell me that I can't do something. I wanted to prove that I could take care of myself upon entering college. After I moved into my own housing unit, there was a lot of readjusting around my physical limitations. I had to learn how to dress myself, bathe myself, and prepare food. It was my first time living independently, and I had been heavily dependent on my family's caretaking. This made my family very nervous. If they called and I did not answer the phone, I knew I would have ten minutes to call back before my mother would be on the way. I answered her calls quickly, telling her I was fine, breathing, and not on the floor.

I had to use an electric wheelchair to get around the campus. I could walk a little, but not very much. People stared at me, yet I was never bothered by their gawking. On the first day of classes, I would try to break the ice with whomever was sitting next to me in the class by making jokes about how I looked and how I walked in order to ease the tension.

One of my biggest accomplishments was founding and becoming president of the university's Muslim Student Association. I'm naturally bossy, so the leadership role was almost second nature. I created it to educate people about Islam and invite others outside of the Muslim community to join us. I felt there were too many stereotypes about Arabs and Muslims and wanted to create a place where people could get answers to their questions and interact with us. When it began, I even invited my Christian friends to the meetings, and they came in support of me, which was very nice. The association was difficult at times because we had a lot of different views present, and I had to control the sentiments. I didn't want negative words or thoughts entering our group because it was created to be an open place, promoting positive Islamic values. My open-minded approach to its leadership came from my experiences with the Palestinian culture and my mother's stories of the Holy Land before the conflicts got so bad. Here is one story I often told: My mother went to a school in

Jerusalem where she was taught by Catholic nuns. They would split Muslims into a Muslim class and Christians into a Christian class. During prayer time, they would go into the church to pray. When the Christians would come during Easter and do a pilgrimage to chronicle the birth of Jesus through the crucifixion, they would walk from Bethlehem to Jerusalem. My mother would hold candles and walk with them. She always said it was beautiful to see Muslims and Christians walking together. Christians from all over the world would come for this pilgrimage. Throngs of people would walk toward one spiritual goal. You wouldn't know who was Muslim and who was Christian; they were all one.

Sadly after the Israeli occupation, the Christians were not allowed to do the pilgrimage anymore. At Christmas, the Christians used to fast with the Muslims, and the Muslims would march with the Christians. I was always amazed to hear my mother's stories of these events. We never hear about such unity in the media, and that saddens me. My mother's stories of her youth have taught me how easy it is to be one and share a connection to God through commonalities.

The Christians are the minority in our part of the world, and the Muslims feel a sense of duty to protect their brotherhood and sisterhood with the Christians because that is what it tells us to do in the Quran. Help the oppressed, free the oppressed, and respect the people of the book. Let me be clear that both Christians and Jews are considered people of the book. In Islam, we believe in Jesus. We believe in his miracles, his birth, and all the amazing things he did. We are told to love all the prophets the same, no more and no less. They are all the messengers of God; they are all given certain powers. You will never hear my culture speaking negatively about any prophet because they will fight for any, regardless whether he is Jesus, Moses, Abraham, or Muhammad. The common thought about Islam is that we don't believe in Jesus and don't respect him, which is completely not true. We respect the teachings of Jesus equally to those of Muhammad.

It's difficult to explain that to people who don't know much about Islam or Christianity, but it summarizes my approach to the student association. This is why I welcomed students of other faiths, not just Muslim students. I had to. I believe we are all people of God.

After I finished college and earned my master's degree, my health problems persisted and continue to persist to this day. Although I was told my disease was in remission, the damage it left continues to cause chronic pain every day. I have to take medication to control it. My doctors are honest with me and have told me many times that nothing can be done about it.

I get through each day with reading, music, and prayer. I particularly love Michael Jackson's music. One principle I have learned through his music and through my life is if you raise your voice with other people alongside you, nobody can deny you. I think that's true for me, at least, with my disability, ethnicity, and fighting spirit—challenging the education system and fighting to get the story of Palestinians heard by the masses.

Prayer is another way I deal with the pain. I mentioned earlier my close relationship with God. I was blessed by God with my mother, who is a HUGE part of my inner strength. We have more of a sister-sister relationship than that of mother-daughter because we are always together. I joke and laugh with her all of the time. Our closeness comes from the fact that we have been through hell and back. Being the mother of a disabled child, she has learned a lot through me and my obstacles.

When I look to my future, she is one of my strengths. Despite the pain I suffer, I have many goals: I want to get a job working with children who have been recently injured and are disabled. I want to give them hope and lift their spirits. I believe children in this state can live a full life; they just need extensive support. My mother and I have talked before about adopting children from the Middle East, especially Palestine. There are so many orphans in the Gaza strip. In these situations, I might not be able to help financially as much as I'd like, but I have many ideas for what I would like to do if I had the opportunity. I have always wanted to build a handicap- accessible school back home in Palestine for people using wheelchairs and crutches. Sadly, this dream is a bit of a long shot for me because I'd have to go through Israel and get approval for building and other permits. More than likely, they would not be approved. This is sad, because this area of the world is really where my heart is. It is where my family is, and I really want to help this part of the world because they don't have the things they need or deserve. Financially, the cost would be significant, assuming I could get the necessary permissions.

Building a community college has also been a goal for my mother and me because a lot of people in Palestine can't afford to go to college. We've talked about creating financial aid or a scholarship so people who have the grades to go to college will have the ability to go. The problem is we would have to go through the Israeli government because they control the water, electricity, and building permits. I will never give up hope that one day I can make this a reality. I believe God will help me to accomplish this in some way. When you give, you give for God. For my family, giving is everything. I put other people before myself. I have always been that way and will always continue to be that way because of my religion.

When my mother was growing up, before Arafat came into power, there were no checkpoints and no walls in Palestine. Everyone lived side by side in peace. Although I am Palestinian, I don't hate any other religions or cultures in our part of the world. I honestly don't hate anybody except oppression and senseless killing. I don't understand why we can't just go back to being neighbors. We are all people of God. We are all going to go back to him and we are all created by him. This is what I believe. Alhamdulillah.

WARDA'S ADVICE FOR WOMEN

1. "There is nothing that can't be done if we raise our voices as one." This is my favorite Michael Jackson quote.
2. You don't need a man to justify who you are.
3. Don't let anybody tell you what you can and can't do.
4. Prove the world wrong; go out there and show them what you've got!

SOUTHERN EUROPE

ITALY

SLOVENIA
LJUBLJANA

• ZAGREB

HUNGARY

CROATIA

SRPSKA
KRAJINA

VOJVODINA

• NOVI SAD

ROMANIA

BOSNIA
AND
HERZEGOVINA

• SARAJEVO

BELGRADE

SERBIA

ADRIATIC

SEA

MONTE-
NEGRO

PODGORICA

KOSOVO

PRISTINA

BULGARIA

SKOPJE

MACEDONIA

GREECE

SILVIJA

Croatia

Beginning in the early '90s, a series of wars known as the Yugoslav Wars broke out in the former Yugoslavia. These wars ultimately led to the breakup of the country of Yugoslavia into six republics and two autonomous regions. In 1991, Croatia declared independence from Yugoslavia and denounced the presidency of Slobodan Milosevic. In the aftermath of this declaration, ethnic Serbian populations along the border of Croatia rebelled. In 1997, nineteen-year-old Silvija began working with the United Nations High Commissioner for Refugees processing refugees and displaced persons in her home country resulting from Operation Storm, the largest military land offensive since World War II. The goal of Operation Storm was to free ethnic-Serb-held territory in Croatia known as Srpska Krajina. Silvija narrates her experiences and observations as a field officer.

I F I COULD say one thing looking back on my experience with the United Nations High Commissioner for Refugees (UNHCR), I would have to admit that I was slightly naïve going into my job.

I was in college in the United States when I applied for work with UNHCR. My major was international business with an emphasis on diplomacy. UNHCR was still attempting to resettle displaced persons and quell ethnic disputes in my native Croatia as late as 1997. I wanted to contribute something positive to humanity and believed strongly in the UN Charter. My passion was international relations and my own country was dealing with serious issues. I felt working for UNHCR in Croatia was the best fit for me because I am Croatian and know the culture and language. I was only nineteen years old when I started as a field officer; a very naïve, doe-eyed, blonde girl who just wanted to change the world—little did I know that this experience would ultimately change me.

I returned to my native Croatia in 1997 with UNHCR, just a couple of years after Operation Storm. The last military operation in the Croatian War of Independence, Operation Storm was a Croatian army–led operation to free up Srpska Krajina, a 630-kilometer border area of Bosnia and Croatia that was previously taken over by the ethnic-Serb population living in Croatia.

BACKGROUND: NATIONALISM AND THE CROATIAN WAR OF INDEPENDENCE

Before the series of wars that broke out in the 1990s, the Balkans was one large socialist federal republic known as Yugoslavia.

Yugoslavia used to include a central government governing six republics: Slovenia, Croatia, Montenegro, Bosnia-Herzegovina, Serbia, and Macedonia, and two autonomous regions of Kosovo and Vojvodina. The wars were the result of the stirring up of ethnic nationalism prompted by Serbian Communist Party leader, Slobodan Milosevic, shortly after he came into power. His ultimate goal was to create a unified state of Serbian brotherhood across the Balkans. He set about this goal by sparking nationalism in ethnic Serbians residing in many of the Balkan republics, namely Croatia and Bosnia.

With the dissolution of Yugoslavia, Croatia declared independence in 1991, sparking the Croatian War of Independence where ethnic-Serb populations, in coordination with the Milosevic-backed Yugoslav People's Army, began an offensive against the Croat population across the border areas of Croatia. This is when many of the heavy battles of the Yugoslav wars began and when nationalism reached its peak. Two of the most notable battles were in the Dalmatia-region town Knin and in the eastern border town of Vukovar, where the ethnic cleansing of many Croats occurred. I spent time in both of these regions with UNHCR.

Although the conflicts of the Croatian War of Independence mainly ended in 1992, the ethnic-Serbian population managed to take control of one third of Croatia, declaring sovereignty over two areas, the eastern Croatian border with Serbia and a region of Dalmatia referred to as Srpska Krajina. It was the diplomatic equivalent of declaring an independent country within the borders of a country, and caused tensions between the Serb population and other Croats, although these Serb and Croatian people had been living in Croatia side by side for generations.

In 1995, Operation Storm, the largest land offensive since World War II, occurred. Lasting eighty-four hours, it was a complete victory for Croatia, allowing them to recapture territory held by Serb forces and the ethnic-Serbian population since 1991. The event caused scores of Serbian refugees to be forced from these areas.

MY ASSIGNMENT

When I applied for work with UNHCR, I wanted to go into the occupied Dalmatia region. Although it was two years after Operation Storm, UNHCR was still working with refugees and displaced persons from that region. I was thrilled when I found out that I'd been accepted as a field officer.

On the first day of the job, I was taken to an enormous two-story house where I would be staying. A couple of days later, I came back home after work and suddenly came to the realization that I was living in somebody's abandoned house. I noticed that nothing had been removed from inside and it was just as though it had been lived in yesterday. It did not take me long to figure out that the house belonged to a displaced family. It was an eerie feeling. I was living in their house without their permission, a notion that I could not shake my entire stay there.

When I arrived at the UNHCR field office in Knin, I learned that there was a field officer from Finland and that the chief officer was American, though originally from Nigeria. There were also several Croatian workers who were acting as drivers and performing other support positions. That was the main cast of characters in the UNHCR office.

In the days prior to Operation Storm, the United Nations anticipated mass casualties and in an effort to minimize them, the United Nations Protection Force (UNPROFOR) helped to evacuate the civilian population from the territory under attack, essentially displacing them. The displaced people were mainly those who religiously identified themselves as Orthodox and were considered Serbian. The sudden need to declare one's ethnicity and religion created a massive ethnic divide among the people of the Dalmatia region.

There are obvious challenges to defining nationality and ethnicity when one day you identify your nationality as Yugoslavian and the next you are identified as Croatian or Serbian. When this started to happen, religions became a way to define one's ethnicity or nationality. Very few people were religious because we lived in a communist society. Croatians are generally Catholic and Serbians are generally Orthodox. People declaring their religion as Orthodox were automatically Serbian and were subsequently considered an enemy of the state, even though they'd lived in Croatia their entire lives. Even though religion had not been supported by the communist regime, the media identified the Croatian conflict as Catholic versus Orthodox. No one was religious before the war started.

Operation Storm was a decisive victory for the Croatian Army and in the months that followed, the Orthodox Serbs who'd been displaced asked to be allowed to return to their homes. But while these Orthodox Serbians were displaced, the Croatian government stripped them of their right to return and populated the Dalmatia area with Catholics from Kosovo. Because of the actions of the Croatian government, returning the displaced Serbs became very challenging.

The President of Croatia, Franjo Tuđman, went to a mainly Catholic village in Janjevo, Kosovo, and recruited groups of Catholics to live in Kistanje, a village about ten miles from Knin. The Catholics were given the homes of the Orthodox-Serbian people that UNPROFOR displaced during Operation Storm. Suddenly, these people from Kosovo who'd never seen Croatia were granted citizenship, given homes, and considered Croatian. Kosovo was poverty stricken, so when a political leader came and said, "We have a house for you on the coast of Croatia," of course the people from Kosovo jumped at the chance. Moving the Catholics in from Kosovo created a situation that was untenable. The displaced Orthodox-Serbian people wanted to come back to their homes and could not, because Croatian policy had stripped them of their land rights and their right to return. It also did not help that the UN procedures to reinstate those rights and grant the freedom to return were very time-consuming.

After Operation Storm, UNHCR and other UN offices worked on an agreement with the Croatian government. This agreement, finalized in 1997, guaranteed the Orthodox Serbs the right to return to their property or receive appropriate compensation for their land. All of the displaced Orthodox Serbs were required to register with their local Office for Displaced Persons and Refugees (ODPR) in order to request return and receive assistance from the Croatian government.

The crux of my job with UNHCR was not only processing the return of the displaced but also documenting the violence that arose in property disputes resulting from the spontaneous returns. This processing was supposed to take about fifteen days for those returning, but due to certain obstacles, the process took on average about two to six months or more per returning family. In the meantime, these desperate, displaced Serbs were tired of waiting and often attempted to return home on their own, and, as a result, would lose their displaced-person status. When they lost that status, they were basically in never-never land having given up all the benefits provided by the UN for displaced people.

Many of the displaced were elderly and didn't understand the procedures. Even when you would sit them down and try to explain, they didn't understand. I would say, "Please don't return to your home on your own because we are trying to process your return," but they did not understand. They had not experienced living anywhere other than the village they'd grown up in and the house where they were born and they were too old to start their life somewhere else. They just wanted to go home in order to die where they grew up. For the young people, readjusting to a new environment was much easier because they found jobs and started their lives wherever they were.

A lot of what I did was interview people who were displaced. I saw so many ladies in their black old-world attire coming on foot from miles away and begging to return to their houses. We could not accommodate them. We were trying to keep them alive and give them some food and shelter while we tried to follow procedures and figure out how to get them back into their homes.

When the displaced Serbs began to spontaneously return, high-strung nationalist Croats were on the lookout. After the Serbs would confirm that their houses were intact, they would return to collect their families and begin the journey back to their homes. In their absence, the Croat nationalists would destroy their homes. Then when the Serbs would return with their entire family, their house would be gone.

Another scenario involved Orthodox Serbs returning to find Croatians living in their home. Of course, the Catholic Croatians had been given the houses by the government and they didn't have anyplace else to go. They were not willing to give the houses back. This created a lot of violence and conflict in the Dalmatia region where I was working.

LINGERING NATIONALISM

Although the war ended before 1997, there was still a lot of nationalistic sentiment in the occupied regions. I noticed that Croats who worked for the UN had the least amount of sympathy for their own people because they considered the Serbians to be enemies of the state. I don't know how one could consider an eighty-year-old lady who is trying to return to her home an enemy of the state. Has she ever done anything against your state, your family, or against anybody? If you grew up in a small village or town, chances are you probably knew this lady. She probably gave you candy at some point, and she was probably the old grandmother of the town. In these settings, everybody knows each other and yet suddenly they all became strangers.

Dealing with nationalistic sentiment was one of the most difficult aspects of my job and certainly the most difficult element to come to terms with. I ended up clashing with some of my colleagues. Being born and raised in Croatia, I understood the culture. The foreigners working in the UN office with me neither understood the culture nor the attitude and negative sentiment toward the displaced held by the Croats working for the UN. By the end of my stay there, it was clear that I was not favored much by the Croats. They didn't know what to do with me or what to make of me. I think that I was challenging them to think differently. By rank, I was above them but they didn't like that either because I was a blonde nineteen-year-old girl who suddenly became an officer. My rank created an interesting dynamic.

This dynamic was evident in one incident that happened when a distraught, elderly Serbian lady came to my office begging for help. My heart went out to her so I was pushing my colleague from Finland to work on her case because she came in at nine o'clock in the morning and had already walked hours and miles in the middle of the summer heat. It was a surreal moment for me because this woman was fighting for her life and I was sitting there behind a desk trying to figure out if we had flour or rice to give her so she could eat. I was not doing a job—I was just being human. I was trying to help her in any way I could. I even gave her money from my own pocket. I knew all she wanted was to go back to her house but sadly I could not give that to her immediately. That was the most difficult part of my job: people wanting what was rightfully theirs while I lacked the power to immediately change their situation.

When the elderly Serbian lady and I concluded our meeting, she needed to go back where she had come from. By this time it was 10:30 AM and upwards of 90 degrees Fahrenheit outside. It would have taken this lady four to five hours to walk back to where she lived. I asked our driver to give her a ride back, which would have probably taken him fifteen minutes. He stared at me and said something like, "I'm not a taxi service." I was shocked! The driver was a guy who lounged around the office, smoked cigarettes, and drank coffee. At that moment, we had about four or five vehicles sitting idle, and since there were no missions going on, all the drivers had nothing to do.

Apparently, it annoyed him that I asked him for fifteen minutes of service to the people whom we were supposed to be assisting. He was employed by the United Nations to assist the people of the region. I was shocked when he said he was not a taxi service because I was in the office where all the Croatians sit and they all witnessed it. So

I closed the door and walked into a hallway and sat there to collect myself. I wasn't sure what to do next. I was not used to fighting the good fight. Moments later, I went back and asked him to tell me why he would not give the elderly woman a ride home. He stared at me blankly. He had no sympathy whatsoever, no feelings. To him she was just some old raggedy lady. What really angered me was that five minutes after he said no to me, he came in asking me if he could fetch me something from a bar. He was always making trips to different places because he was bored, yet he refused to drive this woman to a place that was fifteen minutes away. It was not a big deal to go buy cigarettes, but it was a big deal to drive this lady home. He ended up taking her and he didn't get me anything from the bar. I guess that was my punishment for ruining his day. After that, I wondered if he'd become immune to her plight because he saw so many people in the same situation or whether he truly had animosity for her because he considered her to be the enemy.

Where does humanity stop? At what point do you stop caring about what happens to another person? I understand the effects of divisiveness and rampant nationalism. I have seen the blind hatred that it brings out in people. They don't know why they hate, they simply hate. At some point their minds stop working as human minds and start working as tools or machines for another purpose.

Granted, a lot of Croats who lived in the Dalmatia region experienced a lot of horror during the conflict with the Serb population. Many Croats suffered and were expelled from their homes. Each person has their own war story. Each one of them had family and loved ones who were killed in the conflict. Their stories became a blanket excuse for the continuance of the nationalistic sentiment.

I definitely did not have friends from the Croatian side. Although we all worked together, there was an underlying animosity. I think they were uncomfortable with the fact that I was a Croat, more from an objective than a nationalistic viewpoint. It was as though they were frustrated that I would not side with them. They were working for the UN, but in reality they did not support the UN Charter. They were not able to drop their own prejudice and do the job. The war was over, the economy was bad, and they just needed jobs. It was just a paycheck. They were not interested in helping people or furthering the UN's reach.

Every day, I dealt with heavy issues only to return to that huge, eerie house to reflect on the complexity of my situation. I still get goose bumps thinking about crying in the bathtub because I felt powerless to help the people who were coming to me in the UN offices. I suppressed my emotions to deal logically with their situations during the day but alone at night I could not escape my feelings.

There was one Orthodox man whom I will never forget. His head looked like it was covered with craters because he had a hole in his skull. Initially, I'd thought he was deformed until he sat down and told his story. His house was blown up twice and he was shot in the head when he refused to leave. Croatia was the only land he knew and no matter what they did to him, he would not leave. He said to me, "I'm a Croatian citizen and that is my house."

It was shocking for me to see so much suffering. That is why I would cry at night. I had nobody to talk to, in a situation where I needed to talk and process all the heavy experiences. I had no one. I could not call my friends and tell them about what I saw because they didn't know where I was and they would not have understood. They were all on the beach partying like normal nineteen-year-olds.

I felt disconnected and without emotional outlets. What made the experience all the more challenging was being from Croatia, I understood the culture and the nationalism too well. It was easier for my UN colleagues to deal with these cases because they were so removed from the culture. They did not understand what was going on or why it was happening. For example, when that elderly lady said she wanted to go home, I understood her to the depth of my being.

I have a grandmother who did not eat for months in order to save money to buy cement to build her house. Most of the displaced elderly were agrarians. Their land was their life and their homes were their identity. My grandmother's generation put brick upon brick, rock upon rock with their bare hands, soaking it in their own sweat and blood while sacrificing bread on their table. For some people, a house is all they have. It is their wealth and identity and what they pass on from generation to generation. A house is the most important thing in their world. Having greater cultural awareness and understanding added to the complexity of everything because I could see beyond the surface.

There was one particular incident that was indicative of my whole experience. Since I had no one to talk to I would often go running to clear my head. I had to do something. I didn't know the town at all so I just started running. The town was very small so it was not long before I found trails to run on in rural wooded areas.

One weekend, I went out running on a trail. It was beautiful. I was deep in thought expelling all the happenings of the week from my mind. Suddenly, to my horror, I saw a sign with big letters that said DANGER—MINEFIELD. I had heard that there were a lot of minefields in that area, but I didn't know where they were. In fact, after all of the conflicts, unexploded mines are one of the biggest problems. The minefields are usually not marked and civilians wander into the fields and get injured or blown up.

Here I was trying to get away from it all, have a nice afternoon out in nature, and relax in hopes of getting all the horror out of my system, when suddenly, I was in the middle of it all! I didn't know what to do. Everything became surreal. I stood there for a while con-templating my next move. I tried to remember all the stuff I'd seen in the movies where there were bulges in the ground or trip wires exposed, but I could not see anything. The grass was too tall and they were all buried. My first instinct was to run back. Then I wondered if I was just plain lucky that I hadn't stepped on one in my path. All it takes is a small bit of pressure for one to explode. I did not know their size or how dangerous they were, I just knew that I was in the middle of a potentially fatal situation.

I tried taking tiny steps but I was terrified. My emotions cascaded so fast that I could not process anything logically. I started thinking about the flowers and looking around trying to distract myself just to get out. I was alone with no one to help me. If I stepped on a land mine, who would ever know? Every emotion stirred within me until I disassociated myself from the situation. At one point, I started singing to myself and took tiny steps very slowly until I came to the edge of the field. I was very shaken. To this day, I don't know how long it took me to get out of the minefield. I took my time, because I had to. After that, I sat alone in that big eerie house with all of the nightmares swirling through my mind. It was like a never-ending horror.

VUKOVAR

Not long after, I received a mission to travel from Dalmatia to the eastern part of Croatia to a town called Vukovar. The town had been under siege in the early 1990s during the Croatian War of Independence. The Croatian and Serbian population was reduced by half as the battles further strained relations between the Croats and the Serbs. What I saw when I got to Vukovar was unreal. When I drove in, I saw skyscrapers full of holes, yet every now and then, I observed a little light flickering in a blown-out window indicating that people still lived there without walls or roofs. People were still trying to go back to their apartments and homes despite the destruction.

On one particular street, I saw beautiful, picturesque homes on one side, and on the other there were little walls with grass grown over them. I realized that these small walls were remnants of homes and much of this whole village was now gone. Time had allowed grass to overrun the ruins. Nearly an entire village had been demolished. The kids on the remaining side of the street grew up never seeing anyone on the other side of the street. The only houses that were whole were Serbian houses. The Croatian side was still picking up its fragmented pieces after the ethnic cleansing in the beginning of the Croatian War of Independence.

Vukovar was a very odd place. Life was going on, bars had opened up, and people were having coffee and sitting outside smoking cigarettes and chatting. There was no work so all the young people would just hang out. Downtown life was starting to pick back up, yet there were still snipers around causing tension. People living there were trying to put the pieces of their lives back together in the midst of continuing conflict.

Growing up, I remember hearing about Vukovar and the fighting between the Serbs and the Croats. A lot of refugees in my high school were from Vukovar. It was really strange to be in the town and see it for myself. People still lived there after the war. It was their land. They were still dealing with the aftermath of the war and were living in these impossible situations.

REFLECTIONS ON MY EXPERIENCE

In summarizing my UNHCR experience, I have to say that I think it is easier to do humanitarian work outside of your native country. You understand too much of the subtext of your own culture. I remember talking to the head of the mission about all of my observations and he was blown away even though he'd spent ten years in Croatia. It can be an advantage to be detached because you don't get so tied to your work. For me, it felt as if I was being emotionally bombarded and I understood too much to be able to sustain the constant attacks.

I came back to the states to finish my senior year of college. People assumed that I'd had an amazing summer break in a quaint coastal town back home. It was hard coming back to a normal life. I kept asking myself why I'd returned to Croatia to work. Now I know why.

I did it because I find my passion in helping underdeveloped countries emerge and reach sustainability.

If I were to return to work with the UN, I don't know that I would choose to deal with displaced people in my own country. It's too personal. Of course, you cannot predict how an experience will turn out until you are in the middle of it. Considering the atrocities that UNHCR officers often witness, I do not believe it is an experience that a nineteen-year-old should ever have. For many years, I did not speak of my experiences. Until now, I had not talked to anyone about my experiences except one time with one of my supervisors. We met in Zagreb and had a long talk and stayed in touch afterward.

I felt no one could understand the horrors I'd witnessed and struggled emotionally to digest. To me, it felt like a door that I'd closed in my mind. My parents and my friends could never understand what I went through in my role with UNHCR. The United Nations has a lot of different divisions and I think UNHCR is one of the toughest. You don't have any governmental authority so it's frustrating to try to do something positive for desperately needy people, because you can't readily change their situation in an instant. You end up being the shoulder for these unfortunate souls to cry on. I really admire the people who do this for a living. They are special people. They go around the world entering into dangerous situations and are simply there to help. It is a challenge to bear witness without having the authority or jurisdiction to fully transform a suffering person's situation.

I met up with one of my former supervisors again later in New York. We were walking down the street in Manhattan and talking and he handed out money to every single beggar or homeless person who approached him. These UN representatives have so much kindness. You have to be a certain kind of person to see human suffering in that way and then put yourself directly in the line of fire to help the most hopeless people. I have a lot of respect for these people.

I hope one day that conditions in the Balkans stabilize. The situation there is much better, but nationalism still exists. I suppose only time will tell.

SILVIJA'S ADVICE FOR WOMEN

I think women have more strength than they give themselves credit for. I also think women are the first to question their strength. Confidence and inner strength is a part of you. It is inside all of us. We are born with it. It's who we are. It's sad to me to see so many women question that, whether it's because their parents question it or society questions it. It really saddens me to see that weakness in women. We are not born weak. Sometimes we work too hard trying to be strong. Strength is not something learned and it cannot be taught. Strength is something simply to be acknowledged.

LANA

Bosnia and Herzegovina

In April of 1992, war broke out in Bosnia and Herzegovina following the breakup of the former Socialist Federal Republic of Yugoslavia. The capital city of Sarajevo became a dangerous war zone unfit for civilian habitation during a siege led by the Bosnian Serb army camped high in the mountains surrounding the city. Victims of the longest siege in the history of modern warfare, thousands of Sarajevans faced constant bombardment and sniper shooting directed at civilians. Lana, a young girl during the conflict, shares her memories of a more peaceful Sarajevo, the day her family fled, and the resettlement challenges she faced as a refugee.

IF YOU MET me, you would never imagine what I've been through. I am the vibrant personality decorating every room that I enter. I form friendships effortlessly because I am energetic and amiable. I lead a very active life, spiced and colored with different people, places, and cultures. I am continuously finding myself facing interesting challenges and transitions and I'm happy to take on the world every day.

The early experiences of my childhood will always stay with me. I moved several times and faced long periods of adjustment. If I had to name one aspect of my life I am most grateful for, it would be that my family is currently together and managed to escape the siege of Sarajevo, because many other families in my native Bosnia did not.

I grew up in Sarajevo, Bosnia, and my childhood was beautiful. I had everything that I could possibly desire. My parents definitely did all they could to provide my brother and me with opportunities and to give us amazing memories. Sarajevo is still such a beautiful place. It is a living museum of history. There are mosques, churches, cathedrals, and fine municipal buildings built by the Ottoman Turks and Austro-Hungarian Empire. As a young girl, I did not pay much attention to the history of the city, but it is a great place to travel to for those who have interest in art, history, architecture, and culture.

We had an extended family that was very warm and friendly with each other and enjoyed many get-togethers. In fact, those family gatherings created some of my best memories from childhood.

When I started first grade, my parents signed me up at the same little neighborhood school that my father and his sisters attended. We happened to move to the other side of Sarajevo around that time so I had to be driven across the city to school for about the first six months of the year. My father was not always consistent with the timing so when he would drive me, I would always be late. I remember one time driving to school with him listening to the Madonna song "Like a Prayer" on the radio. My dad was always encouraging me to learn English when I was young so he made me learn the words and sing it. I will never forget that. Little did he know English would ultimately become such an important and necessary language in my life. On days where my father did not drive me, I would ride the trolleys. I loved riding the trolleys and was simply fascinated by them. There was a turnstile where two trolleys would turn together and I loved to be in the middle circle because it was almost like being on a merry-go-round.

Instead of taking the bus to go home on Fridays after school, I would sometimes take the bus to my grandmother's house and stay the weekend with her. Then on Sunday afternoon, my mother and father would come and spend the day with my grandparents before taking me home. This was the typical, simple life that we had in Sarajevo and it was beautiful.

In April of 1992, after the war in Bosnia started, life changed dramatically. Everything we used to do became impossible because nothing was safe anymore. I was ten years old at the beginning of the war. It was hard for me to understand the changes happening in the city because my knowledge was limited by what I witnessed where my aunt and uncle lived. My father, brother, and I ended up trapped at my aunt and uncle's home, separated from my mother for three months, when the siege of Sarajevo started.

On the day we were separated, my mother went to work as usual and my father took my brother and me to our aunt and uncle's house. After work, my mother went to our home while my father, brother, and I were still at my aunt and uncle's house across town. We were getting ready to go home when we heard on the news that the siege was beginning to erupt. At that point, we were stranded and had no hope of leaving. It was not safe to go out. No one knew what was actually going on in the beginning of the war. We heard that snipers were everywhere and that there were attacks, but we didn't have much information.

My family home was in the part of town near the Sarajevo international airport that was occupied by the Serbians. The Serbians would not allow anyone to leave, so my mother had to risk her life to reunite with us. A family friend who was active in law enforcement came and told my mother that he could reunite us but told her that she would have to go immediately. She had no time to pack; she just grabbed our passports and her purse and left. She got into his car and hid, crouched behind the driver's seat, while he drove her through the Serb-held area. The Serbians shot at them as they escaped. I will never forget my mother describing how terrified she was.

Once reunited, my family remained at my aunt's house for several months. We were lucky because my dad did not have to fight in the war like many men. I don't know what I would have done without him. There was a lot of destruction in the city as time passed. I remember how sad and shocked I was when the National Library was burned down because it was a special place to me. I also remember one terrible day when there was bombing that carried over into the night. There was a lot of apprehension in the air. We were still with my aunt and uncle and because of the bombing we had to stay in the basement. We were like caged animals. We sat in that old basement all day and night listening to the news updates on the radio. My brother was probably six or seven years old at the time. As we were listening to the radio, the DJs were trying to make jokes to keep everyone in good spirits. My brother turned to me and said in the most puzzled and innocent voice, "How come we can't be just like those tiny people and go inside the radio and have fun. They are not getting bombed and we are." We all laughed because it was really funny to hear him say that as the bombs were falling close to the backyard and down the street. Soon after that night, conditions escalated to the point where we were forced to flee.

We hit the worst part of the war in July of 1992 and had to leave Sarajevo before the end of the summer. I don't remember much about the preparation for our departure. When you are young, you are oblivious to certain details. Being a child in that situation is different than being an adult. Children witness all the tragedy, while adults seem to be caught up in it yet still have to act as caregivers at the same time. I did not feel all the impact of the war because my parents tried to keep everything as normal as they could for us. Though it was not often, they would even take us outside to play when they could. Now as an adult, I sometimes have war nightmares. I can only imagine what it was like being an adult in Sarajevo during the siege. It must have been especially difficult to be a parent with children during the war. I did not understand how difficult it was on my parents but I could see that they were worried about my brother and me. In a normal environment parenting is not easy. But when you place a parent and child in a war zone, the notions of survival and protection become so readily apparent. Children don't understand the severity or the danger and as the parent it is your job to ensure that they are kept out of harm's way.

One evening my mother abruptly told me that we had one opportunity to escape Sarajevo and we were leaving the next day. We were months into the siege at that point and the conditions of the city were terrible. People could not go outside because of snipers and the city was constantly bombed and shelled by the military in the mountains. All the basic services were unavailable. There was no electricity and it was impossible to get food and necessary supplies. Thousands of people were killed and went missing. It was like living in hell.

Since it was decided that we would leave, that next day my father took us to the train station. There was a massive crowd of people and long lines of women and children standing in front of six or seven large passenger busses. I remember my mother helping lift me onto the bus as other mothers and children crowded on board. The most heartbreaking thing was seeing my father crying as we got on the bus. I'd never seen him cry before and witnessing that made me realize the seriousness of our situation. My brother was just a little boy and he was sitting in my mother's lap as she leaned him out the bus window so my father could kiss him good-bye. My father could not go with us because men were not allowed to leave. This was the last convoy that the United Nations sent for the citizens of Sarajevo. There was nothing after that. We were lucky to escape when we did because the situation in the city worsened after we left. The siege of Sarajevo lasted for years and devastated that beautiful city.

It was a long bus trip and I remember all of it. It was hot and humid on the bus and children were crying. I think the mothers were terrified, frightened, and anxious. They did not know when or if any of us would return to Bosnia or whether those we'd left behind would survive. They might also have worried that our convoy would be attacked. To this day, the memory is still frightening to me.

The first stop on the trip was another central area with more busses lined up. At this point, we had to decide where to go. I remember our options were Croatia, Serbia, and a couple of other places. We had family in both but we were closer to our family in Serbia. We knew if we went to Serbia, my father would not be able to join us because he is a Muslim. At that time, Muslims were being persecuted and the ethnic tension was heated. The risk would have been too great for my father, but in the end, my mother chose to go to Serbia because geographically it made more sense.

We waited several hours for our dilapidated bus to leave. When I was younger, I would often become very nauseated riding in a car for long periods of time. So after riding the bus for a while, I started feeling sick. The driver was very kind and let me sit on the steps near the door. I don't know how long the trip was because it was such a surreal experience. I'm not sure whether the realization that we would not be returning to Sarajevo made me sicker than the ride itself, but I knew that all of the pleasant times I'd spent there were finished.

The entire day passed and we continued to drive long into the night. While going through the mountains, we were stopped twice and men with machine guns and big, thick beards boarded to search the bus. I didn't understand why. They knew the bus was full of women and children. I remember asking the driver if I could get off the bus and step outside for a second because I was ghastly nauseated, but my mother kept telling me to be quiet. She was very upset with me. I just did not comprehend the danger. All I wanted was to get some fresh air. I think my mother was petrified. Knowing the history and the potential danger, my mother was doing all she could to try to stay calm for my brother and me. I can only imagine that she must have wished the ground would open up and swallow her.

When we arrived in Belgrade, Serbia, we called my mother's aunt from the station and she came and picked us up. She had an apartment complex and lived on one of the floors. The first floor was always rented to diplomats and consultants of foreign countries and at that time she had a Spanish diplomat living there whom we became friendly with. Through several dinners shared in broken English and broken Serbian he let us know that the Spanish government was accepting refugees through a lottery system and that my mother could go and sign us up for it. She immediately did. We spent about five or six months in Belgrade until we won the lottery and left to resettle in Spain. We knew this would give my father a chance to join us.

For my brother and me, moving to Spain was not difficult because my mother did all she could to make sure that we adapted quickly. We learned Spanish within a couple of months and integrated quickly into the schools. We made some fantastic friends, people whom we remain good friends with today. We were living in a little town south of Valencia on the coast and it was a beautiful place. Everything would have been perfect, except that we were still without my father. For three years, he was stuck in Bosnia. There were fifty other Bosnian families living in our town and they were all fatherless. Bosnian women and children kept coming, so we all banded together in support of one another.

Eventually my father was able to get out of Bosnia and join us in Spain. I will never forget the night he came because two other fathers arrived with him. The town hall organized a little welcoming event for them, even though they arrived late at night. It was so amazing! I remember my father getting out of the car with tears in his eyes hugging my brother, my mother, and me. This was the first time I had seen him in three years and I was so relieved that he was there with us alive, but I could not help but notice how thin he was. Now we could finally be a family again like we were before.

We settled into a little house initially and then found a huge beautiful apartment. My father worked as a handyman because it was one of the easiest jobs he could find. During the six years we lived in Spain the country was going through an economic crisis. Our family was living paycheck to paycheck and my parents eventually realized that this was not the life they wanted for us. It was really hard for them. Eventually, my father started getting in touch with his former coworkers. One of them was living in the United States in Georgia and he told us about another lottery program that the United States government was hosting through a Christian organization. We had to apply and complete medical testing to ensure we were healthy and not long after we heard we'd been accepted. So we resettled in the United States and within a year received our citizenship. My parents were particularly excited about settling in Georgia because they saw the United States as the land of opportunities. My parents felt that having the opportunity to go and live in the United States with papers in order was the chance of a lifetime for a family from war-torn Bosnia.

Initially, I was excited about the move because I was already watching all the American television shows in Spain. I thought moving to Georgia would be like living in Beverly Hills 90210 though I would discover that Lawrenceville, Georgia, was far from that! When we started to sell things from the house, reality sunk in and I realized that we were leaving Spain and I didn't want to go anymore. The transition was quite a process for me and it took several months. I was sixteen years old and that is a hard age to start over again in a new country and learn a new language.

The move was inevitable and I realized I had no other choice. It was total culture shock. I spent the first two months crying all day because I wanted to go back to Spain. Although I'd studied English before, I did not speak it very well.

Communicating with people was very difficult and frustrating so I grew very shy and timid. I lived in a community of other Bosnians in Lawrenceville so I had friends from my own culture, but since I'd spent six years speaking Spanish it was just as challenging for me to communicate with my Bosnian friends as it was with Americans.

When you relocate to a foreign country, I believe it is very important to have a supportive community structure and be surrounded by people who have been through similar situations. However, it is not positive to limit your exposure and focus only to that community. Many refugees do this and tend to isolate themselves within the safety and familiarity of that familiar structure. I think my own parents would have assimilated and prospered more if there was not such a big Bosnian community where we lived in the United States.

That said, we left Spain at a time of fiestas and parties and arrived in Georgia where there was a grocery store and a gas station. It felt like the middle of nowhere for me since I had grown up in cities. It was summertime when we arrived and school was not in session so there was nothing for me to do. I got through that summer thanks to my mother. Without her, it would have been extremely hard. She made us feel like we had everything we wanted and needed even if we didn't. Honestly, there is no way I would be where I am right now without her. She is such a strong woman who carried my family through two resettlements as well as surviving that horrific bus trip out of Sarajevo. She even braved snipers, running through the streets during the war just to reunite our family. She is one incredible woman!

After moving to Georgia, we didn't have much money and could not afford nice clothes, so my mom would sew something decorative on the plain T-shirts we would buy from thrift stores. She would prepare these big feasts even though all we had to eat with were plastic forks and knives. She proved to me that fancy things do not really matter, that the four of us sitting together at a table sharing a meal was the most beautiful thing in the world. The fine china and fancy wine glasses would come in time, she would always emphasize. That is a common pattern in life.

After what seemed forever, school finally started. High school in Georgia was very weird. It was nothing like what I saw on the TV shows. I was very shy at that time because I did not speak English and I was not interested in learning it. I was part of an ESL program with most of the other Bosnian kids where we incorporated English into our studies in an art class and a math class. I did surprisingly well and everyone was very impressed, but for some reason at the time I was completely oblivious to my success. It was hard to speak English so I secluded myself. It took me two years to grow into myself and feel comfortable enough to be a teenage girl. Being a teenager is hard no matter what ethnicity, country, or culture you are from. It's awkward and emotional and very uncertain.

I became an entirely different person my senior year of high school. I came out of my shell and was more outgoing and later made great friends in college. I was disciplined about my studies and about finding opportunities for myself. I figured there was a reason I made it out of Bosnia and I was determined to find out what my life's mission was. I began to feel more a part of the American society in college. I was finally living in a city again in downtown Atlanta and felt more at home since I was more accustomed to city life, though I was not settled yet; I was destined to move again. After college, I was recruited to be a store manager. One night while dining, I met people from California and jokingly said to one of their managers, "Is there anything in Los Angeles for me?"

Four weeks later, I moved to Los Angeles. I packed my car and drove across the country with my mother. A lot of Americans have had this experience and honestly it made me feel closer to the notion of the American dream. After several years in Los Angeles, I wonder where my next home will be. Every day, I go back and forth on the subject of moving but I think I will remain here for a while. I feel like my life is finally stabilized. I have started to do charity work with an organization that helps kids in Bosnia and have found that in this work my outgoing personality and talents are assets to me.

My approach to life is simply embracing what comes. It's been something I have had to do since I was very young so I fully intend to remain open to life's changes. I was lucky nothing happened to my family or me during the war. I will never forget how fortunate I am. Every day, I embrace everything because life is too short and vulnerable. Honestly, it's a simple fact: Life is not long enough; enjoy it while you can.

LANA'S ADVICE FOR WOMEN
Don't wait for things to just happen. Make them happen for yourself. This is the one thing my mother always told me.

EASTERN EUROPE

MASHA

Moldova

Having grown up under the guise of the former Soviet Union, Masha narrates her earlier life in the former Soviet Republic of Moldova. She details the changes after the collapse of the Soviet Union and the rare misfortune that led to a new life in the United States.

I WAS A CHILD of the former Soviet Union, and since I left home, my world outlook and my life have dramatically changed. I have a strong belief that the places and families we are born into, as well as all stops and people we meet on our journey, are all part of the bigger plan and our mission on this planet.

I was born in the city of Tiraspol of the Moldavian Soviet Socialist Republic in 1980. After the breakup of the Soviet Union, many of us living in the former republics including Ukraine, Moldavia, Kazakhstan, and Belarus found ourselves in different places with shifting governments.

We led a fairly modest Soviet life. We didn't have much, and connections played a very important role in our lives so we could get clothes, shoes, appliances, special foods, tickets to concerts, long-distance train rides, or just get paperwork done. Everything depended on who you knew. My grandfather was well-known across the Soviet Union because he worked as a deputy director of a plant that produced wine and cognac in Tiraspol. He could easily get things in exchange for wine and cognac, which were considered high value items and were essential to social life, important events, and festivities.

In my first years of school, the emphasis of Lenin as the most wonderful, intelligent, hardworking and kind man was instilled in us. We looked up to his image, and nothing negative was ever said about him. We were groomed to become pioneers and then Komsomol youth. Ideally, we were being prepared as future members of the communist party. I became a pioneer at the age of nine in 1989, two years before the collapse of the Soviet Union. Today, people have a lot of negative things to say about communism. I completely understand the criticism. However, we had principles, rules, and standards of behavior that played a very critical role in the character building of my generation. We were to respect the elderly and our teachers, help our parents, work hard in school, and be responsible members of the community. We had strict discipline. If we were late to class, we would be publicly shamed by the teacher. It was also a very conservative society, and sexual talk never occurred in families or in general; we were very sheltered. However, I am really grateful for having had those principles and discipline. They shaped me in so many ways.

The '90s brought economic and political instability, and it became a very chaotic time for the former Soviet Union. Despite the perception that there was a rise of democracy and freedom, at the same time, there were no longer core principles for the kids born in the late '80s and early '90s, so they didn't have the same sense of discipline or built-in respect toward the elderly as my generation. Their parents were too distracted trying to survive the upheaval to hold them accountable.

Yet there was one element from my upbringing that has heavily affected me as an adult and others raised in the former Soviet Union and Russia. This is exemplified in one distinct memory from my youth: As my mom and I were leaving one of the local markets one day, we walked behind a woman, possibly forty years of age. I didn't notice anything different or shocking about her but my mom quietly murmured, "Can you believe she is wearing that at her age!" There was something in my mother's words that went beyond a simple opinion. It was a judgment and obvious disapproval, almost as if my mother was mentally giving this woman a scolding.

This appears to be a deep-seated trait that has permeated most levels of the former Soviet societies. I call it "babushka-on-the-bench" syndrome referring to an elderly woman who sits on a bench in front of her house and engages in judging neighbors as they pass by. As an adult and in my youth, I have always experienced an ongoing struggle with my self-esteem and sense of self-worth due this common Soviet society behavioral pattern in the form of judgment, gossip, and disapproval.

Throughout my youth, I found myself constantly yearning and waiting for that external validation or approval regarding my choices (clothing, boyfriends, profession, etc.). God forbid, if I should wear a skirt too short or have one too many boyfriends during my teen years, then my immediate social environment would become quickly inundated with some sort of rumor that I was "a girl of easy virtue" which would bring shame to my whole family. I was expecting to be looked at and judged every day of my life as I was leaving home for school and returning back home. Before leaving the house, I would always think of who might have been sitting on that bench at the entrance to our apartment building and what they would have thought of me, and, more importantly, what they then might have told other neighbors about me. I was experiencing this anxiety every day of my life, and naturally it conditioned me to project my sense of self-worth onto other people's view of me.

I have been held back in a sense of self-realization. In fact, it appears, the whole society has been holding back from expressing themselves fully and is hostage to this debilitating need for external approval and validation. One modern consequence of "babushka-on-the-bench" syndrome is this national drive for expensive and luxurious things that Russians and those in post-Soviet societies are acquiring as status symbols. The public appears to be in some kind of a race within.

I am not sure if this is a relic of the Soviet past and the era of informants, or perhaps this goes deeper down into the history of the Russian society, but this practice of judging others has been prevalent for as long as I can remember. I recall my grandmother telling me how she was so anxious about going back home after work every day, because the female neighbors were sitting on a bench and gossiping as she was returning home from work. Were they doing this because there was some satisfaction in it? Because they were unhappy and seemed to feel better about themselves when they were putting her down? Or because, in their eyes, my grandmother had more than they did and they wanted to demonize her for that reason? My grandfather is another example. He was one of the most honest and reputable men in town. He became very successful and earned a title of a deputy director at a large wine factory. Back in the Soviet times, he repeatedly refused to buy a car, because he was afraid of what the workers would think of him; whether he would be perceived as corrupt.

The "babushka-on-the-bench" effect appears to be waning these days, compared to the '80s and '90s during the reign and collapse of the Soviet Union, but it's still there. I am hoping that the more Russian people travel the world, they will start letting go of the vulnerability. I believe this cultural phenomenon may be one of the reasons behind a low national happiness index.[1]

When I was eight years old (1988), we took a trip to Bulgaria for one month. Trips abroad were unheard of at that time, and Bulgaria was considered "abroad," even though it was part of the Eastern European communist bloc. Neighbors and my parents' coworkers and bosses gave us lists of things to buy for them. It was a time of scarcity. There wasn't much merchandise in our stores, and people wanted to buy books, stereos, apparel, or other big-label items, which, interestingly, were more available in Bulgaria. In the public perception, we got to go where few people went and had access to things that weren't available in the Soviet Union; therefore, everyone wanted to be our friends.

Before the collapse of the Soviet Union, Moldova was one of the most prosperous Soviet Republics. It had a nice climate, fertile land, a low cost of living, and an abundance of food. But things were to change dramatically. The collapse of the Soviet Union in 1991 resulted in a rise of ethnonationalism across the former Soviet republics. Russia is frequently perceived as *the* former Soviet Union, but in reality, Russia, formerly the Russian Soviet Federative Socialist Republic, was one of the fifteen Soviet republics within the larger union. It was the largest and most economically developed. As Russia was at the helm of the collapse, most former republics didn't wish to identify with anything Russian, and in search of their own national identity, they pursued and declared independence, and passed various language laws dropping the use of Russian language as the official language in their regions. Since many of the republics were ethnically diverse, ethnic conflicts ensued across those republics with the collapse. It was really challenging for that part of the world. Language, as one

---

[1] "Among the more than 150 countries ranked in the survey, Russia has been given the 76th place with a 'happiness index' of just little above five points out of 10, same as for Moldova and Peru." Alina Lobzina, "Russia in the Middle of World Happiness Rankings," The Moscow News, May 4, 2012, http://themoscownews.com/russia/20120405/189593174.html.

of the most distinguishing ways to promote an ethnicity, became the way for these former republics to differentiate themselves from Russia. Moldovan nationalists followed that example. After decades of Russian rule, Moldovan nationalists saw the fall of the Soviet Union as an opportunity to assert the interests of the republic's ethnic Moldovan majority. In the late 1980s, Romanian-speaking nationalists of Moldova found a voice, which extended to calls for reunification with Romania. The strongest cause of the disagreement between Moldova and Transnistria was passage of the Language Law on August 31, 1989. It made Moldovan the official language and required the use of the Latin script instead of Cyrillic. The Language Law was largely seen as a weapon against Russian domination, which gave ethnic Moldovans an advantage over the Russian-speaking population of the Transnistria region, where I resided. It was understood not only in the context of possible reunification with Romania, but also seen as purposefully discriminatory and a means to gain administrative control over economic assets concentrated mostly in Transnistria. As a result, Transnistria separated from Moldova and became one of the four de facto states that resulted from the collapse of the Soviet Union.[2]

The strained relations between Transnistria and Moldova resulted in a military escalation in 1992. I remember a big funeral being held in the center of our town. Dozens of people in caskets were buried in a central memorial complex, which held victims of the Second World War. It was very powerful.

Although it's been over twenty years, Transnistria is not recognized to this day and exists as a de facto state only.

The economic effects of the political changes were fast and rapid. Our entire currency system was completely dysfunctional. When other former Soviet Republics began issuing their own currencies, Transnistria was flooded with Soviet rubles. In an attempt to protect

---

[2] The other three de facto independent but internationally unrecognized states were Abkhazia, Nagorno-Karabakh, and South Ossetia, the latter gaining partial recognition in 2008.

its financial system, in July 1993, the government bought used Soviet notes, dated 1961–1992, which they modified by gluing stamps bearing the image of General Alexander Suvorov, founder of Tiraspol, my native town and Transnistria's capital. These stamped notes replaced unstamped Soviet and Russian notes at par. We still had hyperinflation. In the late '90s, a loaf of bread was 700,000 rubles. People carried stacks of money in bags because it was worthless, requiring a large amount to purchase anything. Finally, they were replaced by new Transnistrian rubles. A Transnistrian ruble did not hold much value either and also suffered from high inflation. Eventually they regulated it, and in 2000 a new ruble was introduced at a rate of 1 new ruble equaling 1,000,000 old rubles. The Transnistrian ruble is still being used.

Hyperinflation plagued other post-Soviet states as well. Having seen their life savings lose value after the breakup of the Soviet System, people didn't trust banks anymore and chose dollars as a way to save money. In Transnistria, we would use different currencies: U.S. dollars and German deutsche marks along with Moldovan leu, Ukrainian grivnas, Russian rubles, and Transnistrian rubles. Remarkably, we were automatically converting them and knew how much everything was in each currency.

The primary concern was to put food on the table. We were living on about $20.00 a month for a long while. To make matters worse, people working real jobs stopped getting paid. My father, an engineer, was paid in items that were produced by his plant. He might bring home a stove or a freezer instead of a paycheck. Once he was given two sacks of doorknobs, which my mother took to the market and sold so we had money to buy food.

The centrally planned economy of the Soviet Union resulted in an excessive surplus of certain goods and a deficit of others. For example, factories were supposed to produce X amount of goods, no matter what the real supply and demand were for the goods in question. It got to a point where, for instance, there were too many tires, yet not enough cars until production stagnated. Companies were not selling and getting money for what they had produced. People had jobs, but were not being paid for months.

People were desperate for income and were forced to sell anything they could. My mother worked at a textile factory and was being paid with fabric. She made bed sheets, robes, and cotton nighties, which we would take to a market in Odessa (a port city on the Black Sea sixty miles southeast of my hometown). After spending the day selling our cotton goods, we would then go straight to the produce market to buy food and take it back home. This is how we were able to survive.

MOVING TO RUSSIA

In 1997, the year I was graduating from high school, my dad took me to Russia (one thousand miles northeast of my hometown), where his mother and his sister lived. He was with me for one month, while I was preparing for and taking entrance exams. In the Russian school system, you only get one chance, and if you do not get into a university, you lose a whole year. The stakes were pretty high. But I got into Ivanovo State Power University to study data and information management, and then my dad left and went back to his job in Tiraspol.

I lived with my grandmother in a Russian town called Ivanovo. It was the first time I lived away from my parents. The next five years spent living and studying there were another challenging chapter of my life.

I need to share that my father had a drinking problem. In a way, he represented a whole generation of men who felt unappreciated and lost at the time of the collapse. Turning to alcohol was a common way of dealing with hardship. With an alcoholic and abusive father, my dad grew up in a very unstable environment himself, which, I believe, deeply traumatized him. He had a serious case of depression, but we didn't have a grasp of the concept of mental depression or therapy in

Russian culture at that time. And there was no AA in our region. I remember him frequently saying: "I need to drink in order to forget." He wanted to commit suicide several times.

My father was a brilliant engineer by education and, quite frankly, by nature. He often created microchips at home and launched, maintained, or repaired industrial machinery at work. He came up with something new all of the time. Our house was like an engineer's studio. He was so very gifted but did not realize his true potential. This came around the time when the Soviet system had no support for such bright minds and those who were strong left, a phenomenon known as "the brain drain." Many of the Russian immigrants in Silicon Valley, California, became very successful. Yet, my dad did not appear to have the strength or courage to pursue his dreams.

That summer my father took me to Russia in 1997 was the only time we ever really spent together. I wasn't close to him, and he was almost like an enemy because of his violent tendencies when he was drunk. When we spent a month together, it was like I suddenly realized I had a father and that he loved me. I crushed a lot of emotional barriers and forced that kind of connection to him. When he was about to leave to return to Moldova, we were at a train station, and we both cried . . . I had rarely seen my father cry, so it was an emotional moment for both of us. That was the last time I saw him.

He went back to Moldova and resumed drinking. He died from a heart attack in January 1998, six months later. I left immediately and went to the funeral, then spent a little over a month with my mother. My mother and I were worried about my Russian grandmother's health after my father's death. She had problems with her heart, and all of us were afraid that she wouldn't survive her son's death. Had she passed away, I would have not been able to finish school. A month later, I went back to Russia to continue to live with her in a studio-size flat where my cousin and her baby later moved in due to marital issues, and, shortly after, I began to apply to visit the United

States, an interest I had held for reasons I cannot quite explain since I was eleven or twelve years old. Perhaps it was a sense of fascination that I had with the country.

In the meantime, I had financial challenges, and my mother could not help me. I was getting 240 rubles per month (equal to $40 in early 1998) from the state due to the loss of my father. Later that year, it was worth $6 due to the Russian financial crisis, which resulted in debt default and the devaluation of the ruble.

I was also getting a monthly student stipend of about 80 to 90 rubles. It was not much, but it was a little helpful. My grandmother and I lived off of her pension so we always had a little food, but, bless her heart, she told me not to eat eggs because they were too expensive! So, I looked for some opportunity to make money and found work canvassing for political campaigns. This work paid for the application fees for two programs I hoped might help me get to the United States: the Camp Counselors USA program (CCUSA) and the Freedom Support Act (FSA) Undergraduate Program.[3] My work also paid for train tickets to Moscow to do the subsequent formal interviews.

On one of these train rides to Moscow in 2000, I remember thinking of one incident that had happened when I was working for a local electoral campaign that infuriated me. A person in charge of the campaign also held a high-ranking position at a local construction company. One day, we were having a conversation at the campaign office when he suddenly asked me what I was going to do for a job when I graduated from the university. I just replied that I didn't know yet. He suggested that I work at their company. How exciting, I thought! So I went to meet with him at his formal office to further discuss the job opportunities. We exchanged some niceties and campaign talk, and then he started throwing sexual content into the conversation,

---

[3] Programs of the Bureau of Educational and Cultural Affairs of the United States Department of State, the American Councils for International Education, and the United States Information Agency, administered by ACTR/ACCELS.

which became extremely uncomfortable. I was only twenty years old at that point, and this man knew my background, where I was coming from. He also knew that I lived with my grandmother, that I did not have a father, and that I had no money. He wanted to take advantage of me.

In the course of the campaign, which I couldn't leave because I needed money so badly, he tried to make passes at me and pressure me to sleep with him. This man was in his fifties, married to a young beautiful woman who worked for the campaign as well. He once said to me, "You don't know life. I do. I have experience. You will regret this." At one point I said that I was planning on going to the United States. He dismissed it and replied: "Well don't you know how people get into those kinds of programs?" In his vision, young aspiring women like me didn't have a chance unless we "got close" with someone powerful or famous. So, he just brushed me off—my worldview, my virtues. I wanted to prove him wrong. In my view, this episode is very representative of the work environment in Russia where sexual harassment is rampant and asking for sexual favors by male bosses is common practice. Women have to quit their jobs and they have a very hard time moving forward.

I became a semifinalist in the Freedom Support Act program and was among fifty people who had been selected out of a pool of over fifty thousand applicants nationwide. I was so very hopeful! After participating in the finals and an interview in Moscow, I entered the longest waiting period of about six months. In May 2001, I received a notification that I was not chosen. I vividly remember the day I received that letter. I was sobbing on the balcony of the apartment feeling devastated.

But the universe had another plan, though after that FSA notice, I was worried as I still had not received anything back from CCUSA.

On June 22, 2001, I was studying for my last summer final exam at Ivanovo State Power University when I got a call from the CCUSA

Moscow office. They told me there was a camp that I had not chosen on the application, but it needed more staff. The camp was for handicapped children and adults in California. However, I'd have to leave for the United States in less than two days and attend an orientation in Moscow prior to that. My visa and plane ticket were ready and waiting in their Moscow office.

I asked them if I could think about it. They told me if I decided not to go or they didn't hear back from me in fifteen minutes, they would pass the opportunity on to another student.

I always say the biggest decision of my life was made in fifteen minutes. I called my mom, a friend, and my grandmother. No one answered. The decision was all mine.

I left for Moscow that same day. I packed my bag quickly, went to the bus station, and took an overnight bus, arriving on time for the orientation.

ARRIVAL IN THE UNITED STATES

I arrived in New York on June 25, 2001, along with eight young women from different parts of Russia. It was late when we landed and we got on the bus to travel to Columbia University to spend the night in the dorms. When we arrived, they handed out information packets, which were to contain a ticket to our final destination. I opened mine and saw no ticket. They told me not to worry, that I should rest and then come to the orientation the next morning. Nervous because my arrangements were not working out very smoothly, I could hardly sleep that night. The next morning, I went to the orientation, devastated because the girls I traveled with all had tickets. After the orientation, I went to the CCUSA office at Columbia University and was told that they still didn't have a ticket for me and that I would have to spend another night there. They told me to come back later that day.

Columbia University happens to be on Broadway, and I was getting quite hungry toward the afternoon. I went out on Broadway and went into a store. I looked at the prices, automatically converting everything into rubles, and the prices were absolutely unreal to me. I picked up a hot dog and a small bottle of apple juice for about $2.50 and thought, *Wow! Forty rubles for this!* I had only brought the equivalent of 50 U.S. dollars with me for my entire trip, which in Russia was a lot of money. I prayed they would let me have breakfast the next day, determined to take as much as I could even if the food looked strange and unfamiliar to me. Scared, I went to my room and cried myself to sleep. When I went to the office at 4:00 PM, they had my ticket to fly out from JFK airport to San Jose, California, the next day. When I asked how to get to JFK, they told me I could take the bus for $12, but then they said I could also take the Metro, which was cheaper.

At the train station, there were two trains with the same number, and I couldn't figure out which one to take. I was afraid to ask directions because I didn't trust anyone and wasn't confident in my spoken English. Finally, I asked a conductor which train was going to JFK airport. After arriving at the airport, I received my ticket and was horrified. I had seat number 13! I wondered how much worse this situation would get.

I settled down on the plane and sat next to the window. After about two hours in flight, a woman took the aisle seat, leaving a vacant seat between us. She asked where I was going, and I shared my story with her for the rest of the flight. When she inquired about the camp, I told her I remembered reading about it being in the forest and that we would sleep outside. She asked me if I had a sleeping bag. I hadn't thought about that! She handed me a card and said, "My name is Betty. If you need one, here is my card. Call me."

Her kindness was startling. I came from the Soviet mentality. If a stranger offers a selfless act, people wonder what he or she has to gain. Of course, I had a few suspicions, but she was an interesting, sweet, and kind lady. Intuitively, I did not feel any ill will from her.

After we landed, she introduced me to her husband, Bob. No one from the camp was there, so Betty stayed with me and helped me contact them. When Betty left, she told me to contact her if no one showed up. The people from the camp arrived after I picked up my luggage and took me to the camp in Cupertino, California. As soon as I arrived, I called Betty to thank her for being so very kind and to let her know that I got there safely. She then volunteered to show me around. I was amazed! That Saturday, she took me to Stanford University and to her house. I was anxious about seeing her husband again, not wanting to impose on his space. On the contrary, we had an in-depth conversation. As I told him about my life, he researched everything on the computer. Afterward, he told me that he thought I was so different and had such an amazing story. That was the day when we became friends.

The camp did not provide us with food on the weekends; they only provided us with food during the sessions. There was no Internet there, either. The compensation was not adequate, but those were the conditions under which we came. They only paid us 500 dollars for two months of work, which was given to us as pocket money. We would also have to buy our return ticket to New York City on our own. I was planning on taking the greyhound bus, but Bob and Betty took care of my airplane ticket to New York. They converted their TV room into my room, and I spent weekends at their house. They introduced me to California in so many different ways and had a profound impact on me. They cared for me very selflessly and had a strong sense of compassion. My family and friends in Transnistria and Russia questioned why they would do these things for me. I just explained that they were simply kind people. That is what America is based on: sharing, giving back, and helping. I went with Bob to his Rotary Club, and later became more involved with Rotary in my work. We became very close, like a family in those two months, until I had to return to Russia to complete another year of school.

Returning to Russia was a culture shock. I was torn, but I was determined to finish school. Staying in the United States illegally was out of the question. It was a principle for me to do it the right way, especially since I learned that many Russian women had married to stay in the United States. I decided that I would not fall into the same stereotype. If I was meant to return, it would work out on its own.

When I parted ways with Bob and Betty, they told me they would help me come back. I left on September 5, 2001, just a few days before 9/11. Interestingly, I was in New York, standing in front of the twin building several days before the attacks. After 9/11, it became very difficult for me to get a visa.

I finished my senior school year in Russia, while Bob and Betty helped me figure out a way to return. Bob talked to everyone he knew; everywhere he went he shared my story. There were possible leads, but they were hanging in the air. I felt like I belonged in the United States.

For the first time, I felt I needed to give something back to the world and share the goodwill I received. I almost felt guilty for having had such a fortunate experience in the United States. It was the first time I believed in something spiritual, and now understood that a spiritual connection could be as strong, if not stronger, than one's connection to a blood relative.

Time went by, and I completed my degree in Russia. In June 2002, I returned home to stay with my mother in Moldova for four months. All I could think about was the documents that would be necessary to get a U.S. student visa. My mother signed her apartment over to me on paper so I would have something to show to the U.S. visa officers. I also went to St. Petersburg, Russia, and found work. I was living there with a friend when Bob wrote to me, saying he had a connection in the American embassy in Moscow who would try to help me. This new connection came from Sharon, the president of the Center of Citizen Initiatives in San Francisco, who would later play a crucial role in my life.

I got my student visa to attend City College in San Francisco, and in January 2003, I was on the way back! Bob asked his mother, Libby, if she would be willing to host me for a while. She agreed. I lived at her beautiful San Francisco home for the next few years and developed a very close grandmother-granddaughter relationship with her. I felt so blessed to have met her and Betty, and, later, Sharon. These strong, wise, generous, kind, and dedicated women had a great impact on me and became my role models. I was getting an education on so many different levels and transitioning into an international citizen. I was becoming an empowered young woman.

In May 2003, I passed the TOEFL exam and later that summer got accepted into the International Relations Master's Program at San Francisco State University. My master's degree work was geared toward presenting the political conflict that I came out of and its intricacies.[4] I even received the opportunity through the Center of Citizen Initiatives to travel to Washington, DC, where I had the chance to discuss the situation in Moldova with a number of congressional representatives and to also brief the regional office of U.S. Representative Tom Lantos on several occasions.

With an international relations emphasis, I learned about key global issues, one of them being poverty in Africa. My desire to be involved with poverty alleviation in Africa led to the opportunity to start a project with one of my former schoolmates, Srijana. She had volunteered at the El Shadai foster home in Uganda and sent out photos and stories of the children residing there (who have been orphaned due to HIV/AIDS), proposing that we do some fund-raising for them.

Our first fundraiser was at Libby's house, where we later hosted a lot of events. After several fundraisers, we had raised enough money

---

[4] Maria Maslova, "Paradoxes of Recognition of Statehood and Self-determination in Post-communist South Eastern Europe: Situating Transnistria in Regional and Global Political Order" (Master's Thesis, San Francisco State University, 2005).

to purchase the land in order to build a house for the kids. We also started looking for sponsors for education.

We have most of the house built now. Slowly but surely we are building a safer place for these thirty kids who will have a permanent home and a sense of belonging. The four of us who cofounded the project are from all different parts of the world: Nepal, Moldova, El Salvador, and the United States. It has been really special to work together toward one common cause.

Now, I am about to have a baby, and after all those experiences, I wonder which of them will make me a good mother. When I am working on a project or have a big responsibility, I always question myself. I am a different person now compared to who I was five years ago. I bring a lot of my own experiences to motherhood. I want to encourage education, because this was my own mantra when growing up. It was always my number one priority. I also want to emphasize the importance of compassion, love, and kindness toward others. I want our child to be internationally minded. Seeing the world and learning about different cultures is key to becoming a complete person.

When I think of being a mother, it scares me in many ways because it is the beginning of a whole new chapter in my life. But I have faith. My experiences have proven to me that everyone has a calling. I think my story proves the existence of destiny in our universe.

My journey consisted of many layers of experiences; each shaped me as an individual, with people I barely knew helping me each step of the way. I have wondered before what would have become of me had I not chosen to come to the United States when I did. What if I had opened that packet in New York and had a ticket the first night? I never would have met Bob, Betty, Libby, and Sharon. I never would have participated in the fund-raising for the El Shadai foster home or worked in the field to improve U.S.-Russia relations.[5] I would have

---

[5] From 2006 until 2010, I worked as an executive assistant, program officer, and special projects manager at the Center of Citizen Initiatives of San Francisco (www.ccisf.org). I worked

not met my wonderful husband and soul mate, Brandon Jones. As my story proves, everything happens for a reason.

MASHA'S ADVICE FOR WOMEN

I really hope that the young woman in a small town who is reading this book realizes that everything is possible. The fact that you are a woman should not prevent you from doing things in your life that you want to do. If you have the right idea and the passion and put your heart into something, work with your conscience, and pour all your energy into it, it will happen. Stay really connected to your sense of purpose and your mission and do it with 100 percent commitment. Believe in yourself and that in this world of opportunities, anything is possible.

---

closely with the CCI's president and founder, Sharon, on projects designed to help build and foster understanding and constructive U.S.-Russia relations.

CAMELIA

Romania

Journeying from Romania to the United States as an immigrant woman, Camelia was unsure which career she could pursue so she created a care home for elderly women. Her story discusses her experiences in caring daily for women afflicted with Alzheimer's disease, dementia, cancer, and other health issues.

I SEE LIFE AS a journey—a legacy we all create for ourselves and our descendants. Everything we do and all that we experience are part of that legacy. My work as a care provider allows me the unique opportunity to help usher other women from this world to the next; it allows me to care for people, often in their final days.

My journey is a fascinating one that amazes me with all of its blessings each day. My name is Camelia and I am originally from Romania. Although immigrating to the United States had its unique challenges, I have found my path in life and purpose from God. As an immigrant woman, I had to start over when I moved and quickly realized I had to create my own means. My English was limited, so it was challenging to find traditional employment.

At the time I was contemplating what kind of job was possible for me, my in-laws had a small care home, where elderly patients lived and received around-the-clock medical care. I volunteered in the care home for two months to see if this would be suitable work. I knew owning a care home involved a heavy amount of responsibility, and I learned a lot while volunteering. At the end of those two months, I told my husband, "I think we can create a care home."

I had done similar work before and very much enjoyed it. I once owned a cleaning business, which also entailed taking care of elderly clients, mostly women. I would even call ahead before going to their homes and ask if there was anything I could get them from the store. I developed special relationships with these women, and they depended on my company and attention.

I reflected on those relationships as I considered this new job possibility. I realized owning and operating a care home involved the same elements of work I had previously enjoyed. I knew it was something I could do very well—I like cooking and taking care of people. To me, these things are very rewarding.

I made the decision to take this new path in my life and opened a small care home. We bought a nice house and started with four residents. It was difficult at first. When you are new in a business and new to a country, there are a lot of worries and stress. I learned so much in this time and very quickly. One of my biggest lessons was learning how attached I became to some of the residents due to the love and care I gave them. That's a very powerful thing.

We had a lady who was close to one-hundred years old. Her name was Granny. One evening, I went to church, and she asked my husband where I was as my husband put her in bed at 9:00 PM, her usual time. I did not arrive home until later that evening and immediately went to bed. In the morning, I checked on her and she was still on the side of the bed, waiting for me. I said, "Granny, didn't you go to sleep last night?" She said, "Oh, Camelia, I waited all night for you." I could not believe that someone would wait all night to make sure I came home safe. That is the caregiver attachment. When you care for other people, they, in turn, care for you. I see this same attachment at our current care home with our residents.

This attachment is something that builds relatively fast. It is so strong, as though you are their family member.

Eventually, I realized the first home was not exactly what I envisioned. It was nice and the residents were wonderful, but I became creative and envisioned myself building a nicer, newer one on my own.

At the time, I had so many plans, and the most amazing aspect is that I could visualize the home completely finished before it was even built. I think it is important to really see your dream as you imagine it so you can begin to achieve it.

My path began with the question: "What kind of job can I do in this new country?" I think a lot of immigrant women struggle with this question. It's hard on your self-esteem when you know you are capable, but no one wants to hire you because you are an immigrant and there is a language barrier. As a result of this, I started my first cleaning business many years ago. In that position, I didn't need to speak fluent English. I just needed to be hardworking. I had a yearning to do more and learned that I had to be creative. In fact, I have always found my way in life by simply saying to myself, "I've got to be creative."

I was certain if I used what I knew and was thinking creatively, I would not have to worry about someone hiring me. That's the problem with the language barrier for many immigrant women. If you are in my position and apply for work, it is almost certain that you will get a very low-level job.

This is why I made the choice to create a larger care home after our first. I always liked to work and wanted to accomplish things. I was the kind of person to look ahead to different possibilities. I had confidence in myself that I could do a really good job as a caregiver. In this job, you have to be very dedicated to the residents. It's not just a job; it's a way of life. You cannot simply look to it as a business; you must look at it as caring for other people and their needs.

Over the years I have learned so much about the women I care for: their backgrounds, how they lived, their families, their achievements, and the dreams they had in their lives. I viewed their pictures and shared their memories. They love to share these things with me, and I enjoy it, too. Especially since most of them are nearing the end of their lives. I get to witness their journey come full circle.

This work has improved my English as I have spent time with the women in my care home. I like to involve them in my work and life. One day, I wrote out a fax to send to someone and asked one of the ladies how my writing looked. She replied in a teacher-like voice, "Oh, Camelia, perfect."

MANAGING THE HOUSE

When residents move into the house at seventy, eighty, or ninety years old, they all come from different lifestyles. Living in a group situation is also a different lifestyle for them. They are coming into a new house with new people, so we have to try our best to make them part of the existing family unit in the house.

We instill in the residents that we are all a family, especially when people with such different personalities move in together. We tell them that we all need to care for and love each other, respect each other, and be kind. I believe it is the caregiver's job to promote this energy. I show kindness and respect, no matter how upset they are when they move here. Many of them are coming into this situation unhappy with having to give up their independence. I am always mindful of that.

I remember when one lady moved in some time ago with a very mean and disrespectful demeanor, I had to tell her, "Honey, you cannot act this way. At your age you have to still show kindness. You can't talk to people like that because you can change a person's life by the way you talk and by your demeanor." She eventually became calmer and adjusted to living with us. I knew it was hard for her at first and tried to help her adjust.

Another one of our residents is very hard to transfer to the bed because of her health issues. I always ask her to help me and thank her when she does. I thank every person I take care of, for even the smallest things. This is out of my respect for these women as human beings. When I thank them, I receive respect back from them.

Some of the women I care for may not always remember my name. I care for women in the late stages of Alzheimer's disease, and these residents have a great deal of difficulty remembering who people are on a daily basis. As their caregiver, I have to learn to work around this, which takes a lot of patience.

I never want to have regrets. I am so happy doing what I am doing and that I had the chance to do this, even on the most difficult days. My children are proud of me and my husband, and they are also very supportive. It's a blessing from God to be able to take care of people, and at such a special time in their lives. This is the last part in the journey of their lives before they go. I always try to do the best I can for them. I treat their stay here like a celebration by being cheerful and happy for them. I am never grumpy. If I walk in a resident's room in a positive and cheerful way, I will reflect that positivity on the residents. I try not to become upset, because those I care for will know right away that something is wrong. I don't want to create that environment for them. I like the home to be peaceful and be surrounded by kindness.

I am happy, and I'm doing exactly what I want to do. You may just have one career in life, or you may reinvent yourself many times. As a young woman, I never thought I would be taking care of elderly ladies in my life. Your journey may not be like mine, but you never know where it will take you.

CAMELIA'S ADVICE FOR WOMEN

One thing I've learned is that it is amazing to see how you can be involved in and change other people's lives. Make the best out of every situation and every day.

There was a lady I was caring for who was terminally ill. The doctor told her she had six months to live because she had cancer. Six months later she is still doing well. I told her the only thing she could do is think positively and look ahead. Honestly, no matter what is left for you, you can make the best out of that situation. Why worry about tomorrow when you have today to enjoy? You cannot control what will happen tomorrow. To be positive, you have to be happy today. It does not matter what is going to happen, just be happy on the inside. When you feel this way, you will reflect positive thinking, enjoy today, and leave tomorrow in God's hands.

It's awesome to have goals ahead of you. Those are part of your forward journey. We have to have goals ahead of us at all times. Even if you do not accomplish 100 percent of the things you look forward to, you don't have to stop. There is always going to be something ahead. You never know what that will be, so enjoy today!

For immigrant women: Moving from one country to another absolutely means that you can still have goals and a career. There are so many opportunities and possibilities ahead of you and so much out there to explore and enjoy. Don't stop with one thing—keep going and do whatever you think fits your life or what you desire.

I think women are adventurous and creative. We are so creative that we can even invent careers. When we are creators, nothing can stop us. When I first envisioned my care home, I did not know how to start the business or where to get help. I just did a little bit of research and kept telling myself that I would not stop until I had finished what I started. I didn't know any of the processes in the beginning. Being an immigrant woman, no one told me where to get a license, what to do, or what schooling I needed. I learned along the way and didn't let anything stop me from doing what I wanted. If you put your mind to it, you can do anything you want. Just because the first door closes, it does not mean that you can't keep going forward. One of these days, the right door will open.

You will amaze yourself with the things you do when you are being creative.

JOLA

Poland

Jola presents important advice for women all over the world about how they view themselves, their goals, and secrets to finding happiness and meaning in each day of their lives.

I AM A PERSON who believes in living life to the greatest extent! Although I am from a small country with a very diverse history, I can promise you that my personality is anything but tiny. I have goals, dreams, and desires that are monumental, a trait many would not expect me to possess, since I come from such a small country.

I could tell you about so many things: my past, my relationships, my childhood, and my work. Instead, I will give my advice and recommendations to women all over the world from my life experiences and the lessons I have learned. I feel that is how I can best serve them, by encouraging them to appreciate the wonderful people that they are.

YOUR BEST FRIEND

The most beautiful word in the world is love, and the most beautiful form of love is between you and your best friend.

Think for a moment about your best friend. Who is he or she? Very often, we would choose someone we truly love, trust, and rely on when asked this question. Perhaps, you have many best friends or just one. Yet, there is someone else we rarely think about, someone who is always with us and wants our desires and dreams our dreams. We want nothing more than to see, accept, love, and trust this someone. No matter what, this someone will always be with you. Are you ready to meet your closest best friend? Look in the mirror, and you will see her. Yes, this is YOU! You are your best friend! So, love yourself! Love your beautiful face, gorgeous eyes, and amazing smile. Love every cell in your body! Love yourself just because you are who you are. It does not matter what anyone says about you—you give yourself the amount of validation that you want.

Human nature is creative, and very often we find things we do not like or do not accept about ourselves. But we should keep in mind that whatever we think about ourselves, it is only the image we created in our minds. Therefore, it is an image that can be wrong. Until we look closer and change it, we will have little chance to grow. Think about it this way: if you want people to love you, you'd better love yourself first. So, fall in love with yourself! Enjoy your own perfect being and give yourself love—every day! You deserve it because you are perfect already! All your power comes from within. It gives you strength and confidence. If you accept yourself for who you are, then you accept people in your life and the things happening around you. Your inner love will allow you to love everyone and everything. When I learned how to love myself, it changed my life.

ATTITUDE VS. FEAR

One of the key elements of achievement is attitude. No matter what, you always need to see possibilities and opportunities, rather than obstacles. Attitude is the measure of this insight, and it dictates how we react to every situation in life. I have learned that our fears can shape attitude and outlook, which can be positive or negative.

Fear can be a blessing and a curse. It can motivate us or discourage us. It can even cause us to have a wrong image of ourselves, one that will hold us back from achieving great things and reaching our dreams. We must discover that fears are really a collection of images that we create in our mind because we think they will protect us, when, in reality, they stop us from reaching our goals and possessing the courage to do the impossible.

When we are afraid, it is good to look closer and examine the way we think. By undergoing this process, we might find that we identify with the wrong ideas and beliefs and that the knowledge we obtained somewhere during our life might be wrong, as well. That's okay. The most important step is to acknowledge it and be aware of it. Begin with yourself first. Many times, you'll find that knowledge and instilled beliefs are the causes of your fears.

There are certain things in life that we cannot change, but we can change our own reactions toward everything that is happening around us. The right attitude allows us to look for the brighter side and look for opportunities and creative solutions in even the worst of times. There is always a way to make something positive out of any situation, if you believe in it strongly. Miracles happen every day, but we need to allow them to come by having an optimistic attitude, rather than creating negative outcomes with our fears. We always have a choice concerning our attitudes; and if we give into our fears, we are choosing the negative path. The next time you find yourself saying, "I can't do this," or "I am not good enough," please replace these negative fear-based sayings with, "I will do whatever it takes to achieve it," and "I deserve this."

GOALS AND JOURNEY

Every day, I write my goals and dreams down in a little journal. It gives me a lot of joy, but it also helps me focus on the little steps I can take each day to get closer to my main goal.

There is a strong difference between goals and thoughts. Your goals should be things you are passionate about and think of with complete obsession. Always write them down as if they are already yours; feel you have them already. See, enjoy, deserve, and appreciate them now rather than in the future! You have to own them completely. Set your goals big and watch what happens. You will be surprised!

Each time you create a new goal, you begin a new journey. It's interesting that the whole road, those little steps you need to take to achieve your goal, are more fascinating than the achievement itself. Even if those small steps require you to fight past your own limits, it is worth it because this is how you grow, develop, and get closer to the goal.

Every journey from point A to B is an amazing way to learn about yourself and discover the unlimited power within yourself. Setting your goals is the first step of any journey.

OBTAINING THE IMPOSSIBLE

You need to feel you deserve everything you aspire to. If you don't believe you deserve it, why should it be given to you? In my culture and religion, we were taught that we needed to be holy to deserve anything good. With this belief came the belief that it is wrong (a sin) to deserve great things and to be worthy of the best. They would say it is selfish to want things, and if you express too much desire, you will find yourself in hell.

I remember when I started to question that belief. It was a huge discovery, because I had no idea this belief was influencing my life on almost every level. I felt guilty to deserve, to be loved, to have and want more, and to be successful. Worst of all, I felt that I was not a good enough person, daughter, sister, and friend, so I didn't deserve the best and to be worth all wonders. It really scared me. I asked myself why I felt so guilty. That was the moment when I realized that one wrong belief I caught as a child was limiting me and making me a fear-based person. It was giving me a poor attitude and outlook on life because I was always afraid I was doing something wrong. To change it, I stopped identifying with those beliefs and changed my way of thinking from telling myself, "I am not good enough," and "I don't deserve this," to "I deserve it," and "I am worth it." This attitude turned my life into a miracle. I finally felt I deserved great things just because of who I am.

Many of these negative beliefs find their way in through the course of our lives. We are not even conscious that we act according to them. They stop us from becoming what we want to become. They stop us from having an amazing and abundant life and relations. The moment we realize them and stop identifying with them is the moment that will change our lives.

SELF-VICTIMIZATION: DO NOT PLAY THE VICTIM

We have a tendency to blame conditions, people, economy, religion, government, and even society for not having what we expect or want. We also blame ourselves for not being the person we want to be. We look for excuses. This way of thinking puts us in the role of a victim. We allow others to create our own world, instead of creating it ourselves; we allow others to have power over us, instead of taking it in our own hands and becoming our own boss.

Being a victim is definitely not the way the winners think and do. If you think you can't do something, in reality, it means you won't do it. It is an excuse. Winners have no excuses. The champions win because they overcome limitations; they don't have excuses and keep on trying over and over again even when they fail.

You are the creator of your own life and the world around you. You are the only one who can change your situation. You have to believe you can do this. You are a winner if you believe you are. Whether you think you can, or you think you can't—you're right either way.

Do not blame or look for excuses; give yourself a chance to discover your unlimited power. Listen to your heart and your intuition. Quiet your mind of all the negative thoughts that are spinning in your head and listen to your inner voice and follow it. Whatever you do, feel like a winner. Be a winner before you even start with any idea. Feel you deserve it, and love yourself because you do.

That is my advice to women everywhere because these things have always made me successful. If my advice can help one woman somewhere in this world, then it is worth everything.

JOLA'S ADVICE FOR WOMEN

Love yourself! Think big and dream bigger! Feel you deserve only the best! Feel great about yourself, and feel you are worthy to do anything. Have the attitude of "I am a winner" all of the time, because you can do anything. Never, ever give up! Never!

NORTH & SOUTH CAUCASUS

RUSSIA

INGUSHETIA

CHECHNIA

N. OSSETIA

CASPIAN SEA

DAGESTAN

BLACK SEA

SOUTH OSSETIA

GEORGIA

TURKEY

ARMENIA

AZERBAIJAN

RUSSIAN FEDERATION

ABKHAZIA

N. OSSETIA

ZUGDIDI

SOUTH OSSETIA

BLACK SEA

GEORGIA

AJARA

TURKEY

ARMENIA

AZERBAIJAN

RUSUDAN

Georgia

As the Soviet Union began to disintegrate toward the end of the 1980s, ethnic tensions grew in two major regions of Georgia: Abkhazia and South Ossetia. Following the 1991–1992 South Ossetian War, disputes arose between the Abkhaz and Georgians over Abkhazia's desire for independence leading to the 1992–1993 war in Abkhazia. As a result of both conflicts, Abkhazia became a de facto territory and more than 250,000 Georgians fled the region to nearby border cities, becoming internally displaced persons (IDPs). In 2008, conflict ensued again in the South Ossetia region, resulting in an additional 26,000 internally displaced persons.

Trapped between closed military borders in the town of Zugdidi following the 1993 war in Abkhazia, Rusudan observed thousands of internally displaced persons (IDPs) resettling in

abandoned warehouses and schools. Without any source of work
in the months of the war, Rusudan created the non-governmental
organization (NGO) Association Atinati to rehabilitate IDPs in
her region. She discusses the conflicts, their impact on Georgia,
her work with IDPs, and recent political changes in the country.

PERHAPS YOU HAVE never heard of my country, Georgia. It is a land with very beautiful nature located in the southern Caucasus region. Although we have a very unique history and a multicultural nation, we have experienced two wars in the last few decades. Yet, there are many positive changes happening here and I am very proud of them.

My name is Rusudan and I was born in a town called Zugdidi in the historical province of Samegrelo, and graduated from the university in Tbilisi with a degree in chemistry. I currently live in Zugdidi with my husband and two children. Zugdidi is not far from the Abkhazia region, which has been in armed conflict since the 1990s.

I am the executive director of the non-governmental organization (NGO) Association Atinati, which works with internally displaced people (IDPs) in Georgia. Association Atinati's mission is to support democratic society, provide education, and to help rehabilitate the internally displaced.

The story of how Association Atinati was born is a beautiful one and one I am very proud of it because it arose from very difficult times.

ABKHAZIA AND SOUTH OSSETIA

A lot of things were changing in Georgia toward the end of the Soviet Union that led to two wars in two different territories of Georgia. The territory of South Ossetia erupted into armed conflict that lasted from 1991 to 1992 because South Ossetians declared independence from Georgia in 1990.

The war in Abkhazia followed in 1992 after Abkhazia also declared independence from Georgia. We essentially had two conflict zones occurring at the same time. Russia was the key player in both because it wanted to have access to the Black Sea and control over Georgia, including the rest of the South Caucasus region, namely Armenia and Azerbaijan.

Borders were created to separate these two regions from the rest of Georgia after the conflicts in the '90s, so Georgia currently has no influence within both regions. Abkhazia considers itself an independent state and is recognized as such by Russia, Nicaragua, Venezuela, Nauru, and Tuvalu, although the Georgian government and all other countries in the rest of the world consider Abkhazia to be part of Georgia's territory. South Ossetia remains a disputed territory.

In 1993, more than 250,000 Georgians became internally displaced as a result of the war in the Abkhazia region. Unfortunately, this problem persists today. Although there are no current war actions, there is still tension and a border separating Samegrelo and Abkhazia. It is not a stable situation and those who live in the area are haunted by the notion that violence could erupt at any time. There is always a very high amount of tension in the air around the borders and in these regions.

This political conflict influences our economy, especially since a lot of IDPs from the Abkhazia region are living in the Samegrelo region. Our government plus local NGOs and the United Nations are doing a lot to try to resolve this conflict and help the IDPs.

Although the situation is more stable now, when the IDPs first started to come to the Samegrelo region from Abkhazia in 1993, they experienced many hardships. Most of them had to walk across the greater Caucasus Mountains to get out of the region due to border closures. Although it's less than a two-hour drive from Abkhazia to the Samegrelo region, the borders were occupied by military and the only way to leave was to trek across the Caucasus Mountains. This was a very difficult journey for them and many women and children died along the way. Within a couple of days, the population of my town, Zugdidi, doubled. The town was not prepared for this to happen.

When they arrived in Zugdidi they occupied old factory and school buildings that did not have restrooms, electricity, or running water. Now their living conditions are much better due to government assistance and the intervention over the years from international aid organizations. Many of the old buildings were renovated for them. They needed a lot of humanitarian and psychological help since they had fled a war.

After the August 2008 war between Russia and Georgia for control of South Ossetia, we had about 26,000 more IDPs flooding in again from South Ossetia. We were confronted with similar challenges in 2008 as in 1993, as we scrambled to help these new IDPs.

SUNRISE IN DARKNESS: ASSOCIATION ATINATI

When I was a young girl the Abkhazia and South Ossetia borders were not closed. I am a Soviet child who spent her earlier life in a Soviet country. When I was young and attending the university in Sukhumi it was very popular to go and drink coffee at a café and socialize. We were also only a one-hour drive from the Black Sea and we had beautiful nature all around us. When my husband and I married, we went on a honeymoon to Abkhazia. He even worked in a town in Abkhazia for eight years since he loved this part of Georgia. Now there is too much border control in the areas outside my region of Zugdidi to be able to enjoy these things.

After my children were born in the '90s, two borders were formed that closed access to Abkhazia. We felt like we were locked in a room after they closed because we could not leave Zugdidi. This situation lasted several months during the war in Abkhazia in 1993. I had small children, we did not have much food, and nothing was coming in from either side of the borders. Soldiers were everywhere.

It was hard to survive during that time because we had no income. I was working in a university since my major was chemistry, but during this period, everything stopped. There was no university, entertainment, or schools. By nature I am a very active person so I wondered what I could do. I decided that I wanted to start a program or business. My husband told me if I did, he would support me. I was a young woman pregnant for the second time when I created our NGO, Association Atinati, after the war in Abkhazia in 1995. After seeing all of the IDPs come into my town from Abkhazia, I decided to reach out to them. When I started Association Atinati, we had no money for rent or anything else. We received a grant from the Open Society Georgia Foundation and another from UNICEF to conduct our first program, a social rehabilitation for IDP children.

My husband started working with me too because the factory he worked in was closed. After all these years, this is our work. Now we have more than fifty staff members, depending on projects, and are very proud to still be existing after eighteen years. Our former students are all leaders, active in their communities, and are in good positions. One of our former IDP students is now working in a bank. She just got married and graduated from a university. Our former students always say that Association Atinati was one of the brightest areas of their childhoods. My husband and I even call it our third child and have celebrated its birthday every year on October 31 since it started in 1995. This was when we officially registered Association Atinati as an NGO.

Atinati means "sunrise in darkness." I called our NGO "Atinati" because it was a light for us and the IDPs in a time of darkness. Our activities were and still are very important for so many displaced people and our local population. Over the years we have helped the displaced rebuild their lives and their children get an education.

After spending years working with other IDPs, my family was forced to run from our home on August 10, 2008 as the Russians came into Georgia with trucks and tanks, bombarding nearby cities close to the Black Sea. They also bombed the mountain where we had the tower and transmitter for our NGO Association Atinati radio station and took some of the equipment away. Fortunately with support from the international community and the U.S. embassy, we were able to regain the station after one month.

Although we had experienced other aspects of war before, my family had never experienced displacement. During those two days we lived in another part of Georgia with relatives because we thought it was safe, but nowhere is safe during a war. After thirteen years of helping others who were displaced, we became displaced ourselves. Fortunately, it was only over a period of two days, but it was still very terrifying because you just never know what can happen in that situation.

During those two days, I recalled memories of when we had started to work with the IDPs in October 1993 after the war in Abkhazia by providing them with some food and supplies. We asked them if they had any heat or electricity where they were living and they told us, "Thank you, but we don't need anything because we are going back to Abkhazia." They never went back and remain in Zugdidi to this day. You never know how many days or how many years you will be an internally displaced person after you become one. It is common to believe it will only be temporary, but most of the time it is permanent.

After we returned home to Zugdidi on August 12, 2008, there were more IDPs flooding into our region whom we had to help. We provided psychological rehabilitation, education, and economic development opportunities. We received support from United Nations High Commissioner for Refugees (UNHCR) to implement two projects that still exist for IDP women: one is an economic empowerment project and the other concerns sexual and gender-based violence.

The first project empowers IDP women economically by teaching them how to start a business and write a business plan. We also try to give some grant money to those with the most successful ideas. Within three years after the launch of this program, more than three hundred IDP ladies started their own business and more than 90 percent of these ladies are working today. This success is very important. Although most are not earning large amounts of money, they are earning enough to feed their children and families.

The second project aims to reduce sexual and gender-based violence. Not only did such violence occur as a result of military actions during the two conflicts, domestic violence is also very prevalent in the culture. Rarely do women speak out if they are experiencing it due to cultural stigma. We try to raise awareness with the women in the IDP community regarding what violence is and how to respond to it. Many of these women do not know that certain treatment from a husband or other family member is violence. They see it as normal, regular behavior.

In our association we have a crisis center that acts as a short-term shelter where a woman can safely stay with her children and receive legal, medical, and even psychological aid. This is mostly for IDP women but we still accept local women when they come to us for help.

Most Georgians are Orthodox Christians so we created cooperation with the local church to give these women the option of talking to a priest openly about all of their problems. In our culture it is easier to go to a priest as most people are more comfortable speaking openly and freely with a member of the church. For our anti-violence program, we work with local NGOs, government, the church, hospitals, and the police. Violence is one big cycle and stopping it involves the cooperation of all levels of society. All the different groups must work together against it.

Our police in Georgia used to be very corrupt, almost like mafia. The last two to three years have revealed many positive changes in Georgian law enforcement. Police became friendlier and very helpful. Now we trust them. Our NGO even provided some training to local law enforcement regarding gender-based violence to teach them how to work with us in preventing it. There are a lot of traditions in my country and sometimes, traditions have more power than law and even religious beliefs. The traditions are the most difficult to navigate and to break because they are so ingrained in the culture. Although our laws dictate that women and men have equal rights, for example, the domestic violence in our society comes from traditions.

When I was younger there was a very popular practice of kidnapping girls for marriage. It was such normal behavior that the society did not react to it. Even when the girl didn't want to be with the man who kidnapped her and would return home, her parents would not allow her to come back because her return would be shameful for the family and shameful for the girl. The kidnapping act itself was very casual—they would just take the girl off the street with machine guns in their hands. These women were not kidnapped for prostitution, rather as an act of creating families. Ten years ago in my country, it was not considered safe for a beautiful young girl to walk down the street.

I knew several women who were kidnapped and taken as brides. It was so common. I also knew several strong girls who came back and said "no" to that tradition. I knew a woman from a wealthy family who was kidnapped and did not want to stay with the man who took her, but her father told her she had to stay with him. These girls often had no support from their own parents!

In the last few years an existing kidnapping law became stricter and is now enforced often. After 2011, offenders who kidnap a girl receive about four to eight years in prison. Remarkably, I have not heard of any cases of kidnapping in the last four years. There are actually a lot of good things happening in Georgia right now and personally, I love this new kidnapping law.

Georgia is a very European country with a lot of tolerance for diversity. Most would perceive it to be a country that is moving backward because of the recent 2008 armed conflict in South Ossetia. This is not true—we are moving forward so positively with changes in laws, policies, and our law enforcement.

I am a very realistic person and know my country has a lot of problems. I know we have a long way to go to develop our country, our laws, and many other things. We still have these two borders in Abkhazia and South Ossetia and scores of IDPs from these conflicts. But, if I compare how Georgia was with how Georgia is now, there is a very big difference and every day I am grateful for that.

I realize there are many issues in my country that need attention, but when I look at the scope of what I can do, I realize that I can help internally displaced women and children. I realize by helping them gain more in their lives, I am also helping Georgia. That is why I do the work that I do.

RUSUDAN'S ADVICE FOR WOMEN
Have solidarity with all women and support each other. If we stay together, we will prevail.

AYSHAT

Republic of Ingushetia

The Republic of Ingushetia is a federal subject of Russia and is one of its poorest and most restive regions. Ongoing military conflict in neighboring Chechnya has spilled into Ingushetia, destabilizing the region through corruption, crime, Russian military presence, and a withering human and women's rights situation.

Soon after the fall of communism, Ayshat was kidnapped by a stranger who wanted to marry her. Such bride kidnappings are not unusual in ultra-conservative Ingushetia, or in any of the North Caucasus republics. What is rare is Ayshat's courage in speaking out. She tells the story of her violent marriage, breaking her silence in the hope of persuading other women to resist abuse.

While telling this story, Ayshat sat in the small basement office of a women's NGO in Ingushetia. Pale, determined, articulate, she looked older than her forty years. With no relatives to support her, she is raising her son alone, on her small income, which is extremely

unusual in Ingushetia. Her thick hair was cut fashionably short—
also a rarity in Ingushetia, where women pride themselves on their
long locks. It had to be cut when she was first treated for a brain
tumor. Since that treatment, she has learned at the hospital that
the cancer has returned, and she needs an operation in Moscow
which she cannot afford. When she broke down after hearing the
news, a kind nurse referred her to the NGO. Ayshat is clear that
her tumor is the result of her ex-husband's violence.

I'D BETTER START with how I met my now ex-husband. I was a nurse, working in the resuscitation department. One day a colleague told me about a man who had just returned from Barnaul. She said he was a great guy, and that she would like to introduce me to him. I agreed. The next day he turned up when I was on my shift and we talked. I didn't like him at all; didn't like the way he talked or behaved. It was quite clear—this was not my kind of man. I refused him, politely. I was about to take my entrance exam for medical school and I had a lot of studying to do. I wanted to study gynecology. We only had that one conversation and he seemed to have gotten the point that I was not interested.

The next morning, I was on my way home after the night shift when he came up and asked if he could walk with me. I said I'd rather he didn't; I thought I'd made my position clear—I wasn't looking for a husband. Suddenly a car drove up, two men leaped out, dragged me in, drove me off to Nazran, and locked me into a fifth floor flat!

I resisted, of course, and said I'd never agree to marry him. Yet, he took no notice. I did try to escape by way of the apartment balcony since the adjoining apartment had one, too. I asked my kidnappers, who were keeping guard in the next room, if I could close the door for five minutes. Then I climbed onto the neighbor's balcony. I thought, "I've done it, I got away!" Imagine—being in my situation where you're going to have to live with a man you don't even like! I was in such a state of shock, shaking from head to toe. I banged on the neighbors' window but there was no one there.

That was when I understood that no one was going to rescue me. I was going to have to go back. For a moment, standing on that fifth floor balcony, I thought, "Why not just throw myself off?" I was distraught. I lay down again quickly in case they came to check on me. When they did, I pretended I was all right. I lay there thinking of how to escape. I knew I had to, somehow, but I never managed to.

Then the men took me off into the depths of Chechnya, as my relatives and friends were all saying "Give us back our girl!" The men then told the Chechen clan elders I was fine with the marriage. The elders said, "Bring her here, so we can ask her ourselves." So they thought up a scam. They took some other girl and presented her to the elders as me! None of my close relations were there, and the clan elders are so distantly connected to me that they wouldn't have known what I looked like. The elders asked the girl posing as me, "Have you agreed to this?" She said yes. The elders then gave their blessing, marrying me off in my absence.

But the older among the elders suspected something wasn't right. They demanded the men produce the real bride. My kidnappers were very cunning. They decided to keep me overnight, in the hope they'd be able to win me over. That night, they piled on the pressure; stood over me, going on and on in monotone voices: "Come on, come on. It'll be fine. He's a great fellow."

The next morning, I gave in. I guess I was just so exhausted. I felt I was offering myself as a sacrifice. I do that. I've been like that since I was a child. Wanting to please anyone no matter what it costs me has done me so much harm.

So this is how my married life, if that's what you can call it, began.

Right away I knew he had problems. To begin, he drank a lot. After they stole me they sat in the next room and drank. The next day there they were again, getting drunk, and the day after. I hated it. But I thought maybe it would pass, that he was drinking because he was so happy.

We were married a week later and a woman from Barnaul came to the wedding. People said she and my husband were old friends so I never suspected a thing. I was very trusting. I believed, and still believe, that men and women can be friends. So I welcomed her. I was so young, so inexperienced! Yet the way she talked and the things she said breathed jealousy. She hated me. She'd say to my husband sarcastically, "Look what a beauty you've chosen!" She even tried undressing me, saying, "Let me see your breasts, your legs—my, what a girl!" If I'd been less naïve, I'd have realized she was his lover. I was surprised when I found this out because I didn't suspect a thing.

A few days later we all went to Barnaul, this lover, my husband, and I. That's where my married life began and it was awful. His lover wouldn't leave him alone. She was always picking fights even when I was there. I was so naïve—even then I didn't realize they were lovers and because she was always yelling at him, he would lash out at me. She'd be there every day, asking me these questions, about how things were in bed with him and I'd tell her. She was consistently bringing me presents and cakes. When I ate them I'd feel terrible. Yes, it sounds weird, but it's true. After eating anything she brought me I'd feel bad. I couldn't understand it. Maybe it had something to do with her jealousy. I lost ten kilos in three months. I got so weak, though usually I was full of energy from racing around the house, cooking, never sitting down, and trying to please my husband. That's how I was brought up. I wanted to be a perfect wife.

Today, I wonder how I could have behaved like that. It goes back to my childhood, I suppose. I grew up in a very conservative family where our father was very strict. Sometimes he was nice, but he was always criticizing us. He never praised us, no matter how much we tried to please him. As a result, my sisters and I grew up believing we had to please everyone.

My husband soon noticed that trait in me, and took advantage of it. I was afraid of him right from the start. He'd get this terrible look in his eyes, and start shouting and throwing things at me often for no apparent reason! He would throw saucepans, ashtrays, watches, and anything that was around. Once he threw a pan of hot fat at me. He'd also grab these big knives and threaten me with them. I'd burst into tears. I could see he was sick. I was scared. When the rage died down he'd be sorry and would say things like, "I'm a fool, and I don't know why I do these things. I love you more than anything in the world." Then I'd forgive him. I pitied him and used to think, "Poor man, what must they have done to you to make you like this."

Pity. My capacity for pity is like a bad joke. It's played a fatal role in my life. I should have looked after myself better instead of pitying others so much.

I was a long way away from my parents. If they'd been there, maybe I'd just have run away when he started beating me up. But I didn't know how to. For a start, he never gave me any money. Maybe he was afraid I'd run away. It wasn't that he was mean to me in this way, he just he never left any money at home. Yet, considering how he lived—the lovers, the restaurants—he must have felt he needed it, just in case. He'd never let an opportunity slip to have a lover. After spending the whole evening with one woman, on the way home he'd manage one more "bit of skirt." By the time he got home at two o'clock in the morning, I'd be exhausted yet then he'd start coming on to me. That's what he was like. Relentless. A compulsive womanizer.

When he beat me I wouldn't say a word. Then he'd beat me because I didn't say anything. He didn't know why he was doing it. He just beat me. Then he'd be sorry. At other times he'd yell, "You're a nobody!" He would say anything to make sure I didn't leave. He wanted me to feel dependent and vulnerable. As time when on, I got bolder—I'd yell at him to try and stand up for myself. We'd have huge fights because he had a temper, too.

After five or six years I got pregnant. Then he left by making some excuse about having to earn money that was not true. Instead, he was gone for months, with his lover. I didn't hear a word from him. He turned up when I was eight months along. That same day he beat me up so badly I had to escape. I scrambled out of the window, barefoot. I kept walking and walking. I had no idea where I was going. Then I reached some woods where I wanted to end my life. I just wanted to die. I never wanted to see that man again. I was furious. How could he beat me up, knowing that I was pregnant with his child?

I didn't kill myself, obviously. I sat there for twenty minutes or so, thinking it through. And realized I was wrong for wanting to end my life because I was pregnant and didn't have the right to kill another life. I pulled myself together and set off in the direction of home, still barefoot. Finally a car stopped and gave me a lift. I had this neighbor, Aunt Katya, who was a very nice Russian woman, and I went to her. She knew about my life and was always telling me to leave my husband. She put me to bed, prayed over me and went to discuss the situation with my husband. He was all smiles, denied we'd had a fight, though it was obvious he'd been really worried since I'd been gone all day until dark and refused to talk to him. I was hurting all over. I returned home the next day.

A month later, when I was about to give birth, he left again. He had this very young lover in Barnaul. He went to her and left me without a ruble. Throughout my pregnancy I hadn't had enough money to feed myself properly, to buy baby supplies or to pay the doctor. I had to turn to his brothers for help.

After the birth I came home. I had no milk to feed the baby. I spent these sleepless nights alone with the crying baby, who was very weak. I cried, too. I was afraid for the baby because he was having convulsions and we had to call an ambulance. My husband's brothers would bring food, but then they'd expect me to cook for them. They'd be there every day with their friends and I'd be cooking with one hand, holding the baby with the other. Around midnight Aunt Katya would come and take the child and I'd run out to the bathhouse and wash the diapers. The child was having diarrhea so I had to keep changing him. I was like a robot. I will forever be grateful to that woman.

My husband turned up again when the child was two months old. To be honest, I was very happy to see him. I took him into the child's room and exclaimed, "Here he is, our son!" He'd told me more than once that if I gave him a son he'd cover me in gold. Yet, he took one look at our son and said, "He's not very much like me!" I was hurt that he could say that after everything I'd been through during the pregnancy and after, when he was away! How ashamed I'd been to have to leave the maternity ward without paying the doctors. Of course, I couldn't pay them back later either because I had no money!

Something broke in me at that moment. I realized that man couldn't even share our joy of having a child. It was as if he was saying the child wasn't his. Had his lover put the idea into his head? I don't know. Well, he spent two months at home and in all that time, though he could see how much the baby was suffering, from pain, from illness, how wretched I was, he never once came and helped.

Now I am divorced after twenty years of marriage. I still have some financial problems and severe problems with my health. I have a tumor in my head and I need another operation which I cannot afford because it is expensive. I hope I can find a way to take care of it…

This story was contributed by the Center for Psychological Assistance and Post-Crisis Rehabilitation located in the Republic of Ingushetia.

SOUTH ASIA

KASHMIR

NEPAL BHUTAN

NEW DELHI

INDIA

CALCUTTA

BANGLADESH

KERALA

PADMA

India

An engineer by trade, writer by passion, Padma is the author of several books and the cofounder of the nonprofit organization, Vanitha. A native of Kerala, India, she shares her experiences growing up in a traditional caste system and the fateful occurrence that allowed her to attend school as a young woman and continue to pursue her passions into adulthood.

KERALA CULTURE

I GREW UP IN Kerala, which is the southernmost state in India. It is a very tropical, green, and beautiful land that had a traditional social structure called a caste system. It wasn't something that I was happy about in my youth, but it was an important part of our culture in Kerala. The caste system began many thousands of years ago and was referred to as a Varna system. The idea behind it was that

214

all people in a society fulfill specific roles and perform different types of work, based on their "nature." Some of them must, for example, be in charge of the body of governance of a kingdom, state, or county. They would ideally manage the society and make sure basic needs were being met. There were other groups who would offer spiritual guidance, those who built things, those interested in trade who were merchants, and others who did the farming and manual work.

People in the Brahmin caste system category are still considered superior because they started learning the Vedas, the old Indian Hindu scriptures. They became priests in temples. Due to the nature of Hinduism, they don't have any authority or control over other people. In Hinduism, no one can tell another person what to do, because it is a very democratic religion. Anybody can do whatever they want and worship whatever deity they want. That is one thing I have always appreciated about my religion. These Brahmins became the upper caste people, maintaining a place at the top of society, because of their knowledge in spiritual matters.

The second category or level of society was the Kshatriya. They were the kings and ruling parties in charge of society. There were many kingdoms in India, and each had its own king, who ruled the entire kingdom and had ministers to help them.

The third was the Vaishya, the merchants who did the transactions, trading, buying, and selling. These categories are actually still present in India. Even now, there are certain communities that have the knack for trade. They know how to conduct business in banking or import/export because these acts were family customs and a way of life for generations.

The fourth caste level was the Sudra, who did all the leftover work of the society, including various forms of manual work, such as domestic help or taking care of cattle. After thousands of years, these four main castes are still operating in the same way, although the categories are no longer strictly applied.

There is another group called "the untouchables." This group did not belong to any of the four castes and was considered so low in the community and society that they were seen as untouchable. They were farmers who manually plowed and harvested the fields, made leather goods from cowhides, or caught snakes to make shoes from snakeskin. There were thousands of menial jobs upper caste members did not want to do, so they fell to this group of people.

I was always so puzzled by this way of society that in my adult years, I wrote a book, called *My Mother's Daughter: Memories of Kerala's Matriarchal Culture*, which refers to the caste system in Kerala. I belonged to the second from the highest caste, which was known as the Kshatriya, or the "Ruler Caste." We had a matriarchal system of land ownership where women owned all of the property. I was born in the same house where my mother and grandmother were born, and my great-grandmother was still living in another part of that property.

In about the 1960s, that matriarchal system became completely extinct. Now, anybody can own property. The father and mother can give it to the son or the daughter. It became more democratic.

My Mother's Daughter: Memories of Kerala's Matriarchal Culture was written as a memoir. I have three grandchildren. It's difficult to describe my upbringing to them because they are growing up in the United States, but I want them to know how and where I grew up and what life was like so I wrote that book for them.

I felt so good after writing that book. There were many things I cannot describe verbally that I felt and was able to write about. One of the main things was I always wanted to go to school as a young girl, but the matriarchal system did not allow girls and women to go anywhere. We would have at-home tutors come to the house and teach us. I wanted to go out and study everything in the world! It was so painful for me to stay home, and I had to struggle to be allowed to go to school. I wrote about that struggle in that memoir.

Any time my parents told me I could not go to school, I would argue that the boys were going and that I did not think it was fair I could not go. From a young age onward, it was a struggle for me. I just wanted an education.

Above all these traditions, conditions, and cultural structures, there had always been something inside of me that couldn't be shut down. I always knew I wanted to go to school. The easier thing for me would have been to do what everyone else did and forget about the energy, the voice, and the force that I had inside. But somehow, for whatever reason, that didn't happen to me. I had one desire. I wanted to study and go to school. There was so much to learn in the world! I wanted to learn so desperately!

There were no books in my home. I never heard about a library when I was growing up. My father's newspaper would come in the morning, and I used to grab it and read it from page to page because it was all I had. A home tutor taught me and my cousins since we were a big joint family consisting of three grandmothers and each of their families. The boys would go to school, and the girls would stay home and wonder why they could not go. Actually, they all accepted it as a fact of life. I could not accept it! Day and night, I would cry and cry that I wanted to go to school.

To this day, my favorite part of who I am is my unyielding desire to learn. I don't think I will ever finish learning. I will learn until the last day of my life.

BREAKING BARRIERS AND ATTENDING SCHOOL

My mother passed away when I was very young. My mother's death was the main reason I went for higher studies and was able to go beyond high school. In high school, I came out with excellent marks, but that was not valued in my family or my community. I didn't think about any of the things a degree would bring me. I didn't care if I got a fast car or a big house. I just had this desire to study more and more things.

It was traumatic in many ways when my mother passed away, but it also opened so many doors for me. I believe when destiny closes one door, if you are paying attention, another door will open. Yet, if you are not paying attention, you may miss the opportunities being presented. Fortunately, I was paying attention after my mother's death.

I had two brothers who belonged to the "new generation" of India, the generation considered to be independent and energetic with new philosophy. They saw how interested I was in studying, so they really encouraged me to pursue my dreams of an education. They supported me the entire way through my degree program and gave me the opportunity to study engineering. Finally, like a dream come true, I received my degree in engineering in the 1960s. Getting that degree was amazing! It was absolutely great to accomplish. My brothers were the most supportive people in my quest for knowledge. Without them, I would have probably gotten married and had children like all the other women at the time. And I would still be living in India, wondering what I could have done and if I could have pursued my dreams.

My engineering degree forever changed my view of the world and my life. I wanted to write these things in *My Mother's Daughter* and give a copy to my brothers, but my oldest brother died before I was able to publish it. It feels so good to have written so many of my struggles, my pain, and my happiness in book form. It was very soothing, comforting, and satisfying. In one sense, I did it for my brothers, to present them a gift like they presented to me.

I also wanted to remember my parents through the book. My father died much later, but my mother died when I was thirteen years old. That was a critical age, because I was neither a child nor a grown-up, rather in the strange transition of puberty. I didn't know anything about the world and felt as though I lost my anchor when

I lost my mother. There were a lot of difficulties for me that I could not express to anyone, including questions about what it meant to be a woman. I released a lot of those bottled emotions while writing *My Mother's Daughter*, and I felt so light afterward! After coming to the United States, I became more liberated and free of constraints, which is why I think I was able to write my story. If I had stayed back in India, I wouldn't have felt the freedom to express myself. I feel really free here. If I want to write something, I can write it. I can go to the library and read every book if I want to. I was so excited to experience that freedom after I immigrated here to work as an engineer. Just living here has given me an inner sense of freedom. I am so grateful for that opportunity.

The only issue in living in a different country from where you were raised is that you think people don't understand you. The notion that others don't understand your background, where you came from, who you are, what motivates you, or what your problems are can be hard on the human spirit. That is very difficult to handle because everybody wants to be understood. We don't want people to have prejudgment, prejudice, or misunderstanding about us. Of course, I had friends who also came from India, but I interacted with so many different people, too.

I came from a difficult experience, growing up in a very rigid cultural structure and moving to a free society. I struggled because of my mother's passing away so early, without telling me who I was and guiding me through the feminine experience of adulthood. Most young girls have a mother they can go to when they are confused and have questions. Sometimes I think having my mother to guide me is what I've missed most in life. There is nobody like a mother who will understand you when you are a woman. Writing this book helped me process a lot of these feelings.

COMING TO THE UNITED STATES

I was in my thirties and had two children when I arrived in the United States in January 1980. I came after working as an engineer for some time in India. I was also writing a lot. My writing was the most enjoyable part and something that I was doing for myself! I used to write newspaper columns and satirical stories of human follies. I always wrote in English.

I was not living in Kerala as an adult, so I had to use English a lot. For some reason, I just loved the English language and wanted to write exclusively in it, even though I could write in Malayalam. Through the 1970s, I wrote in magazines and newspapers in India. After arriving in the United States, I wrote in Indian-American journals while I worked in engineering firms. While I was satisfied with my career, I had a strange feeling that I needed to do more. I didn't know what it was, and this was confusing. I grew anxious and unhappy, maybe due to my lack of understanding of it.

One day while I was working in Santa Rosa, California, an idea struck me like a thunderbolt. Some people did say, "God gave you a hint!" and "It was a calling!" Maybe it came from my subconscious. Regardless, I wanted to learn psychology. It was strange because I was happy working as an engineer. I was doing hardware and software engineering, which is very interesting work, but I just couldn't stop the new idea from coming.

I had to listen to that "call," so I immediately contacted a university and found out about a two-year master's program in psychology. That changed my life. It ignited a strong instinct already inside of me. Some people would never make this decision, assuming ideas like these are crazy, but not me. After the GRE exam, I applied and was accepted to the psychology master's program. For me, this was the first time in my adult life that I got to pursue a higher education toward something that captivated me.

I learned who I am through my studies in psychology. In each and every class, I got an A, an A plus, or an A minus. I completed the program in two years. I went to peer counseling sessions during my studies and was able to open up about childhood experiences I had never been able to discuss before. It was like I got my childhood back. I had blocked out a lot of it because it was so confusing. My studies in psychology were a big part of opening my mind for the task of putting together my memoir and my first book before it.

FIRST BOOK:
SPICES IN THE MELTING POT

My first book was *Spices in the Melting Pot: Life Stories of Exceptional South Asian Immigrant Women*, and it features life stories and achievements of exceptional South Asian women who had immigrated to the United States. It came out of my longing to affirm and validate the contributions of the many South Asian American women. After getting my psychology master's degree, I was a part-time engineer, part-time counselor, and still shifting.

So why did I choose to write about other women in *Spices in the Melting Pot*? It was an idea that came from inside me. To some extent, I am also a philosopher. Begin with philosophy and the practical things will follow. Human nature happens like that. What is life? Why are we doing this? Those kind of big questions come to my mind all the time, and my writing was a vehicle for some of those expressions and concepts that were struggling to come out. My first book was a search for women, because I can understand another woman better than I can understand a man. Their pain, sacrifices, and ideas are similar to my own. At the time, I was studying a lot of women's history. These were women who discovered who they are and defined their relationship with the American society. They did all the things that they wanted to do. I wanted to learn about them and what they have done with their lives. In some sense, America is the land of freedom. You can do whatever you want. Yet, culturally, it is difficult to break through certain barriers. This experience is very spiritual and not religious. Spirituality is an important part of life, and yet, I didn't experience that here. How to reconcile that or if you even need to reconcile it is a big conflict when you are an immigrant.

All of those practical and philosophical thoughts came to me. I wanted to see how these women dealt with them. Did they even have a conflict? Did they always go with their dreams? Have they fulfilled their dreams? Questions are my way of dealing with many things in life. I wanted to ask these questions to other women and see what answers they had for me and later generations.

I began with a woman I already knew who lived in Washington, DC. A good speaker, she happens to be from Kerala and had been working in the federal government for many years, and also was the head of a political organization. As the first woman to head the organization, she is very influential and has met many of the presidents: Clinton, Reagan, Bush Sr., and many more people in power. I discussed the subject of the book with her, and she loved the idea, saying, "I'm doing so much work here, and nobody is documenting it." That showed me that there was a need for this book.

To prepare myself to write that book, I read the stories of some American women, which I found fascinating. I didn't know that American women could not vote for a long time, could not own property, or be on a jury. There were a lot of things they could not do until they fought for those rights.

There were very few books about Susan B. Anthony. I wanted to read more about her, but it was so hard to find information. Women who have done such fantastic work for the betterment of American women and probably for women all over the world are basically invisible. Where are the stories about them? How are future generations going to learn from them? This really bothered me.

One book I read about American women shocked me. Two women spent sixty years working hard to pass a law dealing with women's suffrage—Susan B. Anthony and Elizabeth Cady Stanton. These two women primarily worked their entire lives on one issue. Then they died before they could even see their impact. There are very few books about these women, and even the author of the book I found had not heard about them until he started writing about women's suffrage. In that context, I wondered what the destiny of immigrant women would be. They study here and work hard to make changes in their communities or villages. Who is going to remember the work that they do? That motivated me to write *Spices in the Melting Pot*.

After reading some of the American women's stories, I thought, *Wow, let me do this!* I was so motivated. So I went to New York, Chicago, and other places in order to interview notable immigrant women. Finally, after talking to many women, my book came into existence. In the conclusion of the book, I explained why I wrote it—because it was a piece of history. These women went through so much to do what they did! They were really open and willing to tell me about their lives and their philosophy of life. I learned so much from each of them.

SECOND BOOK: *MY MOTHER'S DAUGHTER: MEMORIES OF KERALA'S MATRIARCHAL CULTURE*

I have already discussed extensively my second book, *My Mother's Daughter*, as it was a memoir of my childhood experiences and the culture of Kerala. You might think that your own story is easy to write, but I found writing my story to be one of the hardest things I have ever done. I didn't know what to say and what not to say or where to begin and end. There is not the same objectivity I have when I write about other people or issues outside of my life.

The process of writing is an interesting one. While I was writing, there were times when I had to stop and cry. Some parts were painful, and other parts were funny. I felt very light after writing this book, especially after I gave a copy to my brother. He did not know many of these things because he lived outside the family and outside Kerala. Giving a copy to him was one way of expressing my gratitude to him. My parents gave me life, but my brothers gave me an opportunity to have an education and open my mind. Without that opportunity, I don't know what would have become of me. Do you believe in destiny? I think it's very easy to stay in a box and believe what other people want us to believe. In that case, we are missing so much.

After writing *My Mother's Daughter,* I felt really relieved and happy. Not only did it give me an opportunity to record a lifestyle that has become extinct, but it helped me to affirm that, no matter how small, our aspirations come from a deeper, sacred place and they are valuable. While it is easy to ignore them, these aspirations hold meaning not just for the individual, but for humanity in general. I can't close the door on them.

For me, many things come down to one question: Why are you here? As a Hindu and believer in Hinduism, I believe in reincarnation. This is a Buddhist belief, as well. Siddhartha's decision was always interesting to me. Instead of choosing to become a ruler, he, a prince, chose another path. But why did he make these choices for himself? Because of his karma? The reincarnation question is very basic Hinduism, but I had to play with it at first. I didn't want to believe in it just because everybody else believed in it. I challenged these beliefs for quite some time until I was able to come to terms with them of my own accord. You have to struggle with each and every thing. That is the case with the immigrants from India who arrive in a new country. They cannot sit, surrounded by a wall, and say, "I'm Indian—this is what I do." Struggle with new experiences and try to understand every new issue that you face. Challenge yourself and your beliefs. Most people do not. They just become quite comfortable and don't change anything. You have to wrestle with beliefs before accepting them. Whether they are traditions or something that your parents and grandparents followed and believed for thousands of years, you have to come to terms with them on your own and learn to accept them under your own terms.

There are beliefs in Hinduism, but you are encouraged to ask questions. That's how the greatest philosophers of India have evolved and continue to evolve. In Hinduism, unless you are ready for knowledge and wisdom, it cannot be given to you. You need to ask questions about everything in life because that shows you are ready to get the answers.

In Hinduism, there is no rule that you have to go to the temple. You can pray at home, or you don't have to pray at all. My grandmother used to tell me that I didn't need to think about Krishna, for instance. She would say, "Look at the tree over there; you can pray to that tree. It is as sacred. God is in each and every thing and in you, too." It is a not a view where you have to believe in certain things that were written just because they are in a book or in a holy scripture. You have to find your own way to believe.

I like to think about and wrestle with these things. Whatever my belief is, I want to make it mine. I don't want to believe it blindly just because my mother asked me to. I want to know that I made them mine. Knowing that an idea is something I have accepted makes me feel relaxed. Is this my idea? How am I affected by it? Is this something I want to accept? I think these are basic questions that everyone needs to ask themselves.

Coming from strong traditions like those in India, I realized one important fact regarding my struggle to accept them: Traditions should not become a burden. Whatever the idea, religion, or tradition, it shouldn't suppress your inner forces, beliefs, or interests, because they are valid, they are yours, and that should be your guide.

While battling with all these ideas, I think more freely and feel lighter than ever before. I believe studying psychology changed me, because I got a glimpse of who I am and got rid of some of the things that were imposed on me that I didn't agree with. What I was left with is who I am.

That inner guiding voice is not something anyone should ignore and mask. You need courage to go with your convictions. Sometimes you may face opposition, obstacles, and contempt from people. If the conviction is there, you will do what you set out to do because you believe in that force. Somehow, it will open doors. Be open to that pathway and that call. If I had not listened to it, I would have continued to work as an engineer, and be content with it. Everything I did from then on came from within me.

Every day, I sit down at the computer to write. I think about my grandchildren, but it's not just for them that I am writing. It gives me so much pleasure and so much happiness to write. I know that I will write something every single day, at least.

PADMA'S ADVICE FOR WOMEN

Listen to your inner voice. Pay attention to the spark of awareness, because that is very powerful. But make sure it is yours. It's very difficult to distinguish between the voices you heard from somewhere else. The first step is to make sure it's yours genuinely. That takes work and a lot of alone time. Spend some time with yourself every day, do something for yourself, and keep your mind free.

boona

India

A refugee from early childhood during the partition of Pakistan and India, boona discusses the revolutionary ambitions she experienced growing up, a yearlong position in Vietnam during the Vietnam war, and resettlement into a United States community where she found the humbling, spiritual call of social justice work.

I WAS NOT BORN at a celebratory time in history. I came into this world in a city in India called Peshawar, only six hours after the atomic bomb was dropped on Hiroshima. It was a time of political unrest in many nations, including my own. It was the time just before the British partition when the nation of Pakistan was born.

FROM PESHAWAR TO PUNJAB
I don't have any memories of Peshawar, except what I have heard from my grandfather and mother. When I was born, the city was beautiful. Today, it is one of the largest arms- and drug-dealer cities

in the world. We left when I was about two years old and started our journey toward Faridkot, where my father was posted. We knew a partition would occur, but nobody knew where the border would be drawn. For those unaware, the partition is what began the Indian Independence Act of 1947 and ultimately dissolved the British Indian Empire. This resulted in a lot of struggle and the displacement of millions of people, including my family.

I was born on August 6, 1945, but my birthday was changed to Vaisakhi, April 13. Vaisakhi is a Punjabi New Year. The news about Hiroshima was out, and my mother went into labor. There was so much tension in the air for several reasons: the dropping of the atomic bomb, the tumultuous political environment, and the resistance of my paternal grandmother, who hadn't wanted my mother to have a second daughter and did not celebrate. I was small and born with a hole in my neck, and my aunt said I looked like a coffee bean, thus the name boona. My grandmother told everyone they should address me in the male gender, thus I became known as boona sahib.

I was referred to in the male gender until my brother was born eight years later. In India at that time, boys were revered, but girls were not. It has changed a bit, but we still have a long way to go. For a while, my gender issues were very confusing. This confusion did not go away until puberty. Much later in my life, I changed my name, spelling it in the lower case. I really wanted the world to know that I was female and wanted to erase the arrogance that came from male behavior.

My first visual, more picturesque memories come from when I was traveling with my mother to get to the Indian side of the new border. We were coming by train from newly created Pakistan to India, and I saw violence at that time. The train we were on was stopped, and Mother kept both of us daughters shielded. She was wearing the burqa or the equivalent of it at the time, while we were in heavy Muslim areas. A Muslim man stood in front of us and said, "This is my family."

Another memory has always stayed with me: My father told us kids he wanted to show us something. There was a little canal behind the little house we moved into with fifty other people in India. In the canal, there were body parts, blood, and grotesque things. It was traumatic, and I didn't speak for a while. I felt it would never leave me. There became a sense of some early childhood purpose almost telling me, "You're here because you have to do something about this." That feeling always stayed with me.

After the partition, we ended up in a small town in Punjab called Faridkot and had a large extended family. Everyone from Pakistan came to where my father was because he was on the India side when the line was drawn. That was a really fun time, because we children did not realize the devastation of this historical experience. We were just happy that there was family and so many kids to play with. Everyone cooked and pitched in to do their share. It was there that I learned the importance of community and what it felt like to enjoy community. That has stayed with me all my life, and I have tried to live that way, instead of transitioning to a more nuclear family situation. Living in a community dwelling allowed me to see how collective decisions are made and learn the real meaning of democracy.

All my life, my father was my beacon of knowledge. When I was five or six he spoke of a new Indian nation being built and a transformation that was going to happen. India, now an independent new country, was going to thrive under the new leadership of people like Jawaharlal Nehru, the first prime minister of India, a Socialist.

By the time I was seven or eight I was interested in India's new constitution and was lucky and glad to have a grandfather who was able to answer my "big people" questions. My maternal grandfather was in civil service and was up on all the new things that were happening in New Delhi. It was exciting, and I became very interested in history and politics at this time. By the time I was ten years old, I had a master plan for my life. Because I always wrote about what I saw,

I clearly thought I wanted to be a journalist when I grew up, along with an air stewardess and a hairdresser, but my destiny was not that.

I was not interested in academic education but loved to soak up newspapers or books. Having read about Hitler and fascism, I could not deal with anything that was authoritarian. Honestly, I love to learn, but it was always the authoritarian aspect of education that turned me off.

I had a great love for theatre and debating, though I didn't do well at the Irish-Catholic school I attended. I was sent there to get a good education, but I was too busy being a tomboy, and they were too busy punishing me. I hated every moment of it. It was a difficult time. I didn't understand why I had to go to school in Delhi and live with my grandfather, uncles, and aunties. I wanted to be with my parents in Chandigarh. I felt abandoned.

To end the risk of my running away, my parents took me to Chandigarh, the new capital of Punjab. I could not have been happier to get out and live in this great city, whose architect was the famous Corbusier. The nuns were quite happy to let me go, because I would organize other kids to destroy the school water system, splatter paint behind the nuns' white dresses, and try to pull their habits off their heads.

I didn't realize until much later how traumatized I had been as a child. For example, the priest at the church attached to the Catholic school would give us holy pictures if we let him put his hands up our skirts and down our blouses. Holy pictures were like gold; you could show the nuns that you were one of the few girls trying to be a good Christian. We were Sikh, Hindu, and Muslim girls. White oppression was still alive after the partition, and I couldn't figure the Irish out, as they were also trying to be free of England.

I never stopped being a prankster in my youth, until I found out how good it feels to win something. That's when the arrogance kicked in! I realized that I could win the debating trophy or the theatre trophy, but my school academic scores were just *terrible*. I barely scraped through all four years of college. I was too busy winning things, which I thought was much more important than school marks. Winning was great because of the challenge and the competition. Winning meant I got attention. Most kids who feel traumatized, abused, and abandoned find unhealthy or healthy ways to get loving attention. It wasn't until I lived with my parents in Chandigarh that I finally blossomed.

Early thought patterns evolved into politics. I became very excited about current events and decided to get a master's degree in journalism after college. By that time, India had had a couple of wars, one with Pakistan and one with China. Our college had one of the first "antiwar movements," which was revolutionary in India.

Around nineteen years old, I decided I had been born in the wrong country. It was so evident to me that if I stayed in India, I would not be able to breathe and my destiny and purpose would not be manifested.

Before I left the country, I got a job at *Times of India* as a reporter. They had me doing fashion shows, flower shows, and typical family articles. I wanted to do pieces on politics and world issues, but that was not considered the "feminine" thing to do. I once wrote an incredible story, which they loved, but they didn't put my name on it because I never got permission to write it. After that, I realized I could not work there, so I found a way to get out and ended up in Vietnam in 1969.

A VIETNAM EXPERIENCE

I met some people who were with an organization called International Voluntary Services. They preceded the actions of the Peace Corps in Southeast Asia, and I applied to work with them in Laos. I didn't want to be in Vietnam; I wanted to be nearby so I could write stories without the horrors of war, while living in a safer area. However, they thought I was better suited for Vietnam. They probably figured out from the sauciness in my application that I could handle it, so I went.

I had the *best* experiences in Vietnam. That is where I cut my teeth in terms of learning, growing, and building a knowledge base that was bigger than where I came from and who I was. It was when I started becoming more international and multicultural. I can walk into any culture and soak it up, and people will soak me up because I am very open. My desire to learn how people feel and what they think is very objective and very strong.

One of my jobs was working with kids who had been burned by Napalm. I helped run the house they lived in and moved them to a hospital in northern California, where they were treated then sent back to Vietnam, where I then resettled them back in their communities.

I was living in Saigon, but traveling to the borders in the north and the south to go to military hospitals to find the kids who needed to go to Saigon. Some of these children's injuries were horrific! There were terrible face injuries and a lot of amputations and burns—nothing that was totally coverable. One of the reasons I left was that the kids were being used by the media in the United States to show why people should be antiwar. That's fine, but it seemed like the kids were propaganda tools. Even though I am totally antiwar, there was something about it that did not feel ethical. From a Buddhist perspective, I wanted less harm to come to the kids and for them to be healed as much as possible by Western medicine, but to have their souls left intact. They didn't do very well after they returned to Vietnam. The assimilation was hard, and many of them had mental health issues. Their parents had disappeared, and even whole hamlets were wiped out, which was very devastating.

That work changed my life in so many ways. It started the process of humility, while it made me fearless, feeling like I could do that kind of work in the world. I also met my American husband in

Saigon through the course of my work and we traveled extensively together, working through adverse situations.

MARRIAGE AND IMMIGRATION TO THE UNITED STATES

I took my Kentuckian boyfriend, whom I met in South Vietnam, to India to introduce him to my family. They said, "Yes! Marry him. But he is to wear a turban and ride a horse and grow a beard." They wanted us to have a traditional wedding, which I was not crazy about, but we had a blast. Even Indira Gandhi sent us congratulations—how cool is that?

When we returned to Saigon, we were told at the airport that we had twenty-four hours to get our stuff and leave. We were confused because we still had six months of work left, but we soon realized they were throwing us out. We had participated in a few antiwar demonstrations and marched with Buddhists, so we were viewed as a threat. The Vietnamese government wanted us to do the work but not become involved in the politics.

It was time to find my home. We used the money from the wedding and went to Australia, Bali, and different places to see where we wanted to put our roots.

We had a lot of contacts in the San Francisco area because of the work we did with the Vietnamese children, so we came to Berkeley, California. When I first arrived, I stood and said, "This is home." There was something so inviting. It just seemed to be the perfect size, and because there were more people of color there, the diversity made me feel at ease. In 1971, Berkeley was exciting; there were protests, riots, bombings, and a real revolutionary spirit in the air.

The only work I could find was in an Indian store, and I thought, *Wait a minute! I left India because I didn't want to do this stuff!* Even the newspapers rarely hired women. It was very competitive, and I didn't have what they considered to be a basic history and knowledge of this country. They also didn't agree with my opinions because they were not mainstream.

We were living in a commune at the time, and I was pregnant. In fact, I had gotten pregnant around September 24, 1970, in Bali, where we were living at the time. My baby was born June 3, 1971, when I was in the United States. I knew I was pregnant the minute it happened. I came out of the house and a Balinese woman said, "You're pregnant," and I replied, "I know."

At the time my son was born, my husband wanted to go to medical school. He did his pre-med at the University of California, Berkeley, and got accepted at Case Western Reserve for medicine in Cleveland, Ohio. I went with him to Ohio for a year because I still had an internship to complete for the Unitarian church as part of my studies at Starr King Unitarian Seminary, and I could complete it in Ohio. At the seminary called Starr King I learned a lot and broke some glass ceilings. I was the first Asian to go to that school. I now have a Master of Divinity degree and am a Unitarian minister. (At age sixteen, I was also blessed by His Holiness the Dalai Lama. I had a very open mind about religion and spirituality, yet a very clear view of what I was on this earth to accomplish and change.)

After receiving my Unitarian education, I wanted to do a special ministry to the poor and was interviewed by twelve men; the only woman in the room was taking notes. I thought that was significant because Unitarians were supposed to be more liberal. I hadn't done well on my internship in Akron, Ohio, at the Unitarian church because I was not aware of how conservative Akron was! At the time, the senior minister took the summer off, and when he came back, the congregation was very unhappy. The Unitarians are supposed to be open and champion everybody's faith. I believed that and brought in the gay community because they wanted a place to worship. The congregation went crazy.

The twelve men making the decision about my ordination told me they didn't believe I could provide enough support to the congregation because my values were not Unitarian Universalistic. I was blown away! I needed twenty more units to graduate, and I told them to graduate me and I would prove them wrong. I would create that ministry for poor people! I believe any work I do is spiritual. It is not academic or social work, and it is absolutely not religiously motivated. It's deeply Buddhist in nature and is about service.

GOLDEN CALIFORNIA AND LIFE ON WELFARE

I came to California and started volunteering for BOSS (Building Opportunities for Self-Sufficiency) in 1971 until I was named the Executive Director in 1978. (I retired in 2013.) My relationship with my husband was declining. We were great together in Vietnam, but we were not good in the United States or in "normal" life. When we were in intense "are we going to live today or die tomorrow" lives, we did very well, but when it felt too ordinary, we realized we both needed something different. I thought of marriage in the more traditional sense, and he didn't believe in monogamy. There were times when I could not be myself and was expected to be somebody else. I didn't want to be a wife who followed my husband's life path since that was one of the reasons I had left India.

I arrived for the second time in Berkeley, California, as a new immigrant, pregnant, and single, and eventually ended up on welfare. As a result, I learned a lot about myself.

The stigma of being on welfare and being educated was immense. The assumption is that educated people should not need welfare. For me, the more important part of welfare was the medical assistance, because I had a son who was chronically asthmatic. Without it, he wouldn't have received medical care.

I was walking past the BOSS building one day and saw a sign that read, "If you need help, come in today. If you need a miracle, it will take a week." I had no idea how to ask for help, because that had never been my forte. I was really scared because this concept was foreign to me. In India, when you are sick, you go to the hospital and they take care of you. Things were simple, and poverty was everywhere. In the United States, poverty was spilling out into the streets with increased homelessness. After being a person in need, I realized what I really wanted to do.

I was also lucky to absorb great teachings and have the capacity to develop what I'd experienced into a community. That is why working with the homeless is easy for me and working with people who have mental illness was even a step more familiar. I am very comfortable around people who have the capacity, if recognized, to make something out of nothing in their lives. When I see someone whom I can engage in a conversation with kindness and love, the healing begins, and we can deal with case managers, social workers, therapists, and psychiatrists. Whether I had anything to do with it or not, just being able to pay witness to it is very powerful.

I really believe that if a person needs help, if you know where the resources are, it should not take more than a week to connect them to something better. If we could teach social welfare and these ideas in school, the world would be better. It's really important in my work with folks for them to be able to see how good and smart they really are.

I don't play the serious social worker role. I laugh a lot at work with children, the homeless, and my employees. Laughing together is the best social work, because it's about healing. Most people view social work as fixing people. If you fix people, they will break again; but healing will last forever.

I got the ministry for the poor that I always wanted through being one of them. When I was chosen as executive director through much internal debate, I deeply reflected about how I was going to fill the role. I realized I wanted to build a sanctuary where people don't have to go ten miles for food and another ten for a bed. The vision I created took about ten years. I believe four things are necessary to be self-sufficient:

1. A place to live and food
2. Health and health care
3. Income
4. Involvement in social justice

We started to grow programs in those areas, which came as a natural structure because the programs complement each other. Bearing witness to the many personal transformations in the people we serve is humbling. One woman I will never forget from one of our family shelters is Janny. She had four kids and had been a long-term drug user, and was with a man who was mentally ill, a drug addict, and not supportive of her. She went through our programs and turned her life around. I could see all of her beauty and spirit underneath all of the other layers, and it was amazing! There was a level of purity and simplicity that was like heaven. One day, she asked me to lend her $1,000, saying she could prove that she could become successful and take care of her kids independently. I took a chance and loaned her the money for her first business.

At first, she was doing desktop publishing, making cards and flyers. Then she got hired in the school system and slowly worked her way up when a job opened up at BOSS. We hire 70 percent of our clients, and I asked her if she wanted to work for me. Her loan was paid off, and she accepted the job and still works for us. She has since become a Reiki master and teaches a course for homeless people. It's truly amazing how one person has the ability to do so much incredible work after having experienced darkness. I love her so deeply. I have learned a lot from her, and she has learned a lot from me. If you know something, you should teach it to someone who does not.

Janny's journey took ten years. Today, she is basically the glue of the organization. Deep change takes time.

I believe in hiring our participants. How can we tell the world that these are worthy people if we are not willing to work with them or willing to hire them? I believe any person, regardless of where they come from, is worthy of support and encouragement. It is how people stay whole.

I have to do this kind of work. It is spiritual for me. Dealing with people who have lived on the streets and have drug addictions is all about getting the resources to properly help them. There are so many potential possibilities in each human being that might not show because the right resources and support are not present or are unavailable. This is why I do what I do.

A PERSPECTIVE ON LIFE AND DEATH
My son's death was one of the most eye-opening experiences in my life. My son died on September 24, 2004, the same week as when he was conceived over thirty-three years earlier. He came and went full circle. He had lived his life to the fullest but could not see a way out of his depression, betrayals, and heartbreaks.

He was diagnosed with bipolar disorder at age twenty-one. He was a chronic asthmatic until he was about fourteen years old, so he was very emotionally fragile. He could not deal with two or three heavy things happening at the same time without falling apart. Divorced from his wife, he was separated from his child. Then a very close friend of his died, and he started to spiral out of control. We had seen him through that before, and the night before he killed himself, I asked him if he wanted me to stay with him. He said, "I am not a baby. If you stay here, I am going to get in my car and I am going to leave."

The next morning, I found him. It was a very intense spiritual experience. I felt that I walked with his soul to whatever that other side was and is. It was beautiful! We went through a dark blue door that opened into gold light, and we were in the gold light, then I was back. His breath was not in his body at that point. I think his soul was still there because he had just died. When I was thrown back from that light, I realized that hundreds and thousands of children had died in that same moment and my grief was universal. I realized I could not possibly personalize my grief or his death; that would be too selfish. He would have wanted to be seen as part of a bigger pain, where there was a bigger experience, because he did not live small experiences. In fact, being bipolar, he lived grandiose ones. In that moment, he was very wonderful and protective. He was taking me to the other side and then sending me back as he continued on. When I was thrown back to this reality, I felt universal grieving. There were all these perished children, and I was just one of the hundreds of thousands of mothers grieving. We were having an individual experience, but able to see other souls that were experiencing the same thing in that moment. This was so spiritual and uplifting. I got to see this truth, and I thank him every day for that. Individual relationships holding so much pain, sorrow, and grief are taken so personally. I believe this is selfish, because we don't think about other people or their hardship. I found a real solidarity in grief.

I feel he has been at peace for a long time. I feel his essence, but I dream about him sitting next to my father. They were kindred spirits.

So that is the summary of my very humbling life. I have my convictions and my beliefs and some of these I have always held on to. I feel that I am in a great place now because the work I am doing is spiritual for me. That is the most important thing.

boona'S ADVICE FOR WOMEN
Being born a woman is being given the greatest gift. Be aware of that, and when the time comes, know that everything you have experienced is understood and accepted. I believe being born a woman is an amazing opportunity to live life, and we need to be fully accepting

in life and in death. No matter what end comes to each one of us or how we leave this universe, we leave having left our mark. Women leave imprints on the people we interact with in life. I believe we have a wisdom that is ours. We are healers of the wounds men cause in the world.

Author's Note: In 2013 boona retired from her position as Executive Director of BOSS and has started her own business called boonaChePresents. Her first children's book has been accepted for publication. She is a dynamic force in her community and continues close relationships within the homeless community.

ILMANA

India

A gynecologist and public health advocate, Ilmana recounts her experience working in the Middle East in the area of community gynecology and highlights common issues she encountered within a local Bedouin community. She also discusses her upcoming public health project in Pakistan and her hope for better India-Pakistan relations.

ON MY INTERNET blog, Blind to Bounds, where I write music, poetry, and articles about a diverse group of issues, I explain how all of its sections are unique parts of myself. It reads:

If Blind to Bounds represented Ilmana:

KABIR is her soul

MY POETRY, her mind

ART, her heart

MUSIC, her senses
INDIA/PAKISTAN/POLITICS/SOCIAL ISSUES are her gut.

I am many things in this world. I am a mother, a wife, a gynecologist, a poet, an activist, and a public-health advocate. I have worked as a gynecologist in the Middle East and am preparing a public health project in Pakistan. Being from India will allow me to promote good relations between Pakistan and India.

In order to understand where my ideals and education come from, you must first understand my family. My father was from a very religious family in New Delhi and stepped out of his family's mindset. His family is Muslim, and my grandfather wanted him to become a cleric, because he was a cleric in a mosque.

Yet my father was a bit more of a rebel, and at the undergraduate level of his education, he left home. He went to Egypt in the 1950s to study for a PhD on the socialist party, which was a very enlightened party and a leading one at that time. He then completely deflected from the path of his family and became a socialist. When he came back three years later, he was a changed man. He took a U-turn and became a very open-minded person, and started advocating against the covering of the face and other conservative Islam doctrines that his family used to preach.

Born in mid 1960s, I was the first child of my parents. At that time, my father wanted me to have a name that represented his philosophy. Ilmana has a special meaning as "Ilm" in Arabic means knowledge. No one had ever heard of my name when I received it. My father was the first person in the world to coin this name. It was his own special creation.

My upbringing was greatly influenced by my father's ideas. He always said, "My treasure is my books." He had about eight thousand books in his personal library at home. Before the family's expenses grew, my father dedicated 25 percent of his salary to books. He would buy, read, and preserve them. If someone wanted to borrow a book, it caused him distress. He used to say that he knew if he gave a book out, it would not come back.

As a little girl, I was always given books as presents on my birthday, instead of dresses and dolls. My family so highly valued education that they wanted me to be surrounded by it. During my entire life, I did not see any other way than being a good student. I was the first person in my entire family and entire clan to become a doctor. The interesting part was that I initially did not choose gynecology. It chose me.

GYNECOLOGY WORK IN THE MIDDLE EAST

After I finished my undergrad, I got married and planned to pursue a career in radiology. I got a radiology job in one of the hospitals in the Middle East. When I went to sign the contract prior to my start date, the director of the hospital told me that he was short of doctors in gynecology, and they would post me there for a month. I had no problems with this. After taking five years off to take care of two small children, I was anxious to return to work again and get a glimpse into a different medical field.

I began my job in gynecology and soon found I had a natural talent for it. My supervisor commented on my accurate diagnoses and the notes I wrote about each of the patients. He recommended that I make gynecology my profession. I did not realize it at the time but that man was such a renowned gynecologist that his name was in all the textbooks! He was so supportive and encouraging that I started really enjoying it. By the end of the month, I had become so involved in gynecology and started liking my job so much that I would do twenty-four-hour shifts. When I was at work, I had so much passion and did not even think about anything else. When it was time for me to return to radiology, I politely declined and decided to stay in the gynecology department.

I took the exam for a British Master's in Gynecology, in an attempt to see what the exam was like. Most people cleared the exam in two or three attempts, so I figured I would see how it went. To my surprise, I actually passed the exam on the first try! Obstetrics and Gynecology was a journey of love. First, I became involved in gynecology medicine. From there, it was interest with women's issues, both medical and social, and then community gynecology. It has been and still continues to be a wonderful journey.

I was excited with the nature of gynecology work. I felt rewarded when I delivered a baby in an emergency. Sometimes I would manage a woman who has been in labor for twelve hours and be on duty for all those hours, examining her every half hour and praying that she ended up with a safe delivery. Ninety-nine percent of the time, there is a happy ending with a healthy baby.

Gradually, all of the medical elements became less influential on me than the real issues that my patients were having. If a patient came in for labor, delivered, and went back happily, that was great, but it was only one part of the story. The real story behind this same patient might be that this was her eighth child, she was anemic, and she would go back to a household where she was treated about the same as cattle. She was not given the consideration she deserved. Then she would come back again after one or two years with another pregnancy because her husband wouldn't allow her to use contraceptives. These types of issues, which I felt had a greater impact on these women's lives, influenced me. I became interested in community gynecology.

I had another opportunity to work in the setting of community gynecology in a Middle East military hospital in a Bedouin community. It was a family practice setting, and 99 percent of my patients were Bedouins. At this point, I was not doing surgery; I was dealing more with the real issues the women faced. Some of these issues may sound strange, but for these women, they certainly were serious.

It didn't take long for many of the community women to figure out that I was someone they could come to and ask any questions they needed answered. They trusted that I would honor their confidentiality and not judge them by their questions.

One girl, between sixteen and seventeen years of age and who was not sexually active, had not had her period for two months and was suddenly scared she might be pregnant. This was not uncommon. When I asked girls why they thought they were pregnant if they were not sexually active, they would tell me they hung their clothes next to their brother's, sat next to a man, or saw sexual contact on TV. Because of certain mythologies in the culture, I realized I was dealing with a lot of superstition in the community surrounding this issue, so I would explain to these young girls the biological explanation and replace that superstition in their mind. I was very sensitive in dealing with them, so they did not feel ridiculed. I wanted them to understand that these processes are natural and biological.

Another big issue I dealt with in my practice was the notion of the preservation of the female hymen. In the Arab world, this is very normal. All women must be virgins when married, and the hymen is a way to determine virginity. Girls often came to me, concerned that they did not have a hymen. They came to this conclusion minus any logic. They were afraid to get married if they did not have a hymen because their husband would not believe they were pure and not sexually active. I reassured these women and explained to them during the examination that they did, indeed, have a hymen. I would also reassure them that their strength is what makes their worth, not whether or not there is a hymen. In community gynecology, there is no limit to such prejudices.

Every age group had a different set of problems or questions. In that community, there was no dialogue about reproductive health or contraceptives, so these women had no one to talk to about these issues. I became the confidante. The community was so small that it was like a family, and certain women came to me so many times that I remembered their file numbers by heart.

There were a lot of myths about contraceptives, especially contraceptive pills. The IUDs were a main subject of gossip and myths,
and many of the women were fearful of using them. I helped them
understand the truth behind them, as well as menopause. They also
believed menopause meant losing their femininity and womanhood.
A lot of men in the area judged women on that basis. I would tell
them that femininity came from within, not from whether or not a
woman had the ability to get pregnant.

There were mixed feelings about contraceptives in this community. Many were taking contraceptive pills, especially in the younger
generation. They did not want to have many kids. The real issue
was with the thirty-five-plus age group, because they believed contraceptives were a taboo issue. The men they were married to were
often older and did not want a woman taking contraceptive pills.
For many men in that culture, being able to get a woman pregnant
was reassurance of their manhood. So if a woman in her forties
already had six or seven children and could not conceive for several
years, she would come to me, asking for infertility treatment. Her
husband might think something was wrong with her or threaten to
marry someone else if she did not get pregnant in the next year. In
the Bedouin community, it was common and custom for a man to
have more than one wife. These women had a lot of anxiety because
they associated their fertility as a status symbol. Since many of the
women had to share their husband with other women, getting pregnant was a way to keep their husband's attention. The pregnancy
issue then became a race between wives to try to get pregnant earlier
and more often. Even though it's not ideal to have so many children
when many of the members of this community had limited means,
their logic and ideal was that Allah promised to feed every mouth
in the family. When I talked to them, I was always very careful not
to argue with or offend them. I had to be very practical and explain
through examples. I found that the younger wives who had more

education often wanted fewer children than the ones who were less educated. It is an interesting correlation.

Abortion was also a major issue that was not legally allowed. We were forbidden from even advocating abortions, which could be performed only if there were congenital anomalies and in a large hospital setting. Because of the illegal nature of abortion, there were many unhealthy procedures taking place behind closed doors that were unregulated and unsafe.

Many of these women who did not want to continue their pregnancies came to me, crying and begging me to tell them any means to abort. I legally could not tell them about anything, even when I knew of ways. Honestly, I knew of one medication called RU486, a pill women could take to end a pregnancy, but it was not legal where I was working in the Middle East. I was under strict rules to never discuss that medication with a patient. Even if I told them that I was simply aware that the medication exists, this tiny comment could create extensive trouble for me. Sometimes they would come back and tell me that they obtained RU486 elsewhere and had secretly terminated their pregnancy. It was a hard position for me to be in as a woman. I wanted to be able to help them, but I could not. Instead, I encouraged stronger and stricter contraceptive use and explained ways to prevent pregnancy. Abortion is not a mode of contraception; unfortunately, many people are using it as contraception now.

One thing I could not help doing was making those women aware of domestic abuse, which is very common in the closed societies in the Middle East. The women used to tell me that their husband hit them, threatened them, and made disrespectful comments to them. Even if there was not physical abuse, there was always emotional abuse. They were also under strict rules: they weren't allowed to have a cell phone, and they weren't allowed to call outside the home. When the husband went out, he locked the house from the outside so no one else could enter. I reassured these women that they were an equal partner with their husbands, and even in Islam it says that a marriage contract is between two equal partners. I told them that they did not need to be treated that way, they were doing a huge service by looking after his home, and he should be thankful for that service. I was lucky enough to have two other colleagues, young doctors who were very enthusiastic about that issue, who agreed to form an official domestic violence procedure in the hospital in order to see what the various help lines were. If you want to help an abused woman, you have to make sure confidentiality is maintained and take the right steps. If you take the wrong steps and the perpetrator comes to know there is someone helping her, the abuse increases and she can become more isolated.

We had to make the women understand that they were not responsible for the abuse and were not the ones to be blamed. We wanted them to be stronger, but, unfortunately, the abuse would sometimes increase when a woman got stronger. We had to encourage them in a way that the men would not know anyone was standing behind the woman.

We also could not encourage these women to divorce their husbands. Many of these women did not choose divorce because they had five children and could not get a job to support themselves. Our goal was to encourage them to stand up for themselves in order to make their situation better. Most abuse is about controlling the other person. We wanted to teach them how to loosen or break that cycle of control.

By the time I left the Gulf part of the Middle East, a group of doctors had made domestic abuse an issue in that community. They started a helpline in the sense that if any woman was abused, she would know the helpline number and be able to contact it and discuss what was happening. It was confidential, so the woman was not at any risk for contacting the helpline, and she would also be watched to make sure she was not in danger. If she was in danger, she would be rescued. The helpline did not exist on a large scale, only in that hospital, and it took us five years to push for it. It was gratifying to see something that originally did not exist and that could address a societal problem, emerge as an accepted solution.

I eventually decided to leave this job in the Middle East since religious values were held higher than any logic. As a doctor working within that mentality, I had to be very careful about what I would say or recommend. I realized I had to be more on guard to save my skin than to save the patient. This hurt my conscience a lot. At times, I had a strong ethical conflict with issues, but according to the hospital policies, I could not speak out. We decided to move to Canada, where I had to requalify for all of my licenses. In the meantime, I continued my work at the community level with the South Asian immigrant community. I am in a waiting period now for my project in Pakistan to finish.

PAKISTAN PLANS AND PUBLIC HEALTH OUTREACH

My husband and I are now of the opinion that it is time for us to give back to our society. How long can we run away from the realities of the world? We decided we did not want to just live on salaries and luxuries and overlook the hardships the common man in Pakistan is facing. Although I am originally from India, I am married to a Pakistani man. There have been a lot of negative sentiments between Pakistan and India in recent times, so you can imagine how many barriers our marriage breaks.

There are a lot of issues in Pakistan now. There is corruption at every level, and doctors over there are often not honest. There is not a lot of good work over there, and a lot of work needs to be done.

Over the last several years, we have invested much of our money in Pakistan. We bought a piece of land and are in the process at the moment of building a clinic, where we plan to help the sick in a good, ethical practice. We also want to do community level public health activism and promotion. It has been five years since we began the project, and we are continuing to develop it to this day. It's very complicated to do what we want to do in Pakistan. Because there is a lot of corruption at every level, paying bribes is expected. We decided right from the beginning that we don't have the money or mindset to pay bribes. We have enough to make a clinic. We had to sell land for the clinic, and the normal bribe would be required to sell it to someone at a good price. We refused every step of the way to pay bribes, so getting the clinic in the process of construction took five years, instead of the normal six months. Still, we refused to succumb and kept supporting each other. When my husband gets weak, I have to push him and tell him we can't give up; and when I get weak, he pushes me.

We have reached a point where we cannot go back. We have invested all our life savings and everything we have. We cannot turn back now, or we will lose everything that we have worked for up to this point. The only direction is forward. The same people who were known for taking bribes signed the papers for us to go ahead because they saw that we had good intentions. There is good in every human being. If you put that point across and make the person realize what you are doing is for good, that small fraction of the individual wakes up. The same people who were known for being corrupt actually ended up helping us. My husband had to live through taunts and criticisms, but he always told them he could not afford bribes.

In the future, I hope we are confident and stay upright in the face of corruption and stand on our own two feet with strength and moral courage. I really need a lot of good wishes to do that because a project of this nature is so complicated.

One thing I have been doing on the side is working for India-Pakistan friendship. I was born in New Delhi and married a Pakistani. A lot of people ask me how I plan to live in Pakistan with my Indian background. It's very different in terms of cities and culture. I reply that life is not about living comfortably. I could have lived comfortably with a lot of money in Delhi, but I moved to the Middle East. Money is not the only value that I possess. My husband and I value going back to our community and giving back. After being married for twenty years, I have decided that I am going to belong to both of the countries. Both are my homeland. India is my land of birth, and Pakistan is the land of my children. I love both of the places equally, and that is really not difficult. If I can love both Pakistan and India, then why can't anyone else?

There is a lot of animosity between India and Pakistan. It is very normal for India to hate Pakistan. It is common for Indians to believe that any ills that they have are caused by Pakistan and the Pakistanis. Whether they like it or not, they are neighbors, and it does no good to live in aggression with a neighbor. There are thousands in India and Pakistan trying to push for better relations. Through my blogs and my writings, I am trying to contribute to the notion that there can be peace between both nations. My writings are appearing in a peace project that is currently pushing for peace between India and Pakistan.

Once we officially launch in Pakistan, I'm going to do some community projects that will involve both the Indian and Pakistani communities, where we can actually demonstrate to the world that there are thousands of people on both sides who really want to have better relations and better friendships. There are many bureaucrats and top military people who don't want these friendships to occur because they create deliberate misgivings about each other. Generally, though, the common man at the common level wants a peaceful area.

I am working on another project with a company in India that involves one of my father's philosophies, which is to spread knowledge by whatever means possible, as easily and cheaply as possible. Right now, we are disseminating information on various health and social issues through the use of mobile games. They developed the gaming software, and I am doing the medical content development. In 2005, we implemented the game on HIV, and it's still ongoing. By playing the game, the player automatically knows different facts and myths about how HIV is spread. Mobile technology has become an inclusive technology. You find mobile phones in the hands of even those in the poorest community. In countries like India and Pakistan, mobile phones are pretty inexpensive.

These are also small simple games people can play without paying anything, and at the same time, learn valuable information. Our tuberculosis game had about five thousand downloads in India and Africa. They even translated it to Swahili, and it is played in Ghana, Kenya, Mozambique, and other countries where they changed it into their local languages. In Africa, there were 27 million users in three years who have played our set of games on tuberculosis and HIV, which allows players to advance to different levels and progress to a new game, where they learn more information.

The newest game concerns sexual abuse and is aimed at teaching boys and girls what to be aware of and how to prevent it from happening by empowering girls and women with information on how to say "no," so they do not become unwilling partners due to sexual abuse. I believe they had about six thousand downloads in the first month alone. In Canada, all of the provinces now have their own version of the game.

I'd like to take this concept to Pakistan and perhaps translate the current games into Urdu. I want to begin with local issues, such as contraceptive usage and domestic abuse, including gender differentiation in terms of food in the household, where the men eat first and the women eat later. With mobile technology, we can reach everyone. In the Muslim Pakistani society, it's difficult for a woman to come out of her household and to have dialogue about reproductive issues. There would be a lot of opposition from family members about women attending classes, but most of these women have a mobile phone. Through mobile technology, we feel we can create that awareness. I have a nonprofit organization by the name of Tabeer, which means "realizing one's dreams" in Urdu. Our slogan is "unveiling the veil of ignorance," and it targets the younger generation of both boys and girls in order to empower them with the right information.

It's still too premature to provide specifics, but we have a lot of aspirations and plans. Moving forward, it will take a lot of courage, faith, and strength to ensure these plans are completed.

We have the structure for our five-story building already, but the electricity, water supply, and other elements need to be in place. This entails a lot of expenditure, but we are prepared to go forward. I hope we are able to reach our goal in two or three years. A long-term project is difficult because we have to keep holding on and believing in it. Now that we've started working toward it, we will not retreat, no matter what happens.

ILMANA'S ADVICE FOR WOMEN

Please realize that there is more to you than just your physical appearance, and it is women who have always been the strength behind successful men or any successful movement in the world. Unfortunately, many of us limit our worth to our physical appearance, and hence do not realize our true potential.

Always stand up for justice and rights for yourself and for others. No one gives them to you on a platter, you have to seek them. Being an ardent believer of Gandhi and his peace and forgiveness I quote him: "You must be the change you wish to see in the world."

SOUTHEAST ASIA

NWE

Bangladesh-Burma border

Born on the Bangladesh-Burma border as a third generation refugee, Nwe narrates her struggles as an undocumented migrant, her resettlement to the United States as a refugee, her fight for community social justice and her drive to save herself and her children from a desperate situation of ongoing domestic violence.

Nwe is the founder of several nonprofit organizations and social welfare initiatives including Weaving Through Change, Rakhaing Women's Union, and Burma Family Refugee Network. She is also active in various ways with the United Nations regarding initiatives for the indigenous peoples of Burma.

MY NAME IS Nwe and I grew up in Bangladesh, on the Bangladesh-Burma border.

There are various indigenous groups of Burmese who have ended up refugees in neighboring Bangladesh and Thailand. Among the main ones are the Karen, Karenni, Chin, Tvoy, Mon, Rakhaing, and Burman. These indigenous groups have witnessed and experienced torture, rape, ethnic cleansing, and undocumented genocides in Burma for more than two hundred years. My grandparents and the prior three generations had to flee their homeland because the King of Burma took over and killed their people. My generation is one of political refugees as were my parents' and grandparents' generations. We are considered "undocumented" or "illegal" immigrants in the neighboring border countries we inhabit, even after several generations.

UNDOCUMENTED IN BANGLADESH

Growing up in Bangladesh, I was a member of an indigenous group from Burma known as Rakhaing. We faced discrimination by majority groups in terms of race, class, and ethnicity. Being a refugee in addition to a low-class ethnic minority causes numerous hardships in a woman's life. Like most refugee women, I not only did not have citizenship in Bangladesh, I also did not have equal education opportunities. When you are from a family of refugees, everything in your life is blocked. We Rakhaing women were beaten, not just by men, but by an economic and social structure as well.

When I was as young as fourteen years old in Bangladesh, I started writing about these issues. I wrote national articles about the struggles of indigenous people and women in Burma and Bangladesh because I saw that no one talked about our struggles in national newspapers. I decided to be a journalist then because I wanted to create a national strategy for indigenous rights. In college I was a social activist for women's rights and the rights of indigenous people. I understood what it was like to be displaced and to not have citizenship in Bangladesh and all of the economic and social struggles surrounding this migration issue.

When I was attending college, the land of the Rakhaing was taken over in Bangladesh, so I was struggling financially because I did not have any means of income. I learned how to weave and created a company called Weaving Through Change. I was financially independent through my weaving work because there were no scholarships for me back then. I also received money from payments for articles that I wrote. I referred to myself as a "small entrepreneur" because I was able to make a living for myself and get an education, despite the harsh social climate we indigenous women were subjected to.

When I was about nineteen years old and attending college, I saw another wave of refugees arrive in Bangladesh who were forced to flee from Burma to Bangladesh because of the abuses of the Burmese government. They were living in jungle areas and rural areas like nomads with very limited means. I heard that a lot of women and children died due to malnutrition and other health issues. Around this time I cofounded a nonprofit called Rakhaing Women's Union to try to bridge the border area with the resources in Bangladesh so they had education and health-care access. We were part of a Thai-Burma border project called Women's League of Burma. They were our umbrella organization for all ethnic groups I mentioned above. They had a big conference and invited us to it.

I decided to work in the border areas because I grew up in the squalor of the border areas like the rest of the refugee children. In those border areas I opened a school and taught English so the refugees would have more opportunities. The governments of Burma and Bangladesh were not thinking about the indigenous refugees on the border areas; they were more concerned with locals instead. Burma has been unstable for decades now and the refugee problem is not getting any better. I had a strong desire to change that situation.

Maybe I could not change the politics of Burma and Bangladesh, but I knew that I could change the circumstances of the people who were displaced on the border. I would have been born in Burma if my mother had not been forced to run when she was pregnant with me. We Burmese are constantly, as refugees, back and forth between countries. Neighboring countries do not want us because we are not citizens so we try to return home, but we can't because of the violence in Burma. I feel like an orphaned child with no parents because I don't have a country. I wanted to make other families who had to flee Burma feel safer and more secure. Most of the refugees from Burma are indigenous, ethnic minorities and most are victimized. When they run from Burma to Bangladesh or Thailand they are stateless and face discrimination, yet no one is accountable for the violence perpetrated against them. Many small young girls end up prostitutes in Thailand. My question is why there is no empathy for us as human beings. It's not our fault we had to flee our homes. We never asked for violence.

UNDOCUMENTED IN THAILAND

I ended up moving to Chiang Mai, Thailand, from Bangladesh in 2000 when I was twenty to work for the Women's League of Burma and to pursue higher education in diplomacy and human rights at Thammasat University. I wanted to learn to be a good representative for my people. When I worked for the Women's League of Burma, many people in our Burmese community were getting arrested by Thai authorities because they were considered to be illegal immigrants. When the refugees were asleep the Thai police would come and arrest them in the middle of the night to deport them. I worried if I was arrested I would be imprisoned for life because of my involvement in various indigenous equality political causes regarding Burma. I was strongly fighting against inequality in regard to the world, not just my people.

While living in Chiang Mai, I married my husband because it was difficult to be a single woman in my culture and be involved in politics. People gossip about you extensively because they consider you to be breaking too many boundaries. I realized that if I got married, the community would see me in a better light and I would be deemed more credible. As a woman you have many boundaries that are unseen.

After two to three days I noticed that my new husband's behavior was very unsatisfactory. He was not working, he was drunk all the time, and I knew that I had made a mistake. One or two months after I was married, I became pregnant. I noticed that he was not looking for any work or anything to prepare for the arrival of our family. I became a very strong woman because I was working for people, working for myself, and working for the baby for when it would come.

I had two more children with him, three children total. Two were born in Thailand and one was born in the United States. As a husband he was very physically and emotionally abusive—always seeking ways to bring me down—but I was not able to get out of the marriage before I moved to the United States because of my culture. In Thailand, he did not live with me very often and would only come back home every six months, giving me the freedom to pursue my interests and advocate for indigenous communities.

Luckily after my second child was born, the United Nations High Commissioner for Refugees (UNHCR) allowed me to apply for refugee status since I had children. I wanted to ensure that my children's lives were safer and for them to receive the freedom of security and education. The two children I had at the time were still considered undocumented migrants even though they were born in Thailand. I was an undocumented refugee and because of my citizenship status, my children would always remain the same. I knew if we stayed in Thailand they would not have the same opportunities for education as they would in the United States, where we could receive legal status.

In 2005, I traveled to the UNHCR office in Bangkok from Chiang Mai on a train with my second son. I was arrested on the train because the Thai authorities asked for my ID and as an undocumented migrant I could not provide it. I called the UNHCR office and asked for their help and they picked me up from the police station. I had my money in my son's diaper—a total of 3,000 Thai Bahts. That was also the day President Bush came to Thailand. I will never forget that day because it only further confirmed that I needed to find a better life for my children.

LIFE IN THE UNITED STATES

All of the Burmese refugees had a vision of America as heaven. I knew I would face a struggle when I arrived here with my husband and children, but I came so my children could have equal opportunities and would not be forced to live as undocumented refugees like we had been in Thailand. When we first arrived in the United States I began to apply for jobs. I did not speak much English but was ready to learn and establish myself. It was challenging because most companies wanted someone with extensive knowledge of English or an advanced degree and I did not have any of those qualifications upon arrival. I still managed to find entry-level work with about $1,200 dollars a month income. I paid $625 dollars for rent, $400 dollars for child care, $60 dollars for bus passes and most months I did not have enough money for food. I worked long hours, waking up at 6:00 AM and not arriving home until 9:00 PM every night. After my third child was born, my husband's abuse continued. The only reason I was intimate with him was out of fear. I was struggling to hold my family together.

Meanwhile I was helping other refugees from Burma in our local community to help connect them to services by taking them to social services and the hospital for health screenings and for other forms of aid. I was not getting paid for that work and my third child had just been born. I did not have a car and it was difficult for me to work because of my baby. Still, I wanted the people in our refugee community to feel secure in America, their new home. My husband was making everything very difficult for me. When he was home the situation was very bad. I treasured my time with my children when he was gone at work because our home was finally peaceful.

He was not helpful to me at all. He had the car and I did not during the day. I walked everywhere with my baby including the local hospital to help the other Burmese and to pick up my children from school. I tried to enroll in a college but my husband's income was 25 dollars over the limit to receive child-care assistance so I could not go to school because I had to take care of my kids. I wanted to study medical interpretation, so I asked a woman I knew if she could help me and she agreed. My husband said "no," that I could not go to school, but I refused to allow him to deny me that opportunity. I went to school for medical interpretative training so I could help the people in my community with their health concerns.

I had several friends who helped with transportation and child care so I could get an education. I never thought I would pass the difficult examination but I did and now I have a health-care certificate to work as a health-care interpreter for the community.

Not long after that I cofounded a nonprofit organization called Burma Refugee Family Network to help the local Burmese refugee community. I still had three children at home and an abusive husband. I continued to work as an interpreter, which became very strenuous, because they needed Karen language interpretation everywhere in my local area in hospitals and doctors' offices. I knew we needed more help. I would work for hours and then tend to my three children. At night we would have board meetings for my nonprofit organization and I would not get home until very late. My husband was very angry about my work. Anytime I had a social event or was out helping my community he would become enraged. He expected me to satisfy him in the evening and be available to him when he wanted me. He said very demeaning insults to me often and spread rumors about me in the community. When I would attend my meetings he started calling me, demanding that I stop working. He told everyone in our local community that I was going out with other men, that I was a bad mother and a terrible person. People could not come to my home for help with their community needs; I would have to go to help them make calls or fill out forms.

At first, this treatment was breaking me down. I would cry a lot but I realized that I knew who I was and that I did not care about what other people said about me. No matter how much he tried getting in my way, I refused to stop the work I was doing.

Despite my family situation, I wanted to help our community. Most people go through their lives and will only help others when they are comfortable. I am used to struggling through life yet helping others at the same time. It is the best thing I can do for people. I am rich in my heart when I help others and I don't have to be financially rich to help others.

Unfortunately, his abuse escalated so badly that it led to serious consequences.

DANGEROUS CONSEQUENCES

Eventually, I went to stay with a friend for two weeks and was away from ~~my children~~ in hiding from my husband. My friend attempted to negotiate with him to get my children back. I worried whether or not they were safe because he was drunk all the time and they were not going to school or being taken care of, yet it was too dangerous for me to go and get them alone.

After some negotiation, he told my friend that he had improved, and that he would not hurt me or them if I came to get them. I drove to the parking lot in front of our apartment with my car and my children got in. He then came, grabbed my hair and started to beat me. My children were crying. When I left, I didn't know where to go. As a refugee I was not aware of any shelters or places that could help my children and I so I called another friend and asked if I could stay with her. She took us in.

At her house my children were playing games and we were cooking. He came over with a big knife demanding to know where I was. I was in the basement hiding, terrified for my life, and shaking. I could hear him above us searching everywhere for me. I was supposed to be on a conference call that evening for refugee youth education programs that my nonprofit wanted to start, but instead I started texting my friends for help with the address that I was at and they called 911. The police came and I asked them to take him away and take us to a safe place. As they drove off in the police car, he started screaming out the window that he was going to kill me. My children were terrified and crying.

In the aftermath of that horrible night, we received a restraining order against him and he was ordered to stay away from my children and me. My kids and I ended up in a women's shelter somewhat far from where we live. We remained there for about three months. Emotionally it was very hard for me because my children were unhappy there and could not go to school. They did not understand why we were there and I could not tell them why. We were with other mothers in a similar situation and it was a struggle to see how emotional they were at the same time as me. From the shelter I still went to open the doors for our youth tutoring programs to ensure the program was still benefitting the youth in our community. Yet, my husband was stalking me and would appear around where I was. After the first few weeks of working with the tutoring program, I had to stop going because there was no security in that area. I was afraid he would follow me back to the shelter.

Although the shelter provided food during the week, on Sundays we all had to go to church in order to eat. I felt this was a form of religious discrimination. I decided at that point that I did not want to stay in the shelter anymore because I did not want my children exposed to being forced to attend church in order to eat. They were taking advantage of vulnerable people.

It was hard for me to return home from the shelter because my husband was still there and he was still saying terrible things about me in the community. I knew I could not avoid returning home forever, so I moved my kids back into our apartment only to discover there was no electricity. My children were happy to be home no matter what. I cry when I think about our going back home, because I had no money, no electricity, and no food but we were happy together because he was gone. We used to jump on the bed together, sing, and laugh. We were finally back in our house and I felt the true meaning of what it meant to be at home. Yet, I worried if I still had my job and if it would still be safe for me to return to the community I was advocating for.

I went back to work to get our lives moving again. As some time passed I realized how lucky I was to be free at home and realized I had lost that notion of freedom before. Not only was I born in Bangladesh as a child of refugees, I also came from Thailand, a country where I was not free and was again part of the undocumented minority group. I came to the United States as a refugee so my children would be free to pursue their education and lives. But what is freedom if you are not even free in your own home? In that case, it does not matter where you live. After my husband left I got to appreciate that aspect of freedom for the first time since arriving in the United States.

Yet, he was still at large. He went around to our entire community and told all of them I had been with other men in the months we were in the shelter. People were asking me if I had a new husband. I was very upset because a lot of them did not know that I spent months in a shelter. For a few years that followed my stay in the shelter, I could not attend cultural events or other important celebrations and meetings within my Burmese community because he was there all the time. I experienced a lot of humiliation because people who used to respect me turned their back to me. It was difficult for me to conduct my political and social activism with my community because I was always worried if I was in a meeting, he would come and make a scene. I still lived in fear of him and what he was capable of and eventually came to the conclusion that he was shrinking my ability to be who I was—the powerful woman that I am. I was a prisoner during our ten-year marriage. I still continued to work with our community, but to this day my work is a challenge because he is always there. That aspect still has not changed, I have only grown stronger.

When I tried to attend the United Nations 57th Commission on the Status of Women meeting in March 2013 in New York, I received notice from my babysitter that he came and took my children away from home. I was terrified because I had no idea where he took them. After a few hours, my best friends called me back and told me they found my children. I flew back to California early from the UN conference. I called the police and they came two days too late. They told me they could not do anything or arrest him because the prior restraining order had not been served on him. A lot of women in my situation struggle with the legal system. I am constantly writing the police and government to deport him since he is such a menace. My children and I are traumatized by his behavior after so many years of abuse. Why is society giving more power to the abuser? The police and justice system have been unfair to my family because neither have done anything to keep him away from me, to protect me or my children.

When he is gone, I realize the true meaning of freedom. If I had to define freedom I would say that it would be the amount of security I have in my life. Also the amount of human rights I possess. Security comes first, then access to food, and after that— human rights. A person needs all of these things to be free. My life experiences have all challenged my notion of freedom—from being indigenous from Burma and living undocumented in other countries to being victimized by my husband's abuse. I know my day will come to feel this free. When he is gone I will have all my freedom back. I still act as an advocate for my community and work to protect their human rights, but because of him I am not free. He does not stop me, but still I do not feel free. When he is out of the picture, I will then have my freedom because I will have my security.

As you can see, I have struggled a lot in my life. I struggled in Bangladesh as an indigenous minority woman, as an undocumented migrant in Thailand, and as a refugee in the United States. I have struggled as a victim of violence. But I work with all my strength to create a bright community so my children can grow up in a better world and not have to struggle like I have. It is my highest and best use as a human being.

NWE'S ADVICE FOR WOMEN

Number one—be confident in who you are. Be strong for your family and for your community. Work to create a better community because the women who do this create freedom for more women. What does citizenship mean to you? Are you a human from the world? So many refugees are stateless. Global citizenship means you have the right as a human being to live where you choose to live. I want to see the next generation of unborn children fully participate as human beings without regard to citizenship and be proud to say, "I am a world citizen."

OEUM

Cambodia

From 1975 to 1979, the notorious Khmer Rouge regime ruled Cambodia. Its policy of creating a purely agrarian-based communist society subjected Cambodians to radical social reform. An estimated two million Cambodians perished in this period from waves of murder, torture, forced labor, forced migration, disease, and starvation. Oeum describes her family's desperate attempt to flee Cambodia and recalls spending the first years of her life in a Thai refugee camp. She also discusses her personal transformation after immigrating to the United States.

MY STORY BEGINS in a bit of a harsh setting but these were the first years of my life. I am a firm believer that we can make a lot of positive things out of devastating circumstances and I am living proof that this is possible.

I am the fifth child of five and the years leading up to my birth in the late 1970s were very tumultuous ones for Cambodia. It was the time of the notorious Khmer Rouge and my family was in danger for several reasons. The Khmer Rouge's specific ethnicity is "red Cambodian" and they were the ruling party in Cambodia from 1975 to 1979. They were responsible for genocide and devastation in the country including a process of very radical social reform where they tried to make everybody become a farmer or peasant by deporting people from urban areas to the countryside and forcing them to do farm labor.

During the time of my conception—during the reign of the Khmer Rouge—a lot of turmoil was happening and my mother was very afraid for the safety of our family. The Khmer Rouge did not like educated people. They desired to convert everyone to agrarian communism, because uneducated people were easier to control and were less likely to fight back and to voice their opinions. Anyone in your family who was educated could be executed at any time. My mother was born, raised, and educated in Thailand but she came to Cambodia as a young woman and decided to stay; she is ethnically half Thai and half Cambodian. As an educated woman, she posed a significant threat to herself and the rest of my family. The Khmer Rouge was the reason my family had to flee Cambodia and leave everything behind.

My mother told me that she has no birth records from my birth and that she burned all the records they had because these records proved their level of education. Because I have no birth certificate, I don't know what year I was born or my exact birth date. My mother remembered it by the season and told me that I was born during the rice harvest. My birthday on paper is July 7, 1977, but that birthday is constructed to be that way because I am the seventh person in the family. It was easier for my mother to pass our United States immigration interview if we all had specific birthdays. My mother, as head of the household, chose a birth date of 1/1 (January 1st) and my father was 2/2. Mother was head of the household because she was an educated woman and as my father could not read or write, she handled everything.

The story of how I was born is also interesting and through it, I see the first sign that I am meant to be here. My mother was lying on a bamboo mat during my delivery above a fire. In Cambodia, it was customary for a fire to be lit under the pregnant woman for her blood to flow and for her to be heated. As my brother was washing me, I almost slipped into the fire pit, but he caught me by the neck so I did not fall.

When I was born, the entire society of Cambodia was in upheaval. The Khmer Rouge did radical and inhumane things and when they came into power they isolated the country from any foreign contact in addition to closing banks and schools. In fact, they completely eliminated banking and even made all religions illegal. One of the worst things they did was move everyone to forced-labor farms. They were trying to turn Cambodia into a "classless" society and make everyone peasants. Family relationships were forbidden and people could be killed for communicating with family members. My mother told me that my family was spilt up and my brother was sent to the boy's side of one of these camps. It was almost impossible to communicate with anyone once they were gone because there were no phones or mail.

As the oppression and violence escalated, my parents decided to flee to a refugee camp in Thailand when I was about six or seven months old. It was a long, difficult, and dangerous journey to get across the border of Cambodia and through the forest to Thailand. During the trek, my mother heard a clicking sound and realized she had stepped on a land mine while carrying me on her back. The only thing she could do was slowly step off of it and hope that it would not go off. Fortunately, it did not until she crossed it. That was truly a miracle because land mines are designed to explode when stepped on. It's very rare for them to fail to explode until the person is out of harm's way. That incident was always the second indication to me that I am meant to be here and serve a higher purpose.

We finally made it to Thailand and found our new home in a refugee camp called Khao-I-Dang where I spent my childhood. It was a very sad existence and as I grew older, I understood more of what I witnessed. I noticed people were starving and suffering and my sister and I always had to go looking for food. We were lucky because my mother could speak Thai so she was able to go over the Thai border and at least beg to feed our family. Other families around us had nothing at all. It's hard being a young child in that environment because you grow up around suffering and that is all you know and see.

Some of my strongest and most intense memories are of soldiers coming into the camp in the middle of the night to occasionally rampage and terrorize us refugees by robbing us of what little we had and raping the girls in the camp. If you had a teenage daughter, there was a strong chance she would be taken away and raped. We would hear warnings from others in the camp before the soldiers came at night. My parents had dug a hole under our hut for us all to hide in so that when the soldiers came they would think nobody was there. They could not see us because it was dark. My mother was always worried about my older sister because she was over fourteen years old and if they saw her she would surely be targeted. I remember hiding in that hole shaking because I could hear a lot of commotion around me. I remember people screaming, crying, and yelling: "Give me my daughter back! Don't touch my daughter!" The voices of those girls being dragged out from their huts are forever burned into my mind. If I had seen their captures it would be more traumatic for me, but

271

I can still remember the terror in their screams. It is a sound you never forget.

The girls would disappear and would rarely come back. As a child it is traumatizing to hear these things. I am sure my sister was more scared then I was because she was part of the targeted group of girls. I am sure if they could have they probably would have taken me, too. They didn't care. Why would they stop there? We would hide in that hole that we dug until they were all gone; until we could not hear any chaos anymore.

My entire family lived in a small hut and received rice, water, and vegetables when the government would bring them to us. They were just basic staple foods, probably donated from the Red Cross or UNHCR to the Thai government to give to us. This existence was my childhood. When some people say they have gone through a struggle, I look at them and wonder what could be so bad about their situation.

At one point, a Caucasian man who was interested in my fifteen-year-old sister used to come in the camp and tell my mother that he would like to take my older sister first and then come get the rest of the family later. My mother was not okay with that. She told him if he wanted her, then he had to take all of us. So that passed. I don't know who he was, why he was there, or even what power he had to take her out of the camp.

Regardless, we knew there were ways out of the camp via immigration so we got in touch with some Cambodians living in the United States and asked them to sponsor us and they agreed. The whole family was sponsored at the same time. When it came time for us to leave, we left with a group of other Cambodians. We had never seen an airplane before so flying was very funny and strange. Some people were crying because they were happy to leave. They knew they would be safe and actually have a chance to live their life in another country.

When we arrived in the United States as refugees we were blown away by everything. We had no idea what all the houses were because we had lived in only a camp our whole lives. Our clothes were a mess as we were basically wearing rags and flip-flops. We moved into an apartment that one of the resettlement groups had arranged for us and received financial aid. We were so happy to have our own place! The apartment was a luxury for us and we were grateful that we were alive and could live there. Above all, we were all so grateful for the opportunity to get an education. Our sponsor family suggested that we go to the Mormon temple to get help enrolling in school and accessing community resources. They introduced us to the Latter-day Saints' faith and gave us clothes, books, and school supplies.

Eventually, my brother, sister, and mother became Latter-day Saints, but they did not stay with the faith. My family is Buddhist so Buddhism is our deep-rooted belief. I decided to become a Latter-day Saint and continued to go to church until I was eighteen or nineteen years old. The Mormon community was a positive influence in my life. I felt that the guidance and mentorship I received through the faith were very positive especially during critical years of my life. My LDS mother and the church kept me out of a lot of trouble because any activity I wanted to do was always connected with the church. Many children of refugees in the United States get into a lot of trouble in school and in the community because of the language and cultural barriers between their parents and the American culture. The parents often don't understand what their children are getting into so they can't stop them. I was lucky to have a mentor in my teen years because it helped me make the right decisions.

When I decided to go to college, I was introduced to my now ex-husband, an African American man. He was finishing his master's degree at the time and we connected with each other quickly. My college years were always busy because I had to help my family quite often. Throughout my childhood, I was the child who helped everybody translate paperwork and I also served as the interpreter. I spoke the most English of any of my siblings so I became the family social worker. Perhaps that is why I went into the social work profession—because I got my training when I was a child; it came naturally to me because the job duties were family duties I had while growing up.

Against the wishes of my family, I followed this man when he moved to Japan to teach for one year. He proposed to me and we had a traditional engagement in my culture. My family at first was not crazy about the fact that he was African American because they wanted me to marry a Cambodian, but when I told them that I loved him they were more understanding and accepting. Though initially I went to Japan to visit him while he was there, I ended up becoming pregnant with our first child so I stayed. I was always grateful that my life took such an interesting turn because living in Japan was wonderful for me.

My family did not like the fact that I moved there and dropped out of college to be with my husband. They were also unhappy that we did not host a traditional Cambodian wedding lasting three days and featuring fascinating clothes and costumes. My decisions resulted in our not speaking for a while. That was a hard thing for me because they had always depended on me and when we stopped talking I felt that there was a very huge void in my life. When I came back to visit them with my daughter, eventually those things were erased in time. They accepted my husband and they even used to worry about him more than they did me!

While we lived in Japan, we traveled to third-world countries and I had the opportunity to return to Cambodia and see the village in Battambang where I was born. I wanted to see the house that I was born in and explore the land of my birth because I always felt like these elements were stolen from me. It's difficult to describe this but I felt that I was cheated out of my own country and that my family was, too. It was spiritual to be there and see it all. I also went to Thailand, and wanted to visit the Khao-I-Dang refugee camp that I grew up in, but they would not let us back in. I suppose I was not meant to see it in my adult life. I was meant to leave it behind.

Through that trip, I decided I wanted to change the course of my university studies to social work. After moving back to the States, I changed my major, finished my bachelor's degree, and worked as a translator for a Cambodian women's group. Having a college degree was such an immense accomplishment for me and was considered so in my family. Although this work does not pay much money, I consider it my mark on the world. I worked within my own community and had a chance to work with my people. I felt like I struggled through the same things as many of my people have been through living in the camps and the effect of the Khmer Rouge on families. It felt nice to do work that allowed me to reconnect with them and help them; to be that bridge between them and the United States. It was very fulfilling.

In 2004 I worked with a program called "Youth Connection" where we took local kids from Oakland, California, to travel to the land of their families. I had the opportunity to take eight American-born kids who were Hmong, Laotian, and Cambodian back to Laos and Cambodia and backpack our way to their original villages to see everything. Those trips changed their lives forever because they actually got to see where their parents lived and experience their own cultures in the motherland. Unfortunately the program no longer exists, but my dream is to continue to do something like that—to reconnect the kids with the roots of their cultures. The personal transformation they undergo is unbelievable to witness; they really grow up through that process.

I got a chance to work with African American kids who came from bad neighborhoods in another of my previous jobs; it's amazing that most of them have never stepped outside of the city they are from! They don't know what snow looks like or feels like and have never taken a trip to the beach. I got to take them to the beach so they could see that there is something beyond their front yard that is waiting for them to explore. When they received that opportunity, I observed a change in them. Their mannerisms changed, they thought before they said things, and their views on life changed. These are kids who didn't get proper attention. All they wanted was someone to tell them they were beautiful or that they had a meaning, purpose, or talent. Yet due to the chaos in their family circumstances, they never received this kind of attention or any support.

Honestly, my heart is in working with youth and especially with troubled youth because I find that deep down inside, they often have the burning desire to change their lives. They are often just products of their circumstance; just like I was the product of the Khmer Rouge and had to flee my own country and live in a refugee camp. Youth are so pure. It does not matter how old they are, they are pure at heart. That is something that you have to see when you work with young people.

My ultimate goal is to build a school back home or start a program that reconnects kids with their culture because I believe the root of what is missing in our current society is that the culture and the community are not intact. Culture is being slowly devalued and replaced by consumerism. Once our community and family ties break down, then everything breaks down. I strongly feel once a woman is breaking down, the family is breaking down. The woman is the key and the root of everything from the family unit to the community. Once you disrespect your mother or sister, the household is broken. Then, if that happens in enough households, the society is broken.

Sometimes I am surprised that I am still alive. I have seen kidnapping, death, and rape. I have come to the conclusion that there is nothing I have to be sad about in life. There is only one of you—make the best of you in that case. My motive is just to be happy and do the best I can with whatever task I am undertaking. I always felt that the reason I survived and was able to come to the United States meant that I had a mission. No matter how bad things get, you have to keep asking yourself why you are still alive.

OEUM'S ADVICE FOR WOMEN

Keep being strong because you are strong. You have to be strong to be a woman.

VA

Laos

For centuries, the Hmong people have lived in the mountainous regions of China, Vietnam, Laos, and Thailand. In the early 1960s, the U.S. Central Intelligence Agency's (CIA) Special Activities Division began recruiting and training Hmong people for a special guerrilla unit led by Hmong Lieutenant General Vang Pao. This unit was used during the Vietnam War to fight against the North Vietnamese Army intruders into Laos. The Hmong people earned a special place in the hearts of American combat soldiers because of the monumental sacrifices they made for the United States in its fight against the North Vietnamese and Pathet Lao communist forces.

Two years after the U.S. withdrawal from Vietnam, Laos was overthrown by communist troops supported by the North Vietnamese Army. The Hmong people immediately became targets of retaliation and persecution, leading thousands of Hmong to flee across the Mekong River into Thailand, often while under attack. This marked the beginning of a mass exodus of Hmong from Laos. Those who reached Thailand were kept in squalid United Nations refugee camps until they could be resettled elsewhere.

As reparation for their service during the Vietnam War, the United States resettled Hmong refugees in the 1970s. Va shares the story of fleeing her home and resettling in the United States.

M Y NAME IS Va, and I was born in Laos, a country of many mountains and forests that has both dry seasons and seasons of much rain. There are winding rivers, and the earth all around is green and lush for farming, which is how my people, the Hmong, have thrived for centuries. We are a unique culture in Laos with traditions that are very different from those of other countries and lands.

Hmong people actually originated in China and eventually migrated to the Laos-Vietnam area. For many centuries the Chinese people performed similar rituals and followed the same spiritual path that we did. They burned papers to communicate with their relatives who had passed away, because they say that when a relative passes away it's as though they live in another place. We believe this, too, and also believe that they will need money in the afterlife, so we burn paper to send money to them. As in every culture, it is a tradition in our culture to be concerned about relatives who have passed away. I believe that is where our culture is similar to others.

When I was a child, I lived with my mother and father in a mountain village. It was not like the United States, where a person can find a job somewhere. Instead, we had to go out each day and work for our food. Hmong people are very well-known for farming, and we gardened and hunted for our sustenance. There were never any grocery stores in the village where I lived because everything was very basic. We had to work just to survive. We even had to build the hut where my family lived. My early childhood consisted mostly of hard work to help my family so we would have food on the table.

When I was fifteen years old, I was married to my first husband. In our culture, women get married very young because people say when they grow older, their children can take care of them. Where I am from, children do not always survive because there are no hospitals or doctors close to the villages. By getting married young and having children, we are making sure we will be cared for just as we care for our parents when they age. I think that is a universal truth that many people can understand, regardless of their culture or country.

We also have wedding traditions. When a man wants to marry a woman in our culture, he has to pay the girl's family a dowry as a way of expressing his love and desire to be with her. Everybody ties a little wristband of yarn around their hand to bring good luck for the marriage. As an act of kindness, other families will donate money to the couple so they can get started in their life. These are important customs to follow in Hmong culture.

I divorced my first husband when I was about seventeen years old. The story of how I met my current husband is very fascinating. He was once married, too, but the Vietnamese invaded the village where he lived and took his wife away. I had known him for a long time, and we started to like each other and eventually married. Shortly after the birth of our child Pa, we had to flee our village. I remember this time very distinctly. I was carrying Pa, a baby who was only thirteen days old, on my back. Gunshots were all around us. The sounds were deafening as we could hear the mortars falling from the sky. It seemed like the earth was exploding because dirt was flying every-where. Suddenly, something flew up and hit me in the eye, but there was no time to stop. It took me one whole day to run from the top to the bottom of the mountain, where we entered a large village that had houses, stores, and a lot of people. The large amount of people there made me feel safe because I knew the Vietnamese would not start killing us if people were around everywhere.

We lived in that village for five weeks and eventually decided to move back up into the mountains again. When we returned home, we realized the Vietnamese had taken over our mountain village, so we could not go back to where we originally had lived. We had to start over. We burned down trees so the sun would come into the land and we could start planting. Then we cut our own wood, which we used to build our houses. We also had to burn a lot of fields to make soil so we could start planting. After the fields were ready, we planted corn and rice and went hunting. My husband did most of the hunting, as most of the men do in our villages.

Despite staying on the lookout for the Vietnamese after our resettlement, life was kind of peaceful overall. The war stopped for a while, until Vang Pao, the Hmong general who was the equivalent to the president of the Hmong community, fled to the United States. After his departure, the Vietnamese attacked us again, so we had to run all the way to Thailand in order to survive. Walking day and night, it took us sixteen days by foot to get there. I carried Pa and was pregnant at that time as well. We stayed in the woods to make the journey, always watching to make sure we would be safe. It was hard because we did not have any food and had to sleep under the trees. We were determined, though, and we did it to survive. When we made it to Thailand, I was relieved, but terribly sad because I realized I would not be going back to my home.

After Lieutenant General Vang Pao fled to the United States, the U.S. government promised to give the Hmong people freedom and a better way of life because of everything we did for them during the war and the number of soldiers we sacrificed. That is how I was able to immigrate to the United States after the Vietnam War. Yet, my immigration to America was not instant, and it came only after four years of struggling in a refugee camp.

Living in the refugee camp was very hard for us because it was equivalent to living in a city. There were no mountains or farming, and people were everywhere around us. It was a far stretch from our normally quiet way of life. Instead of being able to grow our own food and hunt once a week, we were fed a limited amount of rationed food in the form of rice, a small amount of vegetables, and a very small portion of meat. They gave one ration per family, and we had five people in our family at the time. It was not enough food to satisfy our hunger, and we spent most of the time hungry.

I gave birth to two of my sons in the camp. After the one who was in my belly when I was running away to Thailand was born, I became pregnant again with another son and also gave birth to him. The problem with having a baby in the camp was that a lot of Thai people liked to kidnap kids. The Thai people would hold a newborn child and say he or she was cute, and then they would take the child away. I was always worried about a son being kidnapped and taken away from me without my knowledge.

When my second son who was born in the camp was four months old, he was really chubby, and the Thai people thought he was adorable. They bought clothes and shoes for him with their own money. My people told me, "You better go get your child because they will take him away from you." Scared, I got him and took him back to our place in the camp. My people told me that I better not sleep in order to watch and guard him for the next few days. A few days later, a woman who was not wearing any clothes came and wanted to play with my son, and she took him away. I panicked and searched everywhere, only to find this woman breastfeeding him! I was happy he was safe, and now my family laughs when I tell that story.

Most of the Hmong people in the camp had gone through the same situation as we did and had lost their homes, villages, and families. Living there for four years felt like an eternity because we never knew if we would ever get to leave until the actual day finally came. There was a list of people being resettled to the United States, and my name was on it. At first, I didn't want to leave because my mom and dad were still in the camp. We eventually caught up with one another because their names were also on the same resettlement list, though I had to leave them behind at first, which was very difficult since they were all I had left of my life back home.

I officially immigrated to the United States in 1980, landing in Boston and living there for three years. Then I moved to Fresno, California, and in 1986 I moved to Eureka, California, which is where I still live.

I really like America and the town where I currently live, mostly because I can still farm, raise chickens, and live my life the way I did in Laos without worrying about the Vietnamese coming after us. After nearly eight transitional years, I finally had access to my own land. If I had the choice to go back to Laos, I would stay in America because it provides a lot more freedom and there are no threats. You also don't have to plant food to survive—you can find a job. That is important to me and why I like Eureka so much.

After coming to Eureka, I really had to adjust. I had to put all my kids in the school system and manage our lives, but overall I was really comfortable with it. There were fourteen children in my household. Two of my children still lived in Laos until one of them passed away. Managing their schedules was difficult at times, but I did not mind taking them to school because I wanted to give them a better life than mine. Laos didn't have schools like America does, so I was grateful they were getting an education.

For years, I was able to farm and take care of my kids. Things became difficult when my husband became very sick several years ago and suffered from a stroke and kidney failure due to diabetes. Not knowing if he would live, I was devastated. The most difficult part was not knowing much about the medication the doctors wanted him to take, because a large part of our healing culture is devoted to speaking with the spirits. In Laos, when someone becomes sick, it is believed that a bad spirit is inside him, which necessitates the services of a Shaman, who is a communicator with the spirits and a healer. The Shaman talks to the spirits to reach some kind of agreement so the spirits will leave the person's body. If the spirits agree with the Shaman, they leave; but when they don't, a ritual that can take five or six hours is performed in order to extract them. Sometimes we have to kill a pig or a chicken as food for the spirits. We also burn paper and money so we can send money to the dead as part of an agreement.

Because the American medical approach is so different, I invited the nurses to my home to show me which medications to give my husband and to become accustomed to them. My husband's illness signified a very exhausting time for me because I was caring for my entire large family all on my own, holding everything together.

My life was very busy. I would take my kids to school while my husband watched our two other children. Then I would come back, put the other kids in the car seats, and take my husband to the hospital. When I returned home, I farmed while my husband watched the kids. I repeated all of my daily tasks one by one because I always believe in living life in the present. When you are living presently, your stress melts away. My advice for those experiencing stressful situations is to solve the most immediate problem at hand. If my baby cried, I gave him a bottle and changed his diaper. I was not stressed regarding the children because I have been raising children for a very long time, and I am very accustomed to this lifestyle. After having sixteen children, I became very adaptable.

Many people asked me what I did when one or more of my babies would cry. I never became irritated when a baby cried, because the baby only whines so it can be picked up. If the baby cries long enough and the parents do not pick it up, it learns to stop crying. When you are only one mother dealing with so many children, you don't have time to become stressed. Mothering just becomes natural.

Honestly, time went by so fast. I have so many children, and now I have grandchildren. Over the years, I have learned to deal with any situation that may arise. There were even years when some of my older children were getting in a lot of trouble with the law. Being from another country, it was confusing for me to try to handle that, but I did it because I had to. I raised my children, and they are always my children, no matter what they do. Even when they move out of my house, they will always be my children. My advice to other parents who have children who get into trouble is that, no matter what they do, they are still your children. You should never abandon them. If you are going to abandon your child, you should never have given birth to that child in the first place.

It's been a long journey, but I have a very good life now. The most stressful element in my life is that my husband and I still have a daughter in Laos. She is in her forties and has had seven children, but two of them passed away because they were sick and she was not able to get them to the hospital in time to save them. My daughter wanted to move to the United States with us, but this country is no longer accepting Hmong people for resettlement. So I send money to her in Laos so she can buy medicine, send her kids to school, and hire help on the farm. Their homes are made of branches and leaves, which don't hold up well over time, so every two years they have to build another house. The men usually do the construction, but my daughter's husband is no longer living, so we send her money so she can pay someone to work on her house. The hardest part for me is wanting to help her but knowing we can't do much more than send her money.

Ten U.S. dollars is the equivalent of about eighty thousand Laotian Kip. However, goods are very expensive. For example, a candy bar can cost about the equivalent of five thousand dollars in Lao currency. It would cost about forty thousand American dollars to build a house over there. I hope I can give a new house to my daughter one day. She needs it badly, and it is my dream to give this one thing to her since I cannot be near her. I hate the distance. We are apart, but we are still connected in many ways in spirit.

That is my journey. It has not always been easy, but I am strong and brave. I have a lot of courage and pride in my culture and love to share it with others. I hope you have enjoyed reading about my life.

VA'S ADVICE FOR WOMEN
To all the women out there who have kids, my advice is to stand by them and never abandon them. You need to stay by them, no matter what.

THÙY LINH

Vietnam

Jazz Vocalist Thùy Linh discusses her experiences overcoming polio, her family's escape from their native Vietnam, and finding her path to freedom through her passion for jazz music.

F OR EVERYONE, NOT just women, I would like to offer three bits of advice:

Number one: Never get stuck on the "not haves" of life. One has plenty of lacking and shortcomings in her character and life circumstance. If one gets stuck on what she does not have, she becomes immobilized. Instead we should all focus on our strengths; use them to advance and improve ourselves in life.

Number two: Never take no for an answer. If one can't do something one way, then she must find other ways to do it. There are always multiple roads to the same destination; one must look for them. Always push the borders and try the unconventional ways.

Number three: Jump in feet first and be ready to land wherever the adventure takes you. When one hesitates and is fearful, she ends up doing nothing to get closer to her dreams and perhaps even lives in regret.

These three tenets shape and drive my life's model largely due to my physical disability since childhood. Because of limitations from my disability, through my life I have learned to rely on my existing strengths and build from them. In fact, my disability has been a blessing in disguise, pushing me to strive for a normal life and be more "normal" than a physically fit person. In the process, I have overcompensated for my lacking by pursuing more than an average person.

At age three I contracted polio while awaiting my third vaccination shot that was supposed to protect me from a strain going around in 1973. At the time, it paralyzed both of my legs. My parents took me for many therapies, including water, heat, and acupuncture. Eventually my right leg grew stronger through extensive treatments but not at full capacity. Unable to walk long distances, I often relied on adults to carry me around. I had a metal leg brace that was supposed to help me walk and sustain endurance, but it was so heavy that I never used it. Once I started hearing adults' complaints that I was too heavy to be carried, I instantly became offended and told myself that I would grow up to be self-reliant and never depend on others. My need to be independent grew stronger the more my parents wanted to protect and shelter me from everything.

My family is from the beautiful coastal town Nha Trang, about an hour north of Saigon by flight. At age four, I was sent by my parents to a hospice for disabled children in Saigon (now Ho Chi Minh City) that was run by Catholic nuns. I stayed there from January 1974 until April 1975. I did not like it there and always cried because I wanted to go back home. My mother would have to practically escape when she visited me because I refused to stay. Although heartbroken to see me so sad, my parents believed I would receive the best therapy for my polio-stricken legs there. Frankly, I think they put me there because they were compelled to do something to improve my condition. They wanted to give me the best care possible.

Yet, all I knew at that time remains poignant in my mind: I am not like the other kids; I am not disabled. My arrogance at the age of four stems from the desire to be normal. I often played alone because I did not want to associate myself or bond with the others. Bonding with the others would mean that I would be stuck at that hospice and be like them.

Looking back, I truly believe my polio is really a blessing in disguise. It has given me the fire in my belly to pursue a life of a "normal" person—to do everything that a normal person can do. From swimming and skiing to travels and bearing children, I wanted to experience a full, well-rounded life. As a result, I overcompensated with all my pursuits to mask my disability—to make it invisible. Since very little I have always lived a race against time: I feel the urgency to pursue everything in the now while I still have the physical stamina to do so.

To this day, I don't like to talk much about daily struggles that directly result from my disability. I'm deliberate to not make it the focus when people meet me. Certainly I want and make sure that people see my full identity beyond the limp in my gait. Medical research shows that polio victims face chronic exhaustion after living with the condition for at least thirty years. Chronic pains and fatigue steadily increase as the body becomes an *overloaded circuit*. I never complain to people about my daily chronic aches and pains, even though they have become more intense now especially after bearing and caring for my two children (girl, five, and boy, four). This goes back to my desire to be independent, self-reliant, and normal. The disability is part of who I am, not all that I am. This message is clear to others as I do not identify myself as someone with a disability and have never aligned with disability-related causes. I don't use my disability as a crutch to get hired or priority treatment. This determination

I already felt in my head and heart at age four when I was in that hospice for disabled children.

Fortunately, my parents took me out of the hospice at the start of April 1975 before the city fell on the 30th to communist forces. In fact, my maternal grandparents urged my parents to bring me home as they foresaw the fall of Saigon at the end of April. After Saigon was captured, my parents were still able to make a living with their businesses in our hometown Nha Trang and life was still pleasant. Our town was untouched by the war: we were not bombed nor did we experience armed conflict like inland areas and other towns like Hue. Yet, eventually we had to leave Vietnam because life became difficult in 1979. At that time, the government had a mission to rid the country of "capitalists," identified as the Chinese population in Vietnam as they were great entrepreneurs. Although Vietnamese, my parents got caught in that current. With increased harassment and extortions by local police, my parents realized our family would not have a future in Vietnam so they planned an escape out of the country.

During the first escape attempt when I was sent with my aunt, we were caught and jailed by local authorities. We went to a hideout in a small coastal fishing village where we were going to be picked up by our fishing boat at sea. Because we stood out from the local residents with our fairer skin, the locals turned us into the police. Sitting cross-legged under bright lights overnight, we were interrogated in jail. My aunt stuck to our story: she was my mother and we came to the village in search of a Buddhist temple where the monks had a medical regimen that could cure my leg. The following morning they released us after my parents paid off the local authorities.

Shortly after that, my parents bought off a fishing boat inclusive of its owner and two sons to take our family's thirty members to escape Vietnam by sea. Our trip lasted five days and five nights. Just as our water and food ran out we drifted to the Philippines. We lived in the refugee camps for ten months while awaiting sponsorship from the United States, our resettlement destination.

In the camp, we kids had a theatre teacher who taught us to sing and dance for weekly shows to entertain everyone at camp. As a jazz vocalist now, reflecting on that time is so telling. I always landed the lead role in most productions. Every time I stood on stage with a microphone I always envisioned myself as a famous internationally acclaimed singer. Interestingly, refugee parents forbid their children from pursuing the arts once resettled in affluent countries. For them, the key to success, especially after escaping bloodshed and hardship in our homeland, is a degree in higher education that is perceived to be lucrative in traditional professions like medicine, law, engineering, and business. Now, after forty years of living in the diaspora, refugees in these professions are pursuing the arts.

After living in camps across the Philippine islands, in 1979 when I was nine years old, our family was sponsored by a Catholic Church to resettle in Hastings, a rural town in Minnesota. Having to start our lives over, we reached out to the church as our extended family in a foreign land. Church volunteers would shuttle us around to appointments ranging from school, jobs, and doctors' appointments. I was able to get service from an orthopedic children's hospital with polio experts. With a better designed and lighter weight leg brace, I became more mobile and independent. At school I got lessons to swim, play various physical sports, and prevent atrophy in my legs.

After three years in Minnesota, we moved to Southern California to live near my mother's sister who came in 1976. With a successful manicure business as proof of potential success, my aunt encouraged my parents to settle there for the warm weather and the sizeable Vietnamese community.

At eighteen I moved to Northern California to attend college at the University of California, Berkeley. The more my parents wanted to shelter and shield me from the world, the more I became determined to free myself from their overprotective shackles. They were worried for me on two fronts: my disability and my being a girl. If I had not left when I did, they would have suffocated me. At that age, I knew that I could not indulge their protective urges; doing so would disable me even more and cost me my freedom. I did not want to live like a caged bird or in a bubble. Their overprotective behavior was not the only reason I desired to break free.

Although my parents' manicure business was very successful, I still had to wear the hat of the family administrator, handling legal documents and translating things for them. By default, I ended up with these adult responsibilities because I was the smartest child, being second in rank. As I started working my senior year of high school, I helped take care of my family financially. Even when I went away to college, I had to send money home to them. Many of these responsibilities continued even when I came to the San Francisco area to attend college. These things are all very common in refugee families struggling with their new lives.

In my freshman year, I discovered jazz music through friends. I quickly fell in love with the poetic and romantic lyrics very similar to Vietnamese music I heard and sang growing up at home. Also, jazz's improvisational sounds carried me like wings to the freedom that I yearned for from my heavy adult responsibilities. It was a natural connection. Slowly I started to listen to all the classic voices of the legendary Ella Fitzgerald, Sarah Vaughan, Billie Holiday, Nat King Cole, and Louis Armstrong. I would memorize lyrics, study their styles, and sing the songs in my head. I would get lost in the stories: the romantic ones would take me to a fairy land of castles and unicorns while the sad ones would heal me from whatever physical and emotional ailments that plagued me daily.

In 1995 after finishing my bachelor's and master's degrees, I started to pursue professional jazz singing. I learned from scratch, hanging out at jams and learning songs with my ears. Yet, when I sang with a band, I struggled with tempo. My ears were not used to hearing other instruments, just my voice. It's a challenge very hard to conquer and remains a weakness I continue to hone. In 2014 I plan to make what my mentor calls a "real jazz CD." To date I have a demo called *Then & Now*, produced in 2012. I sell this at community appearances and donate the proceeds to Pacific Links Foundation (PALS: Vòng Tay Thái Bình) for its work to stop human trafficking on the borders of Vietnam. PALS started in 2001 with the mission to support the sustainable development of Vietnamese communities. In 2005 our president learned of human trafficking problems there and decided to take on the issue. At the time she truly believed that the trafficking would end within five years. No one really could assess the actual numbers and depth of the problem because of its underground nature. Since Vietnam has become one of the world's source countries for human trafficking, I got very angry with this and decided to join PALS' efforts.

Since 2008, I have volunteered with PALS, serving as its development officer. In this role, I helped to raise funds to support PALS' flagship project to stop human trafficking in Vietnam: Project ADAPT (An Giang/Đồng Tháp Alliance for the Prevention of Trafficking: Dự án Phòng Chống Tệ nạn Buôn Người). This work has allowed me to stay connected to Vietnam and the outside world while raising my two young children at home. Over time as my singing grew to a professional level, my role shifted to that of a spokesperson.

I am very happy to integrate my singing with my passion for justice. Stirred by horrendous stories of trafficking survivors that PALS serves, I started to compose songs with my best friend, the poet Bashou. "Lotus Child: survivors of human trafficking rise to greatness!" honors human trafficking survivors. This song is a poem written by Bashou to which I added melody. The current melody is the exact first take of the song. This proves the natural connection we share and the mutual understanding of the issue which compelled us to create a song magically out of thin air.

The second series, *Lady Moon: the irrepressible Hồ Xuân Hương— 18th century feminist poet*, celebrates the untamed spirit of HXH's politically astute erotic poetry. "Jackfruit" is the first recorded song in this series. This song, based on the risqué poem "Quả *Mít*" of only four lines, celebrates female sexuality with a boldness not allowed for women in these times. It always elicits great hollers and laughter from American audiences due to its unique and sexually charged imagery. Both of these original compositions are on my demo CD, *Then & Now*.

This year I aim to perform more and compose original music. I am also looking for ways to bring jazz into ethnic communities. Last November 2013, a friend and I launched *Jazz Is You! (Jazz Là Em!)* in our local Vietnamese community. We debuted with a jazz jam with only one week of preparation. On a Tuesday night we filled up the house with over one hundred guests, 95 percent of whom were Vietnamese jazz lovers. We received such an enthusiastic response that we plan to offer ongoing shows throughout the community and also move into other ethnic communities like the Latinos. American jazz began within the heart and soul of a minority population: African Americans in the south.

Music is my life yet I have only reached this recognition very recently. Perhaps if I had not experienced my earlier struggles, I would not have fully realized it. Every person needs to have some pain in order to understand and appreciate happiness. The Vietnamese call it "charm" when two strangers click like long lost pals at a first meeting or when something falls into your lap at the time that it does without your doing.

I suppose I can say that I was "charmed" my entire life.

THÙY LINH'S ADVICE FOR WOMEN

As I said, never get stuck on the "not haves" of life because there is plenty of lacking. If we get stuck on those, we get immobilized and paralyzed. I think that is my life model because of my disability. Stick with the positive and build from it. Second, if you can't do something one way, then you have to find other ways to do it.

Finally, jump in feet first (even if you only have one fully functioning foot) and see where things take you. When you hesitate and are fearful, you end up doing nothing.

Contact Thùy Linh: www.about.me/ThuyLinhJazzVocalist

ZARA

Malaysia

Zara became a chef at the age of fifteen years old in an effort to leave the oppressive, abusive conditions of her home. Her story discusses the importance of self-advocacy and self-reliance.

I F THERE IS one lesson learned from reading my story I sincerely hope it is this: Love yourself. Just two simple words, yet the most important lesson you will ever learn.

I want everyone to know that it is hard for me to talk about the details of my earlier life. I chose to talk about them because I know they will help someone in a similar situation. I also know that my life is a perfect example that self-love and self-reliance is all that we have in this life.

AN UNWANTED CHILD
I am from a small village in the country of Malaysia outside of Kuala Lumpur and was raised by my grandmother because I was

an unwanted child. To this day, I do not have an answer as to why. I would always ask my parents but they never had an answer. They never came and visited me. Sometimes I wonder if it was because they had a hard life. I think they know why they abandoned me but are too afraid to admit anything. I am not ashamed to say that I won't forgive them until they decide to tell me the truth. In spite of everything, I do have a current relationship with them and I just keep moving forward on that.

My grandmother didn't want me yet she was forced to raise me because of our society. It is tradition that if a parent does not want to take care of the children, the grandparents are obligated to do so.

I have had one of the most difficult childhoods one could imagine. I was abused sexually, emotionally, and physically by every single person in my family and I could not tell anyone about it because nobody would have cared or helped me. I think what they wanted was for me to go away and disappear. I was left to fend for myself since early childhood. My health was not a big concern to anyone and my family didn't care if I ate, took a shower, or did my school work. Basically I was in the house but was the invisible, quiet child in the corner. Nobody wanted anything to do with me—not to feed me or talk to me or anything—and the only time they would pay attention to me is if they were touching me in sexual ways or beating me. They did sick things like using a stick to explore my body or snipping my breast nipples with fingernail clippers. It was like they enjoyed seeing me in pain.

As an adult I feel awkward in my own body and I believe it was the result of that abuse. Physically, I was beaten often and during those beatings, I wished they would beat me until I died. I would be accused of stealing things that I didn't take, or if I would ask a question they would find a reason to hit me. I am 80 percent deaf in my left ear because of the abuse I suffered as a child.

I was also ridiculed all the time. There is nothing worse than your own family making fun of you. It is the worst rejection that anyone can experience. That rejection has the worst impact in your life.

For years I tried different ways of killing myself but none worked. For example, I would see something poisonous and start drinking it or eating it, but it was never my fate to die. I did so many terrible things to myself because I believed that I was worthless. When you are abused as badly as I was, you stop loving yourself because you think you are not worth anything and your life does not mean anything. You question the purpose of your existence time and time again. The hardest part was through all this, I could not go to any orphanages because I still had parents. There is no social welfare system in Malaysia to where we could be taken away from our families and placed in foster care if we were being abused. We are just left to defend ourselves. When I think about everything they did to me now that I am a mother, I realize how terrible those actions were and what a life-changing impact they had on my sense of self. My grandmother was also raising the children of my uncle and aunts and they were all well fed and very happy. They would always call me "the ugliest person in the world" because I had darker skin than the rest of them. They would tell me that no one was going to marry me because I was so ugly. My mother would always call me a "whore", too, and I was too young to understand what that meant. She would only see me once a year during the big Christmas-type holiday where everyone gets together, and I would hide when everyone would come, which did not matter because nobody ever talked to me or even acknowledged me. My grandmother would never touch me. She was always so cold. She would call me a "whore" and would never call me by my name. I never understood why.

When I was five years old, I had to attend school as required by the Malaysian government. I was humiliated to attend because I would walk by myself to school and all I had to wear was hand-me-down clothing with holes in them. People used to call me "the jungle kid." All through my youth I was the poorest kid at school with the dirtiest clothes and everyone ridiculed me. If I wanted to take a shower to be clean, my grandmother would have a bowl of water and tell me that was all I could have. The hardest part was when I hit puberty and started menstruating because all I had to use was leaves to stop the bleeding. I had no one that could answer questions for me about puberty, womanhood, or anything for many years.

I only had two friends through my whole childhood and they were a monkey and a blind cat. I built a relationship with the monkey because she was the same age as I was. I never knew the gender of my cat, I just knew that it was blind. The three of us were always together as a "freak family" and I believe it was because we were unwanted creatures. The monkey had been abandoned when she was young and you could always see in her eyes that she looked lost. The blind cat was unwanted because of its blindness so no one believed it had any use.

My monkey was also abused very badly by people in my family. I remember seeing her cry when they would mistreat her. She did not cry like us humans where her shoulders would quake—I would just see tears coming out of her eyes. I would sit next to her on my porch, holding my blind cat and we would cry together. We also slept outside on that same porch my entire childhood because we were not allowed to be inside the house where the rest of the family lived.

My monkey was a brilliant creature! I used to have alphabet books and ask her to show me where the letter *A* was and she would show me. I don't know if she understood what I was saying, but when I would giggle she would laugh, too. It was like having a twin. Then the blind cat would sit there and make funny noises. We were so cute, just like a little abandoned family. On rainy days, we would huddle up together and at night we would cuddle together because I was always scared, due to cultural beliefs about ghosts and spirits. When I had my period as a young teenager, my family would tell me spirits would come to attack me because they sensed my blood. I used to see the image of a ghost and it would be so terrifying but my animals were always there to protect me.

I would never have lived through my childhood if it was not for my monkey. She was my playmate and my best friend. We used to go up the hill and pretend that a bad guy was coming to get us and play hide and seek. The condition of this particular game was in order to save each other we would make special sounds that were our own system of codes. She understood everything that I did. She was very smart. Primates have more intelligence than what we give them credit for and I believe in some parts of my life, my monkey was a role model for me. Sadly she ended up getting very sick and dying in my teen years when my blind cat died in a flood.

For most of my youth I was suicidal. I wondered why I was ever born if no one wanted me. Every day I tried to put myself in harm's way by attempting to drown myself and play with the poisonous snakes but nothing happened. As I grew older I realized that it was not my time—the universe had unfinished business that I had to do that kept me alive. I told myself that I wanted to be a successful person and I would do anything to ensure that happened.

After high school, I got exceptional scores on my final exam. I always did well in school because I knew being a successful student could get me out of my circumstances.

A NEW OPPORTUNITY

When I passed my final high school exam with exceptional scores, I was accepted to a university in Malaysia. I was thrilled because I wanted to be a lawyer. The only problem was I needed money to start off with for books and clothing. I could not wear rags at a university. I was also very thin when I was growing up because I was malnourished. These are not qualities you want a university to see because then they would think you are not the right fit and you will lose the opportunity to attend.

I went to all my uncles with my test scores in hand begging them and asking them for just a little money to help me attend the university. They would tell me: "No! Why should we give you money? Your parents are losers and you are going to be a loser, too." These were the words that they would give me of kindness and encouragement even after I had proven myself academically.

I remember at that point, I went to my teacher and told her that I was going to hang myself. My teacher immediately persuaded me not to and told me that through a contact, she could put me into culinary school. She suggested I attend school in the morning and work ten hours in the evening. I accepted her offer and from that opportunity, I became a chef in Asia and Southeast Asia. Not long after I attended culinary school, my teacher told me about a scholarship at a famous restaurant in Bangkok, Thailand, that would further strengthen my professional skills. I applied and was accepted when I was fifteen years old! It was the best thing that ever happened to me. Working in a hospitality profession was a blessing because I had the option to travel to new places to work. Every few months I got to travel to a new country and be part of the culture and the people. The experiences revitalized me into a cultured woman having emerged from the shell of a girl who grew up on her grandmother's porch. What always fascinated me about being a chef is the degree of importance people place on a position like that. When I would tell people where I worked they saw me in a sophisticated light. Finally, I was someone who mattered to people and was no longer the dirty, discarded "jungle kid" anymore.

I worked in Thailand for two years before I returned to Malaysia. At first I worked as an assistant chef for a celebrated restaurant in Kuala Lumpur, then I got to be a principal pastry chef so people started writing about me, praising the work I was doing. Yet, while working these great jobs, I was still sleeping on my grandmother's porch and my paycheck was still taken by my family. I simply could not say no. If I did they would beat me. I could not do anything about it since they had too much power over me back then. Imagine me traveling to Thailand and then back to Malaysia to the same situation of my family monopolizing me again. It was awful. At least with the culinary school I had a way out.

Although it was an excellent path, culinary school was not what I originally wanted to do. I always felt my true purpose was to be a lawyer and protect people who needed help. All over the world people suffer like I did. I believe there are three things a human should have: love, health, and education. When you have these three things, your life is solid and you will be happy no matter what situation you are facing. I want all people to have health, education, and love because all I had was my education in my life and it is what set me free.

That is why I still don't understand to this day why I allowed my family to still have power over me when I returned from Thailand. I became so dead to myself and was so terrified of them that I formed a habit of doing what they wanted me to. I had fifteen years of suffering horrible abuse at their hands that made me surrender myself to them. It takes time to break destructive patterns of behavior and essentially to realize that you are being abused.

MY NEW LIFE

I didn't stay under the ruling fist of my family forever. Shortly after I returned to Malaysia, I met my husband. He was a British man and we continued to date as I worked small stints in several other Asian countries. At the time I was back in Malaysia, I decided I wanted to get married. My husband was a wonderful man and I knew if I married him and moved away my family could not find me and I would never have to see them again. Interestingly enough, they all started being nice to me when I married a foreigner because they thought he was a millionaire! Suddenly I was somebody special in their eyes.

They all probably wondered what I did to get this foreigner. When I was working as an accomplished chef, I was still nothing to them. Though I was earning my own money, they still treated me like an animal. As soon as I met a man, I was something to them. This is interesting to me. Suddenly everyone came to me asking for forgiveness when I met a foreign man they perceived to be a millionaire.

After I married, I told my husband to leave the issue of my family alone. I did not want them affecting our relationship in any way. What could I say? If I said anything they would just deny everything and then what proof would I have for all that abuse? My scars? There is no physical proof for the sexual abuse. Before my wedding, they all came and asked for forgiveness and wanted me to get married in Malaysia. I told them that I would never forgive them. I look at some of my uncles now who hold high ranks in the government and they tell me that they wished they had given me money back then to get into college. I tell them that I am accomplished now and that I don't need their help anymore. I tell them that I will never ask again. I say these things to them with a smile as I have always taken my challenges with a smile. You can cry, be sad, and fall down one day but the next day you have to get up. Nobody in this world cares about that except for you. Nobody will love you as much as you love yourself. You can have ten best friends and a great husband but he will never love you as much as you love yourself. You have to care about yourself because nobody cares about you as much as you care about yourself. I cannot emphasize that more.

After I got married, I moved to New York City in the United States where my husband lived and worked. I gave birth to my children and I vowed to myself that I would never subject them to the childhood that I had. I did not want them growing up in such a hateful environment. I did all the best I could as a parent because I wanted to be the complete opposite of my parents.

I made the choice to share only the positive memories of my life with my children. When I take them back to Malaysia, they run barefoot and chase after the komodo dragons, poke crocodiles to see whether they are alive, touch the snakes, climb the trees, and swim in the river. My children relive only the best parts of my childhood through my stories. I do not share any darkness with them.

I think in my teenage years, I learned to put the bad and negative stuff behind me and only think about the good things. I only see good things in people and I am not prejudiced toward people because that is not the way of thinking that I have. I just try to love the good memories of my childhood: my blind cat and my monkey, the beautiful, exotic nature and the fruit trees. When I was sleeping outside of the house it was silent at night and I would talk and sing to myself. It was like I was in my own little world.

I now am on decent terms with my parents and financially providing for some of my family back home. They love my kids, but it's very strange for me to go back and see them because I don't understand why they love my kids but never loved me. I always ask questions and they never have any answers. I don't understand why I still give them money and have so much compassion, especially for people who hurt me. Yet, I also have this poisonous side where I don't forgive people. The amusing aspect of all of this is the "jungle kid" ended up being the savior to all these people. I find it interesting that I am giving them money but no forgiveness. Even after all the abuse I endured at their hands, I still can't let them starve. They can have my money, but they will never have my forgiveness. They will never receive redemption for all the harm they caused me.

So that is the short version of my story and through all those things I am who I am today.

I want my children to follow who I am and be good people. I don't like remembering all those bad things from my childhood because it's all in a dark box for me. I don't want to open that box because the effect it has for me is too devastating. I can feel the pain physically that I felt when they would sexually and physically abuse me. I can hear when people said derogatory things to me all over again. When I talk about it, it's very hurtful and I don't want to live in those painful memories. We tend to either fall down and bring ourselves back up or we just fall down and stay down. I choose to get back up and keep moving because no one is going to choose to love me like I love myself.

As you can see, I have always only had myself. I think my story is proof that loving yourself is more important than anything because all you have is yourself in the end. Please do not forget that. It is the single most important lesson in life for any woman. I believe so much in myself and what I do. I love myself and every woman should have that. Nothing should stop them; nothing should break them down because they should be tenacious. The only thing that can break us is ourselves. That is it. Who else can break you? Nobody.

I have been like a Cinderella in some ways, in my own crazy way. That is why I could not die back then even when I tried to kill myself. I had this journey to go through first.

ZARA'S ADVICE FOR WOMEN
If I met a woman in a very challenging period in her life, I would tell her to look for the best in herself. She needs to brush all the negativity aside and stand up for herself. If she needs to crawl then she will crawl and then slowly stand up. When she stands up, she needs to stride.

NAW WAH PAW

—As told to Sarah Matsushita of WEAVE Women

Burma[6]

Naw Wah Paw's story illustrates common challenges faced by the Burmese women of the Umpiem Mai refugee camp that is situated on the border between Thailand and Burma. The military government regime in Burma is one of the most oppressive and abusive in the world. Naw Wah Paw is part of a minority group known as the Karen, a group that has been under attack in its villages by Burmese government forces for several decades.

Many Karen accuse the Burmese government of ethnic cleansing due to mass atrocities against the Karen people, including summary execution, severe torture, rape, forced labor, extortion, and displacement. As a result of the violence over the years, as

---

[6] Burma has undergone several changes in name and in 1989 became the Republic of the Union of Myanmar, or simply Myanmar.

many as 400,000 Karen have fled through the hills and jungles of northeast Burma across the border into Thailand, seeking refuge. This pattern of migration has continued for decades.

After fighting erupted in November 2010 between government troops and the opposition Democratic Karen Buddhist Army as a result of the country's first national elections in two decades, more than 10,000 refugees from eastern Burma fled to Thailand. According to UNHCR, the border areas of Thailand currently host some 84,900 registered refugees and an estimated 62,000 unregistered asylum-seekers from Burma in nine camps along the Thai-Burma border. The government of Thailand considers the refugees to be illegal immigrants, so they are not allowed to work or venture outside the camps. Women who do so run the risk of being raped and exploited.

MY NAME IS Naw Wah Paw and I am fifty-nine years old. I'm from a small town in Karen State, Burma, on the border of Thailand. For many years, there was often fighting in my area between the Burmese military and the Karen army. I was always afraid and couldn't sleep because of the gunshots. Finally in 1984, I could no longer stay and had to cross the border into Thailand to escape.

Although we are safer in these camps, we are still vulnerable at times to raids and other threats. In 1995 and again in 1997, my camp was attacked by the Democratic Karen Buddhist Army, a splinter group of the Karen army that turned against Christian Karen like myself. I came to the Umpiem Mai camp in 1997 after my first refugee camp was burned down. I have been here for over ten years and I stay because I have no choice; the enemy will shoot us if we try to return to Burma. Even after all these years, Burma is still not safe.

In the camps we are stateless people without legal status, confined to their barbed-wire territory. I don't have any papers to live or work in Thailand and I can't go back home again. I'm stuck. At both camps I haven't had work. I was told I couldn't climb the mountain to work or gather food because of my illegal status. Anyone from the camps who obtains work off-site on nearby farms does not receive protection under any laws, and is extremely vulnerable to exploitation, harassment, and arrest. It can be especially dangerous for women as sexual harassment and rape are common. If this happens to us, we have no recourse.

Because it's safer to stay inside the camp and jobs in the camp aren't easy to find, I work through WEAVE. Without this, I would have no income. Through WEAVE, I perform some sewing though there isn't enough work.

I learned sewing when I was thirteen years old and used to go to a neighbor's house in the summer. At first, I learned so I could make beautiful clothes. I never realized how important that skill would become later in life and how it would help me make a living. Now I need the money badly. I'm also happy I can share my talents with other women because I enjoy teaching others how to sew. The only difficult part is that sometimes new sewers aren't careful and their ways can become bad habits. My teacher was very strict and I'm the same.

Now that my children are grown, I use my earnings for church tithing and money for poor families in the camps. When I see that their children don't have shirts for school, I buy some for them. I have income now, so I can share with other women who are like me when

I first entered the camps. They are scared and do not have any possessions since most of them came here to run away from the fighting and violence in Burma. The best I can do for them is to teach them skills to help them earn income. I was them before. I know how scary the camps are when you first arrive.

I'm happy making special products that are traditional and handmade. I like our Karen style of making crafts and clothing—the different patterns, the way of making pieces, and the good thread we use to make them original and special. In the WEAVE program, women can use their own skills and talents. Sewing also helps us preserve our culture since we can't return to our country. In many ways, it is all we have left of who we are. Some people know about the difficulties Karen people face and this can help us explain. People can show our products and be proud of them because we put a lot of meaning into them.

But there's another reason I make the beautiful things I make: I want customers to support our women, most of whom are women who have small children and have no other way to earn money to support themselves. Depression exits here. When women get bored, they lose ambition and don't have anything to do. It starts to destroy them. We are confined within the walls of this place. We don't have a country, a state, or a province. We have a camp. That is all. Once we are here, we can never leave. We will never go home.

I want all the women here to have a better life. Through the programs offered by WEAVE, I can gather more women and fight depression. Our work doesn't just earn us money—it helps us help other women. I have no dreams for the future as I am limited to where I am. I want only to do what I can and help others because that is the best I can do with what I have. But my dream for the women here is to stay safe, have jobs, and keep their families together. My dream for the children of Umpiem Mai camp is to leave this place and make their lives outside these walls.

NAW WAH PAW'S ADVICE FOR WOMEN

Women should do their best, work together, and pray for their communities.

Author's Note: About WEAVE (Women's Education for Advancement and Empowerment)

Founded in 1990, WEAVE is a nonprofit organization that helps and supports the needs of marginalized women along the Thai-Burma border. WEAVE advances the status of women and children to become socially, economically, and politically empowered.

Through WEAVE's Income Generation Program (IGP), women like Naw Wah Paw can earn safe and regular income, support their families and community, and stay healthy, both physically and mentally. This kind of livelihood project is essential because it provides fair and consistent wages in a safe environment.

WEAVE purposely designed IGP to be run by displaced women for displaced women, with leaders selected in each camp to oversee day-to-day activities and gather women artisans together. Naw Wah Paw is a member of the six-woman Quality Control (QC) team in her camp and helps build a network of women who come from similar backgrounds and have experienced the trauma of displacement. Participants can draw on this network for strength and support, and, like Naw Wah Paw, have hope for the future.

GENNIE

Philippines

Born in Manila and raised in the United States in a Catholic Filipino community, Gennie illustrates her struggles as a pregnant young teenager and how she navigated two abusive relationships.

DOMESTIC VIOLENCE IS not just a concept, but a horrific reality that women all over the world live with every day. I experienced it in two separate relationships and now I have decided to tell the truth about my past and to tell my story with the hope that it will encourage other women to leave these situations. For all the women out there struggling, I want to say: *There is hope.*

I was born in Manila, Philippines, in an educated, middle-class family. My mother was a doctor and knew that she and my father would have better job opportunities in the United States so we immigrated here during my childhood.

I grew up in a community of Catholic Filipino immigrants. My family, especially my father, was very strict because of our cultural beliefs. In my teenage years he was vehemently opposed to my dating men and would go to the extreme to prevent me from seeing anyone. On one occasion, he even followed my boyfriend and me and removed the fuses from my car, then called the police and told them that I was an "uncontrollable child." When I tried to return home, I found I was locked out of our house.

To his disgust, I started dating another guy in my high school years to be rebellious and my family did not like it at all; he was Mexican and his family didn't have as much money as our family did. I ended up getting pregnant during our relationship and that was a big problem because I was still in high school at the time attending an all-girls Catholic high school. I remember the school counselors suggesting that I tell my parents about the pregnancy, but I was terrified to tell them. Being Catholic, I thought they would want me to keep the child but that was not the case. Since my mother was a doctor, she believed it was bad for me to get pregnant so young so she wanted me to have an abortion. This subject is very taboo in our culture due to our Catholic faith, so I was shocked. My father was really upset about the pregnancy because I was young and not married. I think in my mind I already knew that they were going to throw me out so I already had my bags packed before that conversation. The day I told them, I moved out. My father didn't want to see me so I started living with the guy's parents until things took a turn for the worse.

My boyfriend was beating me while I was pregnant with my daughter and he became so abusive that I had to move back home to get away from him. It started when we were living together and were always around each other. We were going through life together and that creates tension sometimes. He reacted to that tension in more violent ways than the average person would. He also had domestic violence in his family background and witnessed his own father beating up his mother. I didn't realize he was that way until he would get into arguments with me and he would suddenly become a different person filled with so much rage and anger. My friends were very concerned for me at the time and for the baby. They forced me to go and talk to my school counselor who then went and talked to my parents in order for me to move back home. I had come to school with black eyes and bruises and I would wear sunglasses to cover them up. I was at least four or five months pregnant at the time. He never hit me in the stomach, only in the face. Fortunately it never caused me to lose the baby, in spite of the fact that there was a lot of crying, yelling, and screaming.

There was a time frame of one or two months where I was living back with my family and I didn't see him. I was in the process of getting a restraining order against him because I was so afraid of what he would do.

In addition to that trauma, my father also disowned me and that was really difficult. My mother wanted me to have an abortion but that thought horrified me so I decided to keep the baby. I am glad that I decided to do that because now my daughter is my best friend and my parents love her. Back when I was first pregnant with her, they did not want to have anything to do with me. Even after I moved back home, my father told me that if I started to go into labor I needed to call my friends because he didn't want to take me to the hospital. He would not even speak to me or look at me. It was as if I did not exist.

In fact, I did end up calling my friend when I went into labor and she took me to the hospital. I had some really good friends in high school as there were only a few people that knew about the pregnancy. My high school was predominantly white. There were only a few of us that were Asian, Mexican, and African American and they were my group of friends. They kept my secret and took care of me at a time when my family would not and my own father disowned me.

This group of friends sent a petition to the principal to request that they keep me in school. Generally, they would kick a girl out of school if she became pregnant out of wedlock. The principal told them that she did not want to know who I was and only under that condition would she keep me in school. I hid the pregnancy under big shirts and played it off as though I had just gained a lot of weight.

I ended up graduating in the last trimester of the pregnancy. I was ready to burst out at my graduation and I didn't care. I just let it all hang out. I already had my diploma anyway! Who cared what people thought of me!

After my daughter was born I was living with my parents again. I was not talking to my child's father at the time and I received a call from one of his sisters that he had been in a motorcycle accident and passed away. He was drinking and the driver was smoking marijuana and a car hit both of them. When that happened I was shocked because our daughter had just been born. My baby's father was dead! After the funeral, I realized that I was truly alone. I kept wondering what I was going to do. At that point there was an agreement made with my parents for me to go to school and cut off all contact and communication with the family of my child's father. I had to make a decision regarding what was best for my child. I agreed only because I was going to go back to school and they were going to help take care of her. The day I explained this to his family, I felt terrible. They were fine with it; I think they did not know what to do to help me at that point. From there I worked to get the pieces of my life back together.

MY SECOND ABUSIVE RELATIONSHIP

Several years after the death of my daughter's father and my recovery from a tumor in my thymus gland, I entered the worst relationship of my life. I was very vulnerable when I met him and had no idea who he would turn out to be. We met because he owned a cell-phone company and he gave me one of the phones he was selling. At that point, little did I suspect, he was taking down all of my vital personal information: date of birth, social security number, address, and phone number. He was also researching me and at that point in my life I had excellent credit. Years later, after I found out about a woman from China whom he hurt after me, I would come to the conclusion that he preys on Asian women. Asian women are too trusting. We are established in our lives and know how to handle money because we like nice things. At the time, I felt there was no reason for me not to trust him so I did.

Everything happened so fast between us. After we had been seeing each other for a few months, he suddenly wanted to move into my house. At first he was very romantic and charming and wanted to please me in any way. He presented a façade of having a successful business and living lavishly. All of these things were just illusions as to who he really was.

He moved in very quickly and started wanting to take control of everything in my life. He knew not only my social security number, but those of my family members as well. I had a file cabinet in the house where I kept everything personal; he dug into it and stole all of this information. He stole money sitting in an account that was for my daughter and me from the death of her father. That money was supposed to be given to her when she turned eighteen years old. It was supposed to pay for her education but somehow he got a hold of that and invested it into some stocks, subsequently losing it. When I called to ask where the money went, the person on the phone told me that my name was not even on the account he opened. I was flabbergasted! They would not allow me access to the account yet it was my daughter's money! There was very little money in there compared to what had been in there before.

I freaked out on him after I discovered that it was all missing. I called him and demanded to know what was going on. At that point I didn't know what to do. He was trying to calm me down and he told me he had moved it into the account thinking it would go threefold and that he would just give me back the money. Somehow he was going to invest it and make it amount to more. He was basically gambling my daughter's money. I started panicking and that is when he told me that he wanted us to be together and that he wanted to marry me. I was shocked but I agreed because it was the only way I felt I could keep hold of him until I figured this out on my own. It sounds illogical, but I thought if I cooperated then I could find a way out. Instead, things only got worse.

I opened a women's apparel store in San Francisco, California during the dot-com era. At that time, we were making a lot of money because of the industry, yet I would come home and he would tell me there was no money. I had no idea what he was talking about. I was seeing money fly into the store and had no idea where it was going because he insisted on managing the accounting and I was not very computer savvy. All of our arguments were about money. Before long, I knew nothing about my own accounting books and he would not let me get into the accounts. I asked to see paperwork and he would never show me. Our fights were getting worse and worse and eventually they escalated to his punching me and threatening to kill me. By that time I was terrified of what he was capable of.

We got married in 1998, which was only about three months into our living together. I knew deep inside that it was not the right thing to do. I remember crying right before I got married. My friend who was with me asked me over and over if I was sure about my decision. I still did it anyway and we eloped. I thought I was covered because I went to the notary with him and got him to sign a paper saying that he owed me my daughter's money. I was never able to find that paper again. He married me legally by writing another name on the marriage license. He mixed up the letters in his last name for the sake of anonymity. I tried to annul the marriage years later but found out that it would not help me with my ruined credit. He was so sly that years later I still had to endure the aftermath of this. The bad credit that I ended up with never affected him.

After a while the physical abuse escalated to extremes. The worst thing I remember him doing was putting a pillow over my head in an attempt to choke me to death. He was almost successful. That was when I decided I could not sleep in the same bedroom as he did because I was afraid he would do something to me at night. I went and slept with my daughter and kept a knife under the bed just in case. My daughter was a teenager at this point and I have always felt terrible that she had to go through this with me. He was abusive verbally to her. It was terrible but it had to get to that point for me to leave. My friends did not understand why I didn't just leave the relationship. Walking away from a sociopathic man fills you with fear because you don't know what he is capable of. Some women can't get out of it until it's too late. I went to church and prayed during that time. I tried to understand what was happening. I was buried in his deceit and was terrified of him.

Near the end of this marriage, we were arguing almost every night. He would slap me but I am a fighter and I would fight back. After a couple of big hits, I made the decision to not sleep with him anymore and keep my mouth shut. I didn't need to tell him what I was doing. I knew I just needed to figure out where the money was going and knew there had to be some sort of paper trail or something that he was not telling me about. Once there was a receipt on the table, but he saw me looking at it so he grabbed it right away. I knew immediately that it was an account, because I knew he had accounts open behind my back. When I went to the bank, I was able to see what he was doing. He tried to make my women's apparel store a corporation. He also tried to use my mother's name for another transaction. He told me he would make me sell my house and threatened to commit insurance fraud by setting it on fire if I did not comply.

I finally reached the breaking point when I came home one day to realize that an exercise machine I had in the house was gone! He had sold it. I was furious and started yelling at him, demanding him to tell me where it went. I got in my car that he was using and started looking for receipts and papers when he looked out the window and saw me. He came running toward me and I tried to lock the doors. He pried open the door and got in the car and we started driving around. While he was driving he was hitting me with his fists. Luckily I had just spoken to my girlfriend before that and told her what I was doing and how I planned to inspect the car. I pressed speed dial and called her again and screamed for her to call the police. In the meantime we were still fighting in the car. I remember getting up out of the car to free myself. He came around and was about to punch me when this large man walking by saw him and immediately rushed up to us and stopped him. My ex screamed at me, "Get in the fucking car!" I got back in and he drove us home. When we got home I practically fell out of the car because I was running so fast and he scrambled away because the police were there. Thank God my friends had called them. I had a bloody nose from his fists pounding me. The police took a report and that was the end of it. I decided then and there that this man was out of my life for good! That was the only way I would be able to get him out of the house. The police placed a twenty-four-hour restraining order for me and arrested him later at the police station when he came in to find out if there was a warrant against him.

He had ruined my credit. I was trying to keep the credit-card collectors from calling me. Thank goodness he was not able to take my business and my house, though if I had stayed in the marriage longer I think he would have managed that as well. We went through a divorce and even in court he was acting like he hadn't done anything! This man showed up in court to try to get himself out of the whole thing. In fact, he attempted to brush it off as "Oh, the woman just mismanaged everything. I told her to stop and she just kept spending and spending." This even happened for the hearing on the restraining order. I thought he would not show up for that, and could not believe he would try to fight me on that, too!

For the years following that mess, my daughter and I still lived in fear. I thought he might find a way to come after me. We walked around everywhere with mace. We were on edge. The restraining order was for ten years and since then has expired.

Immediately after me, I guess he met another woman. I only know this because she came to my store one day. It was about five years after the mess subsided. At first she looked like any other customer and then she asked if she could talk to me. She started sobbing and asked if I knew the same man. I watched her trembling as she told me her whole story; one that horrifically sounded like my own. She was from China. This man preys on Asian women. He is a professional con artist. She told me that her family hated her and disowned her because he stole all of their money. I started crying and then I was scared. What if he knew I was talking to her? I realized that I could not continue to interact with her. I was too afraid of what he would do if he found out. Mainly, I was afraid for my daughter's life and I did not want him to do anything to hurt her.

PAYING MY DEBT

In the meantime, I was struggling to get "above water" and keep myself from drowning in the debt that he caused me. He had put everything in my name so all the debt was attributed to me. I had to try to track down all the damage he had done. It was terrible to try to explain to creditors what had happened. He charged so much stuff and I owed hundreds of thousands of dollars. This is how my life led me down the next path.

I am a spiritual person. I was raised Catholic, but I don't go to church every Sunday. I do believe in God and the Catholic saints, angels, life and death. I was very close to two of the Catholic saints growing up: St. Jude and St. Theresa. St. Theresa had answered my prayers a couple of times before and at this point I was going through such a hard time and reached out to her again. I was about to make a decision that in being a Catholic would be seen as very sinful and wrong. I was so desperate that I realized the only way to make the money back quickly was to become an escort. I saw an advertisement about it and although it felt morally wrong, I was drowning in debt and needed to get my head above water.

I prayed and told God that I had to do this and I asked God to keep me safe. I asked that I would meet a good person, the right person to take me through all of this and help me straighten things out.

I was practically shaking when I went to go meet the woman in charge of the escort operation. It was a very ritzy place. The woman was surprised in meeting me because I was a bit older than most of the girls who usually did this kind of thing. I didn't care if they turned me away because I felt so terrible about doing it in the first place but the woman did not turn me away. In fact, she was very businesslike in how she handled the operation. She was telling me that I could be very successful as an escort. They were planning on putting a lot of the girls through a training course of sorts—a course about where the best restaurants are in town and how to entertain a man. They had a sheet of paper of "what means what" in the sexual world. It was never actually spoken, but it was implied that we would have sex with clients. They never mentioned anything directly about sex and I tried to ask them if that is what we had to do and they just said, "It's up to you. It's just a date." They were offering to pay 200 dollars per hour for a minimum of two hours. A driver would pick you up and they would pay you half that money up front.

The first call I got I was very nervous. I was just praying that everything would be okay. I felt an enormous amount of guilt deep down inside. I was supposed to be this nice Catholic girl and here I was about to do what my whole upbringing was against. I met the man at his house, driven by a limousine. Then we went to a restaurant where we had dinner and talked. He said to me, "You don't look like you do this all the time" and I broke down and confessed the reasons I was there. The interesting part was that he gave me a rose. St. Theresa always answers your prayers through roses. That was a shock to me. I felt so safe and cared for after I saw the rose, as strange as that may sound. He was an older European man from Switzerland and most of the older European men calling escorts just wanted company. While we ate and talked he propositioned me. He suggested that I exclusively meet with him once a week instead of going through the agency and that he would just pay me directly. I did not ask him if that meant we would have sex, but somehow I knew that it did. I was right. We became intimate.

He was a very nice man and he ended up really liking me. He took me everywhere: to Europe—Portugal and Switzerland—and I met some of his family. Eventually he wanted me to stay with him and told me that he would take care of me. I just could not do that. I wanted to have my own life and my own job and there were times where he wanted me to tell him that I loved him and I could not. Those words just could not come out of my mouth. He was in his seventies when I was seeing him so I knew he did not want to get married; he just wanted me to be his companion. He also helped me get out of the debt situation that I was in and I will always be grateful about that. This arrangement went on for a while but I eventually had to end it because I met the love of my life and it did not feel right anymore.

It was hard to date other men while seeing him. For me, this was a business arrangement, and mixing business and pleasure was too hard. Finally I sat down and talked to him and honestly confessed that I could not do it anymore. He was an older gentleman so he understood that I wanted a life of my own. He was never angry or disrespectful about any of my decisions. In fact, he really was a wonderful man—very caring and kind, gentle, and compassionate. He helped me out of financial trauma while being someone that I could talk to. He really embodied many of the qualities a "good man" would have. I have never had any negative feelings after walking away from our arrangement.

Eventually I met the love of my life and we are now married. He knows everything about my past and everything I have done and has accepted me for who I am without passing judgment on anything that I did. I am so lucky to have him in my life.

I am in my forties now and I am very happy and optimistic. The man who ruined my life is still out there and at large. I am sure he is still preying on other women as I speak. I am praying that they will leave him before he takes from them what he took from me.

I was once a little girl from the Philippines. My life has not been easy by any means but I have arrived from the traumatic experiences a solid person: a good wife, mother, and still a business owner. I am so thankful every day for what I have now. I can't wait for all the good years that are coming!

GENNIE'S ADVICE FOR WOMEN

Really go with your gut. You will always have the right answer for yourself deep down inside. We want so much to be loved that sometimes we are desperate. You need to also love yourself so that you do not become so desperate.

CENTRAL ASIA

CENTRAL ASIA

HEBA

Afghanistan

Afghanistan has been at war for over thirty years and for various reasons. For three decades, the country has experienced near complete destruction of all infrastructure and a mass exodus of Afghan refugees in neighboring countries. In her story, Heba narrates her struggle to survive after losing her beloved husband and the courageous, yet devastating, choice she had to make concerning her young son. Heba dreams of the day she will be reunited with her son and continue her life in peace.

MY NAME IS Heba, and I am from Afghanistan. Before I tell you about myself, I want to ask you a question: Do you know what it feels like to lose everything? I do. I have lost everything twice in my life, but I am strong because of God and the wonderful family and friends I have in my life. God has always taken care of me; I am a very lucky person.

I was born in Kabul, Afghanistan. My parents were very educated people who worked for the government. Life was pleasant until the early 2000s when the Taliban took over in Kabul and my family had to run away from all of the fighting and violent threats.

I was just a young girl at the time, so were my other siblings. We fled with our parents over the mountains to a refugee camp in Pakistan. Life in this camp, as I remember, was terribly difficult. My family lived in a tent, and the conditions of the camp were very dirty. I remember that the lights would go out a lot and there was never enough food. Sometimes in the night, I could hear girls being taken from their tents. They would scream, and we could hear them, but there was nothing we could do. It was so hard to hear. There were also groups of criminals that would come in and take things from everyone in the camp. This was a very hard life for our family, especially for my parents. It was hard for them to go from having an education, jobs, a house, and food to living in these conditions.

You can imagine that I was thankful when my family moved to an apartment and away from the camp. Even though we had better living arrangements, life was still very hard for us, because we did not have any money and faced a lot of discrimination for being Afghans. For years, there were so many who had fled Afghanistan because of wars that Pakistan became overrun by Afghan people, but the Pakistanis don't want us there. Even though we are educated people, there was no work for my family. We had to sell vegetables on carts in order to survive. One of the worst days I remember was when the police came and destroyed all of the vegetables my father had to sell and then they beat him. Another time, our landlord broke into our house and stole all of our things. It was a hard way to live, because we felt like nobody wanted us there. We had fled to Pakistan to be in a safer place, but we did not feel safe. It was as if there was nowhere we could go. We had no refuge.

We were living in Islamabad, a city several miles from the tribal areas and a territory known as Waziristan.

When I was sixteen, a man came to our house in Pakistan, wanting to marry me. At first, I was a bit afraid of him because I had never dated any boys before. In Afghan culture, our view on dating is very different than other countries. We have arranged marriages, where the parents of both the boy and girl decide they will marry. Women and men do not date; in fact, that is forbidden. When both families agree to marriage, there is an engagement party and then the official wedding party, which is a three-day event with a lot of celebration. The women wear beautiful, vibrant, and bright-colored dresses. There is a lot of food, and people dance through all hours of the night. It is a very exciting time! When I married my husband, our wedding was beautiful. There were hundreds of guests from all around Afghanistan, and all of our family members were there to celebrate with us. At that point, I stopped being shy around my husband, because I was able to see that he was a good man with a kind heart. I knew he would take care of me and be respectful and kind to me. I felt lucky to have such a good man in my life. At this point, I knew that I loved him, too, and I could be very happy with him. Soon after the wedding, I became pregnant with our son and moved back to Kabul, Afghanistan, with him.

When our son was born, he cried so much that the nurse let him come back into the hospital room to see us. That is not normal for an Afghan man, but my husband was an extraordinary person. He had a pure heart and was very kind and intelligent. He was forward thinking and believed in making Afghanistan a better country for our future generations.

Many people living outside of Afghanistan only see very bad Afghan men in the news. They only hear tragic and violent stories. My husband was not one of these men; he loved me and my son. He wanted me to go to school and get an education, and he even wanted me to have a good job. He would buy me anything I wanted just to make sure I was happy.

My husband worked for the American military and NATO for many years. He had many different jobs: cook, restaurateur, and chauffeur. He worked for them because he believed in the future of Afghanistan and wanted our son to have opportunities that we did not have. He was a progressive thinker with many American friends, and he liked the Americans because they had very new and different ideas. He even started celebrating American holidays, like Valentine's Day, when he bought me a necklace one year. American people would come into our house and share meals with us sometimes, and I would get the chance to speak English with them.

I remember when he worked as a chauffeur. He was always worried about roadside bombs and afraid he would run over one of them when he was driving. It was a very trying lifestyle to work the jobs that he did. He was so brave to give everything he gave for what he believed in. Unfortunately, in the process, he managed to anger certain individuals with connections to the Taliban.

I don't remember exactly when the problems with a certain man began. He did not like my husband at all and especially did not like the fact that he was working for the Americans. He threatened us in different ways and distributed propaganda around town claiming that my husband was a bad man, which caused people to turn against him. This man owned a business which he purchased jointly with my husband. Soon, he stopped giving us money for it and started distributing a lot of Taliban and anti-American propaganda regarding activities against my husband. These items described how my husband worked on relief projects with the U.S. Army and NATO forces. Day by day, this made life more difficult for my husband and family. We received threats, until he finally decided to take me and our son back to Islamabad, Pakistan, where he left us and returned to continue his job. He was gravely concerned about our safety, and I had asked my husband many times to stop working in this area. He was traveling to some of the most dangerous provinces, such as Ghazni and Kandahar, but was very adamant to continue his work. He often told me that he was not afraid of the propaganda and had to continue working in order to help his country and relieve the suffering of our people. He would not give up.

Those working for westerners are targeted by rebels and Taliban supporters. This is why the improvement of Afghanistan can be a nearly impossible goal in most cases. There are some people in that country who do not want anything to change. Even the good Afghan people, like my husband, who want things to be better, face many hardships because of what they believe. It is a difficult environment.

On the final night of his life, so I'm told, my husband went to check on his business and then disappeared. A few days later, I received a call from Kabul that his body was found. This was an excruciating day for me and my family. I was devastated. He was a wonderful man and did not deserve for this to happen to him. I cried so much, I feared I damaged my eyes. Why would they do this to him? Why! Worse yet for myself, what could I do to take care of my son? It is very difficult for women to find any kind of work in Afghanistan or Pakistan, and I was forced to move back in with my family in Islamabad, Pakistan, so I would have a place to live. After moving back to Pakistan, I thought my problems would go away, but they did not. They followed me and only continued to get worse.

It was not long after my husband's funeral that the men responsible for his death came to my family's house in Islamabad. The man who was responsible for my husband's death (the one with the propaganda) told me I had to marry him. I was furious. How could this man come and propose such a thing to me? Because of him my husband was gone! I prayed to God, asking him why I was in this situation. I told this man, "Absolutely not," and that I refused to marry him because he was a criminal and a murderer. He told me I did not have a choice and informed me that he would be back in a few days to get me and take me with him. I refused to go.

At this time, I was very afraid for my son. I tried to start a life in Islamabad. I started attending college to learn about business. I tried to continue to do what I would have done if my husband were alive. When I went to school, I would wear a black burqa so no one could see my face. I was always afraid these men were following me and would try to kidnap me.

These men continued to make threats. They came to my family's house and yelled into the door that they were going to kill me. My family was all in one room of our house, and we were all so scared. Worst of all, I worried if they took me away or something happened to me, my son would be in immediate danger. He was my main concern. I didn't want these men to take him from me and hurt him.

Eventually, I stopped leaving the house because I was always afraid that something would happen if I did. I knew these men would kidnap me if they had the chance, and I could not risk that happening. I was very sad staying in the house all the time, but the men would not leave me alone. I prayed all the time that my family and my son would be safe. I did not know what to do to escape all these problems; each day felt more hopeless than the next.

I had some family who came to the United States years ago and they were living in New York. I reached out to them and told them what was happening in Islamabad. They were praying for me every day and doing everything they could to try to help me. They told me I could live with them in New York if I wanted, so I decided that would be the only way out. When I went to get a visa, the man working in the embassy refused to give one to my son. I left crying, devastated because I knew I had to choose between leaving my son behind and remaining in Pakistan. Afghanistan and Pakistan were not options. My son and I would not be safe. So I made the hardest decision I ever made in my life: I had to leave my son behind. I felt horrible and guilty. At first, I felt like a bad mother, but I knew I had to do this for both of us. It was our only chance at a much better life. I do not want for my son to have a life like I have had. I don't want him to suffer and live in fear. I want him to have an education and to be able to live somewhere where he is safe. If I wanted all of those things for him, I had to make the move. I knew it would be best for the longer path of our lives.

I got my visa and boarded a plane in the airport in Islamabad to New York City. I had never flown on an airplane before and was very nervous, but I could only think about my son. I kept crying because he was left behind. I worried if he would have food to eat or if the men would come back and try to take him away from my family. Praying as the plane took off, I knew I was leaving my problems behind, but I still had a long road ahead of me.

I knew I would never be completely free from my worries because my family was still back in Pakistan with my son. Even though I am now more free, my heart and mind are not because they are still so attached to my son. Even when I landed in the United States, I was still filled with fear.

Although I had never visited the United States, I studied English in Afghanistan and Pakistan, so I knew a little bit when I arrived. Everything was so different, and so much larger than Afghanistan and Pakistan. It was a new world and a new beginning, but without my son by my side.

At night, I would lie in bed and cry. My thoughts centered around my husband, my son, and how powerless I felt that I could not send my son money or help him. I had officially lost everything and was even depending on family for food and a place to stay. I prayed a lot—all of the time—and did not understand why God did this to me and why my family was suffering so much. I just prayed to God that he would help me and bring my son to me. I can't wait to see him again.

I met many good friends in the United States. Many American women were very kind to me, and having these friendships is so positive because they help me forget about my troubles and worries. My son and I have been apart for over one year now. Every minute without him is like a breath without oxygen. I am choking slowly with him so far away. One day, we were on Skype and he said, "Mommy, show me your fridge." I walked over and showed him all of the food. He said, "I am hungry; we have only water in our fridge." I cried when he told me that because there is nothing I can do for him as an immigrant woman trying to adjust here. I cannot find work, and it's hard for me to send him money.

At this point, I have lost everything. However, I believe I will slowly put all of the pieces of my life back together. I believe that one day my son will be here with me and years from now, he will get an education and a really great job where he is earning good money. This is what keeps my hope alive—thinking about these things and knowing that one day I will see him again.

I didn't ask for these things to happen to me. Even though I am young, I was strong through each of these experiences. I was strong because God gave me strength and because I had to be for my son. Sometimes there is no warning for what you will face in your life. You just have to find the strength inside and ask God for it.

In America, I can walk down the streets without fear that someone is following me. I am grateful for this. You have no idea what freedom this is until you are in a situation like I was.

I do not know what will happen in my life, but I am sure God will take care of me. I don't know what will happen to my family, and I pray every day that they will be okay and will have food to eat. I pray that one day, in a few years, they will all be here safe with me. This is my only hope right now. It is a hope that never dies.

HEBA'S ADVICE FOR WOMEN
Believe in God. Be strong. Be powerful. Believe in yourself.

Author's Note: Heba is now reunited with her son. They began a new life together where he is excelling in school.

LARISA

Uzbekistan

Uzbekistan is a landlocked country located in Central Asia. A former part of the Soviet Union, its economy depends heavily on agriculture and its predominant religion is Islam. Larisa details her mother's transition to Uzbekistan after marriage and common cultural barriers Uzbek women still struggle to break.

M Y NAME IS Larisa, and this story is about my dear mom. The more I have traveled and met many international people, the more I realized that many of them look up to their parents as role models. For most young women, the main role model in their lives is their mother. Why do we adore our mothers? Because most of the time our mothers are morally strong, patient, merciful, and forgiving. Moreover, they are homemakers, wives, mothers, and working professionals at the same time. In order to succeed, women have to be very flexible and learn how to balance all these responsibilities. This balance becomes more difficult when there are strong cultural limitations and expectations. This story about my own mother is perhaps the most inspiring story I have ever heard. She is an amazing woman.

My mom is Russian. She was born in a warm and sunny part of Russia called Rostov. She was born with partial dislocation of the joints in her pelvic area and was not able to walk until she had an operation at five years old. To this day she walks with a limp. She was always restricted in her activities and under strict parental control. Yet, her family never treated her differently because of her physical afflictions. My mom was raised in the Soviet Union's culture, where woman are expected to be a role model, a good housewife, a caring mother, and a responsible professional. There, women and men had equal rights. There was a strong mindset of idealism, as people in the society were always striving for the best. There were high moral values, but they were based on strong national beliefs in communism, fairness, and decency, not on any particular religion. There were countries in the Soviet Union where the culture was deeply religious such as Uzbekistan, Kazakhstan, Turkmenistan, and other regions in the Caucasus.

My dad is from Uzbekistan, a country with Islam-based culture, traditions, and language. My mother and father met in Russia when they studied together at a university. They dated for two years before they married. From this point, my mother's life changed completely. She became pregnant when she was finishing the last year of her bachelor's degree. My father returned to Uzbekistan to a small village not far from the Aral Sea and told my mother to move there when she finished at the university.

Their first child was a boy. My mother had just graduated from college when she and her newborn son moved to a new and unknown country.

My dad lived with his parents and the rest of his family in a small village about ten miles from the city. There was no natural gas, running water, or basic utilities for comfort. In addition to the lack of modern resources, no one spoke Russian, except for my dad and a couple of relatives. This was challenging for my mom, because she did not know how to speak the Uzbek language. She was also a city girl, so she had to learn how to take care of the cattle, work in the cotton field, cook Uzbek dishes (they did not accept Russian cuisine), and take care of my father's parents. When I asked my mom about this difficult part of her life, she shared the following story with me:

"When I was moving to Uzbekistan, I could not fully imagine how different it would be, since I had come from a city. Although it was a small Russian city, it still had all the basic utilities, a theater, a cinema, and people who had a positive quality of life. Then, suddenly, there I was in a small village without even a basic bathroom. However, these were not the most difficult discomforts. The hardest adaptation by far was when I had to quickly learn that wives of the family's sons, called "brides," didn't have many rights and played a secondary role in their families. There was not much communication with the "brides," because they were more like servants, there to do housework, give birth to children, and take care of the elders in the family. Coming from Russia where men and women both shared equal opportunities, I was new to all of this. I desperately wanted to know why certain things were done and why they were done in those specific ways. Unfortunately, there were not any explanations from the family, and basic communication was challenging because I didn't speak the Uzbek language. I spent entire days with my mother-in-law and other brides without understanding a word. Unfortunately, I cannot say that I have any particular talent for languages, even though later in my life I would understand more of the Uzbek language. Also, I needed clothes, toys, and other common materials for my children after they were born, but I felt ashamed to ask for the money since I did not work. My husband and rest of the men gave the money to my mother-in-law. She kept and managed all the money, so I never saw any of it. I knew I had to do something, so I decided to look for a job so I could get my children what they needed.

Finally, I got a job in a water purification plant. It was not the most pleasant job, but it gave me some income. My basic day was an early start spent milking a cow, then feeding chickens and the rest of the cattle before work. When I gave birth to my second son, I had to return to work from maternity leave early. To my dismay, during this time, nobody within this big family was looking after my youngest boy. Nobody fed him during the day, changed his diaper, or played with him. I could not comprehend the lack of respect toward the brides or even the children. There was not a loving, soft, and affectionate relationship between the mother and children like I was used to in my own family, and certainly not one between the fathers and children. Children are regarded for future support and household and agricultural help. They don't even have a playground or any toys. Also, people are pretty superstitious; if you try to do something outside of their common traditions, it is automatically regarded as a harmful or sinful thing.

When my older son grew up a little bit, he was circumcised; but it was done so carelessly that he became very ill, and they could not do much to treat him in this little village. That was the last drop of my patience. I gathered all my belongings, took a bus to the city, and found an apartment to rent. My husband did not move with me until I got a job and settled down. By that time, I already learned that my husband was incapable of making big decisions on his own, even if they concerned his wife and children, because he was very dependent on his family. Yet, I loved him and wanted to keep our family together, so I forgave him that time and many times later.

My husband's family was very surprised by what I did. It was unheard of that a wife would leave her husband and move to the city with children. They probably never saw anything like that before. I honestly didn't belong there, and I can say that, to them, I always was a strange Russian woman. Plus, I am not Muslim, so it was even more difficult for them to accept me. Finally, my relationship with my husband's family is okay. I still do not speak Uzbek, but my children do, so they are a little bit closer to the family now. I still visit them, but not that often, because when I lived in the village, my health worsened after lifting a lot of heavy things (the men did not even bother to help us) and as a result of giving birth to three children. As a result, there were some days when I could not walk at all, and I could not walk long distances. I am not sure if my husband really understood that I sacrificed my health for him—that I lived and did everything I was asked to do for his family. I gave respect to his parents, even when I was mistreated and disrespected by being a new bride in the house. He never comprehended it, because the same attitudes have existed in the culture for so many years."

This summarizes the story of my mom's first years in Uzbekistan. It touches some problems that existed for many years before, and, unfortunately, still exist now. Sons and their mothers play the first role in families. The wives, until they are in the husband's houses, exist with the rights of servants. Women are generally allowed to visit their parents once a week, but only if the husband gives his permission *and* after all the housework is done. The housework seems to be never ending. Every morning when the sun rises, the wife has to sweep the entire house. She also has to bow to every person that she or the family knows. Brides are never asked for their opinions because they are not regarded as important. Similar beliefs exist all over the world, especially in Asia. The Uzbek culture is not the only one where these beliefs are practiced.

Moreover, in my culture, having a second wife becomes common in a city environment. Of course, for Muslims, it might be allowed only under certain conditions; but my country is ruled by a constitution, so it is against the law. The husbands still do it behind their wives' backs. Imagine how these women feel! They are in the husband's house, suppressed and restricted in many ways, in addition to knowing that their husband has a second wife. I believe this is the result of arranged marriages by the parents and the nonacceptance of divorce in the culture. Until recent years, there were too many obstacles for youth to create their family with whom they want and how they want because parents tend to dictate the way of life, especially to their sons. This aspect of the culture is slowly changing with each new generation.

In my culture, we have a low divorce rate. Most couples will not divorce due to family pressure (children and cultural stereotypes) that acts to keep the family together. This can be a good or bad thing, depending on the reason for divorce. Of course, in rare cases, couples stay together because they love each other. After some time, the husband and wife adjust to each other, and this relationship might turn into a strong family. At the end of the day, the most important thing for women is family, and if the husband is a good provider for her children and the rest of the family, she often forgives him and closes her eyes to many unpleasant things.

Another astonishing fact is that women who once had the experience of being a young bride, who went through all these difficulties and struggles, do the same to the wives of their sons. It is a closed circle. Unless someone comes along and has enough courage to break the circle of these rituals, nothing will ever change. In order to have a strong family, there has to be understanding, respect, and some sympathy for one another. Without these things between all units of the family, the unit cannot thrive together.

Nevertheless, my culture is based on modesty, conservativeness, and patience. In Uzbekistan we have very high moral standards. It has become difficult to keep them up after the Western influence infiltrating the culture through movies and TV shows. Now there is an increased tendency for young girls and boys to become wild and do many things under the covers and behind closed doors. In front of the parents and society, they have to maintain certain standards. This is a side effect of our cultural strictness, but it also might just be one of the ways in which young teens rebel and resist specific traditions, images, and expectations of proper girls, men, and family.

Time will tell if an equilibrium will be reached.

I believe that many obstacles, cultural misunderstandings, and traditions are similar all over the world. Women or men run into the same problems, but each culture handles these issues differently. However, my mother says that the first quality a woman needs to have is patience. In understanding my mother's life experience, I have learned that you can go through and overcome many family and life obstacles when you love. Love is the only thing that breaks through in difficult times.

LARISA'S ADVICE FOR WOMEN
All women should possess patience. It is the number one thing a woman must have.

LENA

Kazakhstan

In many countries around the world, young women are often victimized by men in powerful governmental positions or by those involved in criminal activities. Due to cultural stigma, threats against their families and societal corruption, it is nearly impossible for victims to attain retribution or speak out against their perpetrators. Lena shares her experiences of being forced into a relationship with a powerful criminal and the details of her courageous escape.

I F YOU MET me today, you would never suspect that my journey to the United States took me out of immediate danger. You would never know about the man who terrorized me, forcing me into exile far from my family and the place where I grew up. Today, I am successful and climbing toward my goals and dreams.

Sadly, my story is a testimony of an experience many young women share in my country and beyond. Maybe this is even happening in your own country, and you are just not aware. I am sharing my story because I believe it will help someone in a similar situation. I was one of the lucky ones who escaped.

I am from Kazakhstan, a country in Asia that is very different from most westernized countries. It used to be part of the Soviet Union, but now it's independent. The main religion is Islam, and there are many other minority religions present. My hometown is in the northern portion of the country, close to Russia. In fact, a large percentage of the population in my town is Russian, so it was easier for me to grow up there since my family was originally from Russia. I have nothing but good memories from my childhood. When I was little, I made many trips to my grandparents' house. They live in the countryside, so I have beautiful summer memories of running around in the grass wearing the clothes my mother made for me. She was always sewing and knitting cute little outfits and dresses for me. At that time, it was really hard to get any nice clothes in the department stores because we were technically living in the Soviet Union, so the economy was not very prosperous. We had to be resourceful about our clothing. I remember Mother changing some of my old outfits by buying fabric and making different clothes out of the ones I already had. She is a very resourceful person, as are many people in Soviet countries. She gave me my obsession to create things. During my childhood, I went to all the clubs that were offered: acting club, dancing club, knitting club, sewing club, and even sports. I was always doing something. I was a polite girl, but a bit of a tomboy because of my outspokenness.

Most of my best friends were guys, because I didn't think girls really understood me. I didn't even start to wear high heels until the end of high school.

Since my town was in the north and closer to Russia, we were less conservative than in other parts of Kazakhstan. We are a large Muslim country, so the society is very conservative. We still had more mosques than churches, but people did not show their religion in the way they dressed. Actually, we all dressed the same, Muslim or not, and many girls wore high heels, just like women do in Western countries.

Unfortunately, there was some discrimination against Russians from the Kazakh people. I really became aware that I was a Russian in a Muslim society in high school when the other kids would talk in the Kazakh language and not care that others couldn't understand. In public places, there were signs everywhere saying if you are a citizen of Kazakhstan, you have to speak in the Kazakh language. Sometimes you would go to pay bills, for example, and try to ask questions only to have the attendant start talking to you in Kazakh. If a company wanted to fire you from your job, then they would give you a test in Kazakh, which you would, of course, fail because you did not speak that language. Officially, Kazakhstan is a multinational, multiethnic country where everyone is at peace, but underneath there is a lot of discrimination. I was born in the Soviet Union, but in the land of Kazakhstan, so one would think that I am Kazakh. Yet, on my passport, I am labeled as "Russian."

Fortunately, in my school years, I attended a predominately Russian school. About 60 percent of the students in high school were Russian, and when I went to the university, four out of twenty-five students in my group were Russian.

Even though discrimination existed in our society, I was able to get around it because of my personality. I was the center of attention and made friends with everyone. All of my best friends were Kazakh, and I don't have anything against them at all. I respected them, and I loved their families. It was the situation that government and society created that I didn't like.

My family is Russian and settled in Kazakhstan by way of my grandparents who were biologists and chemists. Kazakhstan was a very underdeveloped country, so young specialists like my grandparents were sent to the country to help elevate it and educate people. Two generations later, it is still more of an agricultural than urban country. Although I love my country, I can never return. I am living in exile in the United States because of a powerful man.

Little did I know how everything in my life would change when I met a man just after high school. I knew very little about him at the time. He stopped his car when I was walking one day and introduced himself. He was very attractive and had a very nice car. In my country these two things are representative of a powerful person. He was much older than I; I was seventeen, and he was about thirty-five. At first, I talked to him because I was young and naïve and enjoyed the attention. In the beginning, he treated me more like a friend, so I did not suspect any harm could come from our interaction. Then he started taking me to fancy restaurants and buying me things. Eventually, he made it clear that he wanted me to be his mistress. He was already married, so I did not want to get involved with him intimately, but he warned me I would have "extensive problems" if I did not comply. We became intimate after that.

Suddenly, my perception of him being a "nice guy" changed. He was doing things you would see in Italian mafia movies. So I left him and told him I didn't want to talk to him or see him anymore because I did not trust him.

He was a Muslim man and involved in a lot of criminal activity from what I could observe of his lifestyle. He was always dealing with higher-up policemen, and his house and cars were very fancy. He always had a lot of money, so it was obvious that something illegal was happening. Normal people did not have the luxuries he had in Kazakhstan, only corrupt government officials and criminal gang members.

He was completely emotionally detached from life and had a large ego, expecting to always get what he wanted, when he wanted it. Later, I realized when he had approached me the first day we met he did not see me as a human being, but as his next toy. This became more and more apparent as our relationship became intimate.

After he threatened me, he disappeared for two or three months. This was a blessing for me, because when he disappeared, I also disappeared and went to the United States on an exchange student program. I was so happy to be away from him in that time span, it was such a relief. However, my mother had my cellular phone after I left, and he called one day. I had not told my mother what was happening with him, so she was completely sincere and told him I had gone to America. When I came back, I didn't see or hear from him and figured he had lost interest in me.

Unfortunately, he had not forgotten. One day, I met him on the street accidentally, and it started all over again. At the time, I was thinking about what I could do to get out of the situation. Every time we slept together, it felt like rape. Yet, this man was not the kind of man you could say "no" to. He was a stealthy criminal. One option was to move to Russia or go overseas to escape the forced relationship. So as soon it started again, I began applying to return to America as a student.

As I kept putting him off with excuses, he became increasingly frustrated. Eventually, although terrified, I told him for the second time I didn't want to be with him. He was not a very emotional person, so he didn't react, and that made me more afraid. After that conversation, he glared at me and harshly said, "You know what will happen if you leave." Although he did not threaten me outright, he just made me clearly understand that something horrible would happen.

About a week after that conversation, I was walking home from work around 8:00 PM. Three cars were sitting in the yard of my apartment building, and I saw his driver coming out of one. Suddenly, the driver grabbed me and threw me in the backseat of the car. The man was there. He started screaming at me, telling me he would do terrible things to me. "I know where you study, I know where you live, I know your family, and I know your sibling. Nothing can stop me. All my friends are powerful, and you cannot go anywhere or say anything to anyone! You are mine!"

I was so shocked and caught off guard that I thought he would kill me right then and there. Instead, he violently threw me from the car and drove away. I was left slumped over and sobbing in the dust wondering what I was going to do and what would happen the next time I saw him.

Not long after that incident, I started having problems with the police. I was working at a preschool at the time, and the police said a group of mothers were complaining against their husbands and that I had organized it. This was not true at all. I had only listened to these women complain about what was going on in their lives. I was so well connected with their kids and loved them so much that I had learned their families' stories, some of which were very sad. The police filed an official case and made me go to the station a few times. Once a police officer threatened me in the interrogation room, saying, "Do you see what you are doing, you Russian whore?" He was very aggressive, and I thought he would hit me, but he did not. Everything was so bizarre and unclear that I didn't know what they wanted from me or what to do. I didn't want this man in my life anymore. Yet I had no one to turn to, because he was connected with everyone in power. I didn't want my parents to get involved because they could not do anything and I didn't want to get my family in trouble. I knew he used his connections to cause these problems for me but I had no way to get out of our relationship or escape him.

One day the police came to my house when I was not at home, so I had to tell my parents what had happened. Meanwhile, my papers were approved for travel to the United States. I was so happy.

A month before I was to leave Kazakhstan for the United States, I agreed to meet with him, hoping he would leave me alone. All the time this was going on, I hoped for the good, for the better. I hoped it would stop. I hoped that maybe he would move on. He hadn't. He again tried to force me to be with him in the middle of a crowded restaurant by pushing himself on me, touching me, and talking sexy. My first reaction was to flee, so I ran out of the restaurant.

A few days after the restaurant incident, the police arrested me at the university and took me to the police station. They put me in a small room with no windows and an ugly sofa. They never turned on the lights so I sat in darkness the entire night and into the next morning.

I spent the entire night alone, crying. It felt like an eternity. My face was hot and puffy from all the tears. I was paranoid that they would harm my family. I thought if he went to this extreme, it would not really matter for him to terrorize them, too.

After they took me out the next morning, they began screaming at me again about that stupid case. They told me more women were coming forward about things I had said to them and that I needed to confess what I had done. They told me there were drugs involved and threatened to charge me with drug trafficking. Then, they forced me to sign papers in Kazakh language. They had a baseball bat and were hitting me with it, calling me a "Russian bitch" and even tried choking me. I had bruises on my neck and all over my body. It was very confusing and terrifying because they were speaking half Russian and half Kazakh and nothing made any sense, because none of it was true.

They were screaming and screaming for hours, then suddenly they became silent and released me. My dad was already at the station, waiting, although they had told him I was not there. I realized my entry to the station was never documented on any reports, so they could have done anything to me and no one would have known. I will never know how my dad knew that I was there, but I was so happy to see him. When I was leaving, I was told I would "receive a phone call." I figured that the guy who was making all the problems would call me. I was right. He contacted me, saying I had to meet him in the same restaurant as before. I absolutely panicked. My parents and I scrambled to figure out what to do before deciding it would be best if I did not meet him.

We decided I should go to my grandparents' house to be safe, so I stayed with my grandpa in hiding for over a month. After getting the visa I was waiting for to leave for America, I decided not to wait any longer. A friend of my grandfather's took me across the Russian border by taking a route where everyone crosses illegally. There, all you had to do was wave your ID at the guard, pay some money as a bribe, and they would let you go without checking your identification. This is exactly what we did.

While leaving, my main thought was staying alive and safe. The more distance between me and that town in Kazakhstan, the better I felt. I was scared for my life, but also scared for my family. I was very afraid he would do something to harm them in my absence.

The journey across the border to Russia took about six hours. I was driven to an airport in Russia, where I boarded a flight to Moscow. I slept in that airport because I felt safer sleeping in a public place than in my own bed at a hotel. I was worried I was being followed.

From there, I flew to Moscow and spent a couple days with a friend. Then, I had a ticket to the United States through Ireland, but there were issues with the ticket at the airport. I was told there was no transfer room in Dublin and I could not fly out of Moscow due to a transfer visa. My ticket was not refundable, so I lost it. This put me in a trying situation. In Moscow, one is only permitted to stay three days without a residency permit, and then they have to leave.

I felt these problems were a continuation of all my others, like the God or the universe was saying, "No, you are not leaving anywhere, ha ha!" I didn't have any money or a credit card to purchase a new ticket. I could not return to Kazakhstan, nor could I remain in Moscow without a residency permit. I went back to my friend's house, but she was leaving the next morning to another city. I was exiled with no place to stay, no money, and no residency. Fortunately, a classmate had some money, and I begged her for help. I was surprised that she gave it to me, because in Russia, it would take five months to earn that amount of money. In total, I spent a bit more than a week there, which was too long without a permit. During that week, I was very nervous that I would be discovered and deported back to Kazakhstan or jailed.

When I bought the second ticket at the airport, sure enough, they asked for my Moscow residency permit, so I played a fool and acted like I didn't have it. I said, "Oh, it was confiscated on the border with Russia. I thought I wouldn't need it here since I am leaving." They told me that I could not fly anywhere without presenting it. I attempted to bribe them, offering to pay a fee to fly. Practically begging one of the female customs officers, I then broke down and cried. This was my last hope, and she was all that was in my way. Finally, she told me to go ahead. I think she didn't want any drama.

Sitting on the plane, I was still paranoid that something else would go wrong. Finally, though, the airplane took off, and the earth was underneath us. Suddenly, all of my troubles were behind me. In this situation, it was a man's ethnocentric pride against me. I was the Russian girl who turned down a Muslim Kazakh man. My parents told me the police came twice after I left, but they told them I was gone and they did not know where I was. I have not been back to Kazakhstan since, and I won't go back until I am sure he is dead.

When I arrived in the United States, I returned to the same place I had previously worked. The same people were there to greet me, which brought me back into a positive realm. The stress I'd been under had made me feel like an animal trapped in the corner of a cage. It took me a little time to get over everything. It also took me a while to realize I was not going back. It was hard to come to terms with the fact I may never see my home again. After a while, though, I was confronted with a new and very serious problem: my visa would soon expire. The easiest option was to get a student visa, but I was told I had to return to Kazakhstan to change my visa status.

I moved to another state in the United States, where I lived with a friend. I spent my first few weeks in my new city at the library, researching ways to get a visa. Because a student visa could keep me in the United States longer, I wrote all of the universities I could find online, telling them that I really wanted to study and had good grades. I found one on the other side of the United States and had to fly to their offices only days later. Everything again became a game of survival. At the time, I didn't know political asylum was an option.

At this university, I was in line with a girl who was applying for political asylum. I don't know how she knew that I so desperately needed to hear her words. Maybe she sensed my desperation. After I told her a little about me, she gave me everything I needed. Eventually, I got an attorney and fought for asylum. Even then, in making my case, I had problems mentioning the name of the guy. Proving my case was so hard because I didn't have any information on him. He was not an overt public figure, rather an underground criminal. When I met with the lawyer, I was embarrassed to admit this. The only thing I could do was tell my story.

I did receive political asylum. I was homeless for roughly two months when I moved to my current city, but eventually life started improving. I am now on my way to a career and have my legal documents. I finally feel like a human being having my freedom back. Without freedom, what do you really have in this life?

There are times when I wish I could talk about this publicly. I can't, though, because I am worried about my family. So many girls living in Kazakhstan are going through worse things than I did. They think it's normal and that nothing can help them. In my country, girls disappear all of the time. Their disappearances are never in the news. They are just gone suddenly, and no one ever hears from them again.

Please do not misinterpret me as being a Russian girl who hates Kazakhs. That is completely not the case. My best friends from back home were Kazakhs and Muslims. I grew up in that culture, and I respect it. The negative attitude, in my opinion, comes from the government. It's a "you live in this country because we let you" attitude. There are no human rights. If you have troubles, you don't have anywhere to go for help, especially if you are female.

There is also no protected freedom of speech in Kazakhstan, so you cannot say anything against this discrimination. If you searched the Internet to find other instances like mine, you will not find a lot of cases. Women and girls affected by situations like what I went through DO NOT speak out. Ever. The threat to their families and the shame they will endure silences them. It's one thing to speak out for yourself, but when your own family could be negatively impacted and at risk by your words, you think twice about talking.

Sometimes, I feel like this didn't even happen to me, mostly because, like most girls in such situations, I don't have any documents to prove my case. I didn't go to a hospital after the incident at the police station because I was afraid they would kill me if I told anyone. There isn't even a police report. I think a lot of girls in my part of the world feel helpless because they can't prove their cases. They have no recourse or money for bribes. It's horrible to go through something like that, knowing there is nothing that can help you. Thank God for my asylum in the United States. I will always be grateful for that because it gave me a chance at a new life. One day I will return to the home I was exiled from. Though I am unsure of when I will get that chance.

LENA'S ADVICE FOR WOMEN
Appreciate life as it is. Right now, I am just happy to live every day. All of this happened unexpectedly. You never know what will happen. Never let anyone make you do something you don't want to do.

CPSIA information can be obtained
at www.ICGtesting.com
Printed in the USA
FSOW02n1437300115
4899FS

9 780990 337508